Model Reliability

Model Reliability

edited by

David A. Belsley
and
Edwin Kuh

The MIT Press
Cambridge, Massachusetts
London, England

This book was set in Times New Roman by Asco Trade Typesetting Ltd., Hong Kong, and printed and bound by Halliday Lithograph in the United States of America

Library of Congress Cataloging-in-Publication Data

Main entry under title:

Model reliability.

 Includes bibliographies and index.
 1. Econometric models—Addresses, essays, lectures.   I. Belsley, David A.
II. Kuh, Edwin.
HB141.M58   1986   330′.028   85-18455
ISBN 0-262-02224-9

Contents

List of Contributors

Lewis S. Alexander
Yale University
New Haven, Conn.

David A. Belsley
Boston College and
Massachusetts Institute of Technology
Cambridge, Mass

Jean-Marie Dufour
University of Montreal
Montreal, Quebec, Canada

Robert F. Engle
University of California at San Diego
San Diego, Calif.

Ray C. Fair
Yale University
New Haven, Conn.

C. W. J. Granger
University of California at San Diego
San Diego, Calif.

Mark N. Greene
Federal Reserve System
Washington, D.C.

E. Philip Howrey
University of Michigan
Ann Arbor, Mich.

Peter Hollinger
Massachusetts Institute of Technology
Cambridge, Mass.

Saul H. Hymans
University of Michigan
Ann Arbor, Mich.

Edwin Kuh
Massachusetts Institute of Technology
Cambridge, Mass.

Edward E. Leamer
University of California at Los Angeles
Los Angeles, Calif.

John Neese
Massachusetts Institute of Technology
Cambridge, Mass.

R. P. Robins
University of California at San Diego
San Diego, Calif.

Stephen Swartz
Federal Reserve System
Washington, D.C.

Roy E. Welsch
Massachusetts Institute of Technology
Cambridge, Mass

Introduction

In the latter part of the seventies, several of us recognized a growing need for a generally improved understanding of notions about model reliability. The result was a five-year interuniversity research project that allowed us to exchange views on different approaches and also to work together on topics of common interest, often using a common computer environment, TROLL. This volume skims some of the cream from the top of these efforts, giving the reader an excellent feel for the directions that the thoughts and ideas of this group have taken.

The seventies witnessed greater criticism of and skepticism about econometric models. And, although much of this was justified, at least some slings and darts partook of maiming the messenger who brings the bad news (economic maladies like stagflation are beyond the power of econometricians to create or expunge). We sought to be more constructive in our criticism. We shared a common belief that the mechanical application of standard econometric methods was not enough and that the solution was not merely more bells and whistles. There was a clear need to evaluate models more intensively from new perspectives, ones extending beyond the confines of Neyman-Pearson hypothesis testing. This volume contains some of these ideas, and although the unifying theme of model reliability is the objective, the approaches toward it are highly diverse. We worked individually, meeting once or twice a year. These meetings fostered continuity in the evolution of our several view points. Sometimes several of our members would cooperate on the same topic or use the same analytical tools. The principal area of common interest was time series.

Robert Engle and Clive Granger at the University of California, San Diego, and Douglas Martin, University of Washington, Seattle, worked with members of the Center for Computational Research in Economics and Management Science at MIT. So did James Durbin of the London School of Economics, who visited the Center for three summers to work with us on related time-series problems. Alexander Samarov, Walter Vandaele, and Stephen Peters at the center worked in collaboration with this group on team research projects. Meetings over a four-year period provided one important means for continuity to the evolution of our individual thinking. Another means of cooperation existed through the TROLL econometric modeling system. This system was accessible over national telecommunication networks to those who were interested in common methods and was employed mainly in the several time-series topics.

Other participants included G. S. Maddala, University of Florida,

Gainesville; Gregory Chow, Princeton University; Edward Leamer, University of California, Los Angeles; Saul Hymans, Philip Howrey, and Mark Greene, University of Michigan; Ray Fair, Yale University, and Jean-Marie Dufour, University of Montreal. John Neese, Peter Hollinger, David Belsley, Roy Welsch, and Edwin Kuh were actively engaged throughout on model reliability issues.

This volume includes pieces evenly divided into four, possibly overlapping, facets of model reliability: specification testing, outside information, diagnostics, and system analysis. In chapter 1 Engle, Granger, and Robins show that the common practice of forecasting on the basis of conditional means while ignoring conditional variances can be misleading both as to the form of the conditional mean and the nature of causality. In chapter 2 Dufour makes use of recursive techniques to analyze the stability over time of various models of the demand for money during the German hyper-inflation. The techniques highlight structural instability and pinpoint the time of occurrence.

In chapter 3 Leamer illuminates the effect different priors can have on inferences about the course of U.S. inflation when applied to the same data set. His hope of aiding the formation of a consensus is frustrated, but the techniques displayed are a model for other research. In chapter 4 Greene, Howrey, and Hymans show how to include recently occurring monthly data to improve the forecast reliability of quarterly models.

In chapter 5 Belsley examines the proper form for data that are to be subjected to conditioning analysis. The "improved" conditioning often obtained through centering or first-differencing is shown typically to be illusory. In chapter 6 Swartz and Welsch make use of bounded-influence techniques to investigate the quality of the data-model fit in an energy model. These robust techniques notably improve certain forecasts.

In chapter 7 Fair and Alexander demonstrate means for comparing the equation-by-equation accuracy of two large-system macromodels. In this case the two models are Fair's own and the Michigan Quarterly Econometric Model (MQEM). In chapter 8 Kuh, Neese, and Hollinger apply their methods for cutting through the complexity of large multi-equation, dynamic models to help understand the main forces at work in producing inflation in the MQEM.

Although there is much diversity among the topics of these papers, they are connected by one important thread: a search for means beyond routine econometric practice to produce more reliable econometric models.

Econometric practice unavoidably incorporates, either explicitly or implicitly, two different sources of prior information: that brought by the investigator on the nature of the process being modeled and that inculcated by econometric practice as to what is conventionally acceptable. The former source arises from the concepts and questions of interest to a particular research topic. The latter source is frequently accepted without much question and is all too often highly restrictive. Thus, having formulated an econometric model on the basis of specific knowledge, it is often routine practice or routine software availability that determines, and limits, the estimator to be used, the hypotheses to be tested, the questions to be asked, and the ways for proceeding when problems arise.

Each study in this volume widens and deepens the set of techniques available to econometric investigation and extends our ability to assess many assumptions that have been traditionally less open to investigation. The combined result represents a dynamic view of econometric practice that we feel increases our ability to understand model reliability and to produce econometric results more relevant to their intended purpose.

Model Reliability

1 Wholesale and Retail Prices: Bivariate Time-Series Modeling with Forecastable Error Variances

C. W. J. Granger, R. P. Robins, and Robert F. Engle

1.1 Introduction

Suppose that x_t is a time series and that one is interested in the conditional distribution of x_{t+1} given some information set I_t available at time t. Using a least-squares criterion, the optimum forecast of x_{t+1} given I_t is the conditional mean:

$$f_{t,1} = E[x_{t+1}|I_t] = m_t. \tag{1.1}$$

If now one considers the conditional variance

$$E[(x_{t+1} - m_t)^2|I_t] = h_t^2, \tag{1.2}$$

there seems to be no particular reason to suppose that h_t^2 will be a constant, although this is the assumption frequently made in time-series analysis. If h_t^2 is not a constant, then a regression estimating m_t will be subject to heteroscedasticity, and ignoring this can lead to inefficient parameter estimates and incorrect inference, as econometricians have frequently documented. Whereas a great deal of attention has been paid to modeling conditional means, for example, by Box and Jenkins (1970) in the univariate case and by Granger and Newbold (1977), Jenkins (1979), and others in the bivariate case, little work has been done on modeling conditional variances. Denoting $\varepsilon_t = x_t - m_{t-1}$, the one-step forecast errors, Engle (1982) has considered the specification

$$h_t^2 = \sum_{j=1}^{q} \gamma_j \varepsilon_{t-j}^2 \tag{1.3}$$

and called the resulting process autoregressive conditional heteroscedastic (ARCH). He found that conclusions concerning the generating process for inflation change in important ways when ARCH was allowed for in the model. In this chapter we consider causality testing between a pair of price series, a wholesale and a consumer price index, with generalized ARCH effects, using a richer specification of h_t^2 than (1.3). Thus h_t^2 will use terms from the information set including both price series and not just past errors squared.

The concept of causation used here is that called "Granger causation" in the literature, as discussed in Granger (1980) and elsewhere. In the bivariate case two information sets are considered: $I_n : x_{n-j}, j \geq 0$, and $J_n : x_{n-j}, y_{n-j}$,

$j \geq 0$, then denoting the conditional distribution of x_{n+1} given z_n by $P(x_{n+1}|z_n)$; y_n is said to cause x_{n+1}, with respect to J_n, if

$$P(x_{n+1}|I_n) \neq P(x_{n+1}|J_n).$$

The definition used in practice is y_n causes x_{n+1} in mean with respect to J_n if

$$E[x_{n+1}|I_n] \neq E[x_{n+1}|J_n] = m_{n+1}.$$

This is clearly less general than the previous definition but more easily tested. It is natural to define "causality in variance" as well. y_n will be said to cause x_{n+1} in variance if

$$E[(x_{n+1} - m_{n+1})^2|I_n] \neq E[(x_{n+1} - m_{n+1})^2|J_n].$$

Clearly noncausality in mean and variance does not imply noncausality using conditional distributions, but if causation is found in mean or in variance, then general causation has been found. Interpretation of such results, using a more careful terminology, may be found in Granger (1980).

Section 1.3 presents the results of an exploratory analysis of the various relationships, and section 1.5 builds bivariate ARCH models, with associated causality tests. A maximum likelihood procedure developed in section 1.4 is used to estimate the models assuming

$$x_{t+1} - m_t = h_t a_{t+1},$$

where $a_t \sim N(0, 1)$, and is pure white noise.

1.2   The Sources of Variance

A variety of studies have examined the relationship between wholesale and retail prices. Generally, these have assumed that changes in wholesale prices precede changes in consumer prices. The economic reasoning is very simply that as input costs increase, the price of the finished good several months later will have to be raised. Popkin (1974) examines a series of wholesale price indexes by stage of processing; Guthrie (1981) looks at the relationship between the consumer price index and the wholesale price index, and Engle (1978) models the relationship between the wholesale price of raw food products, the wage rate in industry 20 (manufacture of food), and the food component of the consumer price index for sixteen cities. In each case he found that there is a lag between the wholesale price and the consumer price.

Economic theory, and many of the large macro econometric models, however, take a different approach as the prices of factors of production may well be determined by the derived demand for factors with an inelastic supply. Thus changes in the demand for goods will lead to subsequent changes in the demand for inputs and corresponding changes in input prices. Recent work by Gordon (1975) and by Engle, Granger, and Kraft (1982) attempts to test or combine these theories empirically.

This discussion is, however, focused entirely on the dynamics of the mean, and tests are based on "causality in the mean." On closer scrutiny the justification for taking the input or the output prices as causally prior hinges on exogenous components of variance. For example, energy prices are often taken as exogenous because OPEC is presumably exogenous and is responsible for the bulk of the variance, even though energy prices are surely influenced by the state of the economy. Similar arguments are given for food prices in terms of the weather. Much of the variance of these input prices is accounted for by the variance of exogenous unmeasured variables. A presentation of the demand pull model reveals a similar structure. Macroeconomic shocks shift the demand for final goods, and this then feeds back to the prices of primary inputs. The variance of the final price is largely determined by the variance of the unobserved macro shock, and the variability of the primary product price follows as a consequence.

To make this verbal discussion more precise, consider an economy with only two commodities: a primary product, such as agricultural produce labeled x with price w, and a final product q, which might be food with price p. The wage rate is taken as numeraire, so both prices are measured in man-hours per unit of output. The supply function for x depends on its price relative to labor costs and on r, which is the unexpected amount of rainfall. The demand for x is derived from the final producers and depends on the price of the final good as well as w. Static model equilibrium is expressed as

$$x^D = x^D(w, p),$$

$$x^S = x^S(w, r),$$

$$x^D = x^S,$$

implying

$$w = g(p, r). \tag{1.4}$$

Equilibrium for the final good is expressed similarly. The supply function depends on input and output prices while demand depends on final goods prices and macro shocks, which are labeled m to suggest that they may be unexpected changes in the money supply. Thus

$$q^D = q^D(p, m),$$

$$q^S = q^S(w, p),$$

$$q^D = q^S,$$

giving

$$p = f(w, m). \tag{1.5}$$

Because of lags in adjustment the model in (1.4) and (1.5) must be formulated with the potential for general dynamic structure. Letting these be linear vector autoregressions driven by the unobservables r and m, respectively, the system becomes

$$B(L)(p, w)' = (m, r)', \tag{1.6}$$

where

$$B(L) = B_0 + LB_1(L),$$

$$B_1(L) = \begin{bmatrix} b_{11}(L) & b_{12}(L) \\ b_{21}(L) & b_{22}(L) \end{bmatrix},$$

and

$$E[(m_t, r_t)|\{m_{t-i}, r_{t-i}\}] = 0, \tag{1.7}$$

$$V[(m_t, r_t)|\{m_{t-i}, r_{t-i}\}] = H_t, \tag{1.8}$$

with H_t a function of the information set. The set $\{x_{t-i}\}$ will be interpreted throughout as the sigma algebra generated by all x_{t-i} for $i > 0$. Assumption (1.7) might appear unrealistic; however, any forecastability of the shocks can be immediately incorporated in the $B(L)$ polynomials so there is no loss of generality. By allowing a time subscript on the covariance matrix of the shocks, equation (1.8) opens the possibility of examining the behavior of the variances over time and thereby deriving implications concerning causality in the second moments. The inclusion of moving average terms would merely complicate the analysis but would not change any of the implications.

Equations (1.6) through (1.8) imply that

$$V[(p_t, w_t) | \{p_{t-i}, w_{t-i}\}] = B_0 H_t B_0, \tag{1.9}$$

$$E[(p_t, w_t)' | \{p_{t-i}, w_{t-i}\}] = B_1(L)(p_{t-1}, w_{t-1})'. \tag{1.10}$$

Causality in mean is therefore summarized in (1.10), but causality in variance cannot be ascertained without a description of H_t as a function of available information.

For simplicity, suppose that m and r are first-order ARCH processes so that their conditional variances depend only on the past squared value of the two series. This is a special case of the bivariate ARCH process described in Engle and Kraft (1983) and of the process later used in this chapter. It is convenient to write this using a matrix product that multiplies matrices element by element. Define $[A * B]_{ij} = [A]_{ij}[B]_{ij}$. Then

$$\begin{aligned}
H_t &= A_0 + A_1 * [(m, r)'(m, r)]_{t-1} \\
&= A_0 + A_1 * [B(L)(p, w)'(B(L)(p, w)')']_{t-1},
\end{aligned} \tag{1.11}$$

with

$$[A_1]_{ij} = a_{ij}.$$

From the definition of causality in variance, one can see that w will cause p in variance if the expression for the conditional variance of p in (1.9) and (1.11) has past w in it and not otherwise. Several sufficient conditions for noncausality of p in variance can be identified. A useful example is given in proposition 1.1

PROPOSITION 1.1 w does not cause p in variance if the following three conditions hold.

1. A_1 is diagonal.
2. $[B_0]_{12} = 0$.
3. $b_{12}(L) = 0$.

Proof The proof proceeds by substituting (1.11) into (1.9) and showing that under these conditions, the upper left-hand element of the conditional variance matrix in (1.9) will contain no lagged w's. Without condition 3 past w's will help explain current m's. $\square$

Because condition 3 is identical to the condition for noncausality in the mean, it appears that the variance notion is simply a stronger version of noncausality. Certainly one may have causality in the variance without causality in the mean if the other two conditions are not satisfied. One can also have causality in mean without causality in variance, for example, if $[A_1]_{11} = 0$.

In this particular example it is plausible to restrict A_1 to be diagonal as both rainfall and macro shocks may have changing variances, but it would be surprising to find any correlation between them. Because the data set is monthly, one might expect little simultaneity, and therefore B_0 would be diagonal as well. In this case causality in variance implies causality in mean, although the converse is not true as there may be no time-varying variances at all.

Thus we expect in this example to find causality in mean whenever we find causality in variance. But the existence of causality in variance is in itself interesting as it indicates how variances propagate through the economic system and shows that one can form better confidence intervals by joint time-series modeling of first and second moments.

A second reason for building models of first and second moments is more statistical. Estimates obtained by ignoring time-varying variances will not have their standard asymptotic distributions, and therefore inference will be misleading. This is discussed in more detail in section 1.4.

1.3   Initial Explorations

The data used in this study are "prices of intermediate materials, supplies, and components" (which is a wholesale price index) and "all items of the consumer price index for wage and clerical workers" (a consumer price index). The data were for the period January 1947 to November 1981, giving a series of length 406, and were taken from the Citibank Economic Database. The series were not seasonally adjusted.

The correlograms on the levels of the series suggested that differencing was appropriate. In what follows C_t will be used to represent the change in the consumer price index and W_t the change in the wholesale price index. Autoregressive models were identified for each series, estimated, and the residuals checked that they were white noise. The univariate models fitted were

$$C_t = 0.023 + 0.41C_{t-1} + 0.24C_{t-2} + 0.15C_{t-8} + 0.17C_{t-9} + ec_t \qquad (1.12)$$
$$\quad\;\, (0.021)\;\; (0.047) \qquad (0.046) \qquad (0.048) \qquad (0.049)$$

and

$$W_t = 0.06 + 0.32W_{t-1} + 0.25W_{t-2} + 0.24W_{t-3} - 0.10W_{t-7} + 0.2W_{t-12}$$
$$\quad (0.045)\,(0.047) \qquad (0.048) \qquad (0.047) \qquad (0.043) \qquad (0.047)$$
$$\tag{1.13}$$
$$+ \; ew_t.$$

The error series passed Lagrange multiplier tests for white noise. Denote

$$mc_t = C_t - ec_t,$$

$$mw_t = W_t - ew_t,$$

so that mc_t, mw_t are the conditional means of C_t, W_t using just lagged terms of the individual series, and each are known at time $t - 1$.

A variety of regression models for the squared residuals were considered. The following lists the explanatory variables used for ec_t^2, with the corresponding corrected R^2 values:

		R_c^2
(i)	Lagged ec_t^2, the simple ARCH specification	0.04
(ii)	Lagged ec_t^2, lagged and current mc_t	0.12
(iii)	Lagged ec_t^2, lagged and current mc_t^2	0.22
(iv)	Lagged ec_t^2, lagged ew_t^2	0.25
(v)	Lagged ec_t^2, lagged ew_t^2, lagged and current mw_t^2	0.37
(vi)	As (v) plus lagged and current mc_t^2	0.51

Twelve lags were used for each lagged variable. The corresponding table explaining ew_t^2 is as follows:

		R_c^2
(i)	Lagged ew_t^2	0.30
(ii)	Lagged ew_t^2, lagged and current mw_t	0.36
(iii)	Lagged ew_t^2, lagged and current mw_t^2	0.40
(iv)	Lagged ew_t^2, lagged and current mw_t and mw_t^2	0.41
(v)	Lagged ew_t^2, lagged ec_t^2	0.40
(vi)	Lagged ew_t^2, ec_t^2, lagged and current mw_t^2	0.46
(vii)	As (vi) plus current and lagged mc_t^2	0.52

The individual lagged values that seemed significant were usually at 1 or 2 and at or near 12.

The regressions only record the predictable part of ec_t^2, ew_t^2. There is some further structure, as the residuals from regression (vi) for ec_t^2 and (vii) for ew_t^2 have a contemporaneous correlation of 0.23. The use of mw_t to explain ew_t^2 could lead to problems as it may lead to negative predictive values of a positive variable and so regressions using squared terms are likely to be more satisfactory.

The results suggest that the simple ARCH specification can be improved by bringing in lagged squared conditional means and possibly also by introducing squared residuals from the other univariate equation.

However, the univariate models used for the conditional means should also be capable of improvement by using the complete bivariate information set. One might, for example, expect wholesale prices to cause consumer prices. Adding W_{t-j}, $j = 1, 2, 3$, to equation (1.12) gives the new model

$$C_t = 0.03 + 0.27C_{t-1} + 0.14C_{t-2} + 0.13C_{t-8} + 0.21C_{t-9}$$
$$(5.2)\phantom{C_{t-1}}(3.04)\phantom{C_{t-2}}(2.9)\phantom{C_{t-8}}(4.3)$$

$$+ 0.06W_{t-1} + 0.08W_{t-2} + 0.04W_{t-3} + ecc_t.$$
$$(3.01)\phantom{W_{t-1}}(3.66)\phantom{W_{t-2}}(1.9)$$

$$(1.14)$$

The sum of squared residuals was 46.6 for equation (1.12) and 41.6 for (1.14); t values are also shown in (1.14), and the new residuals, ecc_t, pass a test for white noise.

The new residuals squared were regressed on various explanatory variables, with the following results:

Explanatory variables	R_c^2
(i) Lagged ecc_t^2	0.08
(ii) Lagged ecc_t^2, lagged and current mcc_t	0.18
(iii) Lagged ecc_t^2, lagged and current mcc_t^2	0.27
(iv) Lagged ecc_t^2, lagged and current mcc_t^2, mw_t^2	0.27
(v) Lagged ecc_t^2, lagged ew_t^2, lagged and current mcc_t^2	0.52

where $mcc_t = C_t - ecc_t$. Again substantial improvement over a simple

ARCH is achieved, and there appears to be causation in variances as well as in means. These results are merely suggestive, but they can be helpful in specifying a more complete model.

When causation from consumer prices to wholesale prices was considered, some weak evidence in favor of this causation was found. Analysis of the new squared residuals (eww_t^2) produced similar results to those given here, with an R_c^2 of 0.27 when a simple ARCH specification was used, increasing to $R_c^2 = 0.50$ when eww_t^2 was explained by lagged eww_t^2, ecc_t^2, mcc_t^2, and mww_t^2.

1.4 Maximum Likelihood Estimation

The preliminary explorations in the previous section suggest estimation of a model of the following form for each of the variables:

$$\beta(L)c_t = \gamma(L)w_t + e_t,$$

$$e_t = hc_t a_t, \quad a_t \sim IN(0, 1), \tag{1.15}$$

$$hc_t^2 = \alpha_0 + \alpha_1 \sum_j d_j e_{t-j}^2 + \alpha_2 \sum_j d_j (c_{t-j} - e_{t-j})^2 + \alpha_3 \sum_j d_j w_{t-j}^2.$$

This expression for the conditional variance synthesizes the ARCH model as originally specified by Engle (1982), the heteroscedasticity model discussed but not estimated by Pagan, Hall, and Trivedi (1983) which allows the variance to depend on the mean, and the bivariate ARCH process presented in Engle and Kraft (1983). These extensions are implied by nonzero values of α_2 and α_3. Further generalizations are easy to formulate; however, these appear to be the most relevant from an economic point of view.

It is essential for the variance to remain positive for all observed data points and desirable for it to be positive for all possible data points. This is implied by positive values for all four α coefficients if the d_j are all positive. To ensure that the d_j are positive, they are assumed to be gradually declining over a finite period. This corresponds to the assumption that the usefulness of past information in forecasting the current variance, declines monotonically. In particular, it is assumed that

$$d_j = 13 - j, \quad j = 1, \ldots, 12. \tag{1.16}$$

The log likelihood of the sample is given by

$$\mathscr{L}(\theta) = \sum \mathscr{L}_t(\theta) = -\sum \left[\log h_t + \frac{e_t^2}{2h_t^2} \right], \tag{1.17}$$

where θ is the set of k unknown parameters $\{\beta, \gamma, \alpha\}$. Denoting the $T \times k$ matrix S by

$$[S]_{ti} = s_{ti} = \frac{\partial \mathscr{L}_t}{\partial \theta_i}, \tag{1.18}$$

the derivative of $\mathscr{L}$ with respect to θ can be written compactly as

$$\frac{\partial \mathscr{L}}{\partial \theta} = S'i, \tag{1.19}$$

where i is the T dimensional unit vector.

The Hessian of the log likelihood is simply the sum of the Hessians of the t conditional log likelihoods, $\mathscr{L}_t$. Under the assumption that the likelihood function is correctly specified,

$$\mathscr{I}_t = E \left[\frac{\partial \mathscr{L}_t}{\partial \theta} \frac{\partial \mathscr{L}_t}{\partial \theta'} \right] = -E \left[\frac{\partial^2 \mathscr{L}_t}{\partial \theta \partial \theta'} \right], \tag{1.20}$$

where $\mathscr{I}$ is the information matrix. Because $\mathscr{I} = \sum \mathscr{I}_t / T$.

$$\mathscr{I} = E \left[\frac{S'S}{T} \right]. \tag{1.21}$$

Under slightly stronger conditions $S'S/T$ is also consistent for $\mathscr{I}$.

The algorithm used to maximize the likelihood function is the Berndt, Hall, Hall, and Hausman (1973) algorithm which can be formulated in this notation as

$$\theta^{i+1} = \theta^i + \lambda (S'S)^{-1} S'i, \tag{1.22}$$

where S is evaluated at θ^i and λ is the step length which is examined through a very simple line search. As the log likelihood for the tth observation is simply

$$\mathscr{L}_t = -\log h_t - \frac{e_t^2}{2h_t^2},$$

analytical derivatives were calculated in all cases. The stopping rule was either a series of steps with little change in the log likelihood or sufficiently small gradients in the direction of each parameter.

As this is the solution to the maximization of the log likelihood function, it will in general have the familiar properties of maximum likelihood estimators of consistency, asymptotic efficiency and asymptotic normality subject to regularity conditions such as those given by Crowder (1976). If these are satisfied, then

$$(S'S)^{1/2}(\hat{\theta} - \theta) \overset{A}{\sim} N(0, I). \tag{1.23}$$

Expression (1.23) also defines inference procedures for the estimates, and it is from here that asymptotic standard errors and t statistics are computed, for example.

1.5 Maximum Likelihood Estimated Models

Using the identifications suggested in the earlier analysis, the following model was considered for consumer prices:

$$C_t = \beta_0 + \beta_1 C_{t-1} + \beta_2 C_{t-2} + \beta_3 C_{t-8} + \beta_4 C_{t-9}$$

$$+ \beta_5 W_{t-1} + \beta_6 W_{t-2} + \beta_7 W_{t-3} + ec_t,$$

where

$$ec_t = hc_t \cdot a_t \sim N(0, 1),$$

$$hc_t^2 = \alpha_0 + \alpha_1 \sum_{j=1}^{12} d_j ec_{t-j}^2 + \alpha_2 \sum_{j=1}^{12} d_j mc_{t-j}^2 + \alpha_3 \sum_{j=1}^{12} d_j W_{t-j}^2.$$

Here $mc_t = C_t - ec_t$ is the conditional mean. A fully general log specifications in hc_t^2 would be highly overparameterized and difficult to estimate, so the set of values used for the weights d_j were taken a priori to be $d_j = 13 - j, j = 1, \ldots, 12$. Experience with other smooth values for the d_j's suggest that this choice is not of critical importance. The model was fitted in six different fashions:

Case 1.
OLS—with $\alpha_1 = \alpha_2 = \alpha_3 = 0$, so h_t^2 is a constant, using least squares.
OLS 1—constrained to have $\beta_5 = \beta_6 = \beta_7 = 0$.
OLS 2—without these constraints.

Case 2.
MLC—with $\alpha_3 = 0$, a constrained maximum likelihood procedure.

MLC 1—with further constraints $\beta_5 = \beta_6 = \beta_7 = 0$.
MLC 2—without these constraints.

Case 3.
MLCW—no constraints on α's, an unconstrained maximum likelihood estimation procedure.
MLCW 1—with constraints $\beta_5 = \beta_6 = \beta_7 = 0$.
MLCW 2—without these constraints.

Thus the OLS models do not take any ARCH effects into account, MLC does not involve lagged W_t^2 in the variances, whereas MLCW does. OLS 1, MLC 1, and MLCW 1 have a mean function that explained consumer prices just from past consumer prices, whereas OLS 2, and so on, also used past wholesale prices. By looking at appropriate pairs of models, the relevance of ARCH and causality in mean or variance of consumer prices by wholesale prices can be tested. In the maximum likelihood estimates all parameters are estimated jointly.

The estimates of the various parameters, with attached standard errors, are shown in table 1.1.

Merely looking at t values suggests the following:

1. Wholesale prices cause consumer prices in means, since β_6 is always clearly significant regardless of the method of estimation.
2. Since α_3 is significant, there appears to be causality of the variance of consumer prices by the squared mean of wholesale prices. When α_3 is introduced, α_2 becomes insignificant.
3. There appear to be important general ARCH effects; introducing these effects alters estimates of the beta coefficients to some extent.

Comparing the two OLS models with an f test, gives a statistic with (3,407) degrees of freedom and a value of 15.59 which is significant at the 99% confidence level, suggesting that wholesale prices do cause consumer prices in means.

For the maximum likelihood models, likelihood ratio tests have been used to compare alternative formulations, so that the test statistic, τ, is minus twice the log likelihood ratio, and this is compared to chi-squared significance levels with k degrees of freedom, where k is the number of extra parameters involved in the less constrained model formulation.

To test if there is causality in means or variances, models MLC 1 and MLCW 2 are compared, giving a τ value of 57, with four degrees of

Table 1.1
Consumer prices

Variable (standard error)	OLS 1	OLS 2	MLC 1	MLC 2	MLCW 1	MLCW 2
Regression equation constant	0.023 (0.021)	0.029 (0.020)	0.021 (0.019)	0.030 (0.017)	0.025 (0.019)	0.026 (0.016)
C_{t-1}	0.409 (0.021)	0.269 (0.051)	0.373 (0.050)	0.260 (0.057)	0.356 (0.062)	0.262 (0.054)
C_{t-2}	0.245 (0.046)	0.145 (0.047)	0.245 (0.048)	0.111 (0.054)	0.220 (0.059)	0.119 (0.052)
C_{t-8}	0.146 (0.048)	0.134 (0.046)	0.130 (0.055)	0.120 (0.050)	0.138 (0.057)	0.136 (0.046)
C_{t-9}	0.168 (0.049)	0.206 (0.047)	0.210 (0.055)	0.220 (0.050)	0.197 (0.060)	0.213 (0.049)
W_{t-1}	—	0.063 (0.021)	—	0.025 (0.021)	—	0.061 (0.032)
W_{t-2}	—	0.079 (0.021)	—	0.100 (0.026)	—	0.097 (0.032)
W_{t-3}	—	0.040 (0.021)	—	0.051 (0.027)	—	0.048 (0.031)
Variance equation constant	—	—	0.038 (0.0035)	0.035 (0.003)	0.039 (0.0042)	0.036 (0.0033)
$\{ec_{t-j}^2\}$	—	—	0.004 (0.001)	0.0034 (0.001)	0.0023 (0.0014)	0.002 (0.0009)
$\{mc_{t-j}^2\}$	—	—	0.001 (0.0002)	0.0009 (0.0002)	0.41×10^{-9} (0.0005)	0.31×10^{-7} (0.0002)
$\{W_{t-j}^2\}$	—	—	—	—	0.0010 (0.00024)	0.00047 (0.00015)
Sum squared errors	46.11	41.59	—	—	—	—
Likelihood values	—	—	296.7	319	304.2	326.2

freedom, which is very highly significant (greater than a 99.9% confidence level). Comparing MLC 1 and MLC 2 and also MLCW 1 and MLCW 2 give τ values that are very highly significant, showing that wholesale prices cause consumer prices in mean regardless of various alternative ARCH specifications.

The results of a similar analysis for wholesale prices are shown in table 1.2. The model considered is

$$W_t = \beta_0 + \beta_1 W_{t-1} + \beta_2 W_{t-2} + \beta_3 W_{t-3} + \beta_4 W_{t-7} + \beta_5 W_{t-12} + \beta_6 W_{t-13}$$

$$+ \beta_7 C_{t-2} + \beta_8 C_{t-3} + ew_t,$$

where $ew_t = hw_t \cdot \varepsilon_t$, $\varepsilon_t \sim N(0, 1)$, and

$$hw_t^2 = \alpha_0 + \alpha_1 \sum_{j=1}^{12} d_j ew_{t-j}^2 + \alpha_2 \sum_{j=1}^{12} d_j mw_{t-j}^2 + \alpha_3 \sum_{j=1}^{12} d_j C_{t-j}^2,$$

where $mw_t = w_t - ew_t$ and the d_j are as before. The estimation methods are OLS 1 ($\beta_7 = \beta_8 = 0$), OLS 2 (no constraint), MLW 1 ($\alpha_3 = 0, \beta_7 = \beta_8 = 0$), and MLW 2 ($\alpha_3 = 0$), MLWC 1 ($\beta_7 = \beta_8 = 0$), and MLWC 2 (no constraints).

The implications of this table are the following:

1. When using OLS, consumer prices appear to cause wholesale prices in mean, but when ARCH is introduced, this causation becomes rather weak.
2. There is no evidence of squared consumer prices causing variance in wholesale prices, since α_3 is not significant.
3. ARCH effects are present, and introducing ARCH can change parameter values by important amounts, particularly β_7 and β_8.

An F test comparing OLS 1 and OLS 2, with (3,398) degrees of freedom, appears to be significant at the 99% confidence level, suggesting that consumer prices cause wholesale prices in mean, when ARCH effects are ignored. The distribution of the test statistic, however, is not F when the ARCH is ignored.

The likelihood ratio statistic when comparing MLW 1 and MLWC 2 is 3.8, whereas the chi-squared with three degrees of freedom has to be 7.8 for a 95% confidence; thus there is no evidence of causation in mean or variance of wholesale by consumer prices. Similarly comparing MLW 1 to MLW 2 and MLWC 1 to MLWC 2 gives τ values of 3.8 and 3.8, respectively, which are clearly less than the 5.99 value required for 95% confi-

Table 1.2
Wholesale prices

Variable (standard error)	OLS 1	OLS 2	MLW 1	MLW 2	MLWC 1	MLWC 2
Regression equation constant						
W_{t-1}	0.08 (0.045)	0.047 (0.046)	0.042 (0.018)	0.02 (0.021)	0.039 (0.019)	0.02 (0.021)
	0.35 (0.047)	0.36 (0.051)	0.40 (0.046)	0.38 (0.049)	0.41 (0.049)	0.38 (0.049)
W_{t-2}	0.25 (0.048)	0.17 (0.051)	0.18 (0.043)	0.10 (0.048)	0.17 (0.049)	0.10 (0.048)
W_{t-3}	0.23 (0.047)	0.22 (0.050)	0.21 (0.045)	0.20 (0.049)	0.21 (0.049)	0.20 (0.049)
W_{t-7}	-0.08 (0.043)	-0.09 (0.044)	0.07 (0.046)	0.045 (0.049)	0.07 (0.054)	0.045 (0.049)
W_{t-12}	0.28 (0.047)	0.27 (0.047)	0.10 (0.041)	0.06 (0.045)	0.09 (0.043)	0.06 (0.045)
W_{t-13}	-0.17 (0.046)	-0.21 (0.047)	-0.10 (0.039)	-0.09 (0.042)	-0.09 (0.042)	-0.09 (0.042)
C_{t-2}	—	0.50 (0.113)	—	0.17 (0.076)	—	0.17 (0.076)
C_{t-3}	—	-0.26 (0.116)	—	0.05 (0.081)	—	0.05 (0.081)
Variance equation constant	—	—	0.04 (0.0063)	0.04 (0.0066)	0.04 (0.006)	0.04 (0.0072)
$\{ew_{t-j}^2\}$	—	—	0.002 (0.0012)	0.003 (0.0013)	0.002 (0.0013)	0.0036 (0.0016)
$\{mw_{t-j}^2\}$	—	—	0.007 (0.0010)	0.006 (0.0010)	0.007 (0.0011)	0.006 (0.0021)
$\{c_{t-j}^2\}$	—	—	—	—	0.00023 (0.0009)	0.00059 (0.0011)
Sum of squared residuals	232.42	221.14	—	—	—	—
Likelihood values	—	—	137.0	138.8	137.0	138.9

dence with two degrees of freedom. Thus the ARCH models had no clear evidence of causation from consumer to wholesale prices, unlike the OLS results.

1.6 Conclusion

The variances of the variables considered appear to be predictable, as are the means, from bivariate information sets. Ignoring this can give misleading conclusions about the form of the conditional means, in particular conclusions about causality.

The results presented are naturally somewhat tentative because the computer programs could not deal with general specifications, the bivariate system could not be jointly estimated, and only bivariate, linear, constant parameter models were utilized. However, modeling the time-series properties of variances is seen to be practical and potentially important. This is a modeling situation where economic theory is unlikely to be helpful with the specification, and so pure time-series techniques are particularly relevant.

References

Berndt, E., B. Hall, R. Hall, and J. Hausman, 1974. Estimation and inference in nonlinear structural models. *Annals of Economic and Social Measurement* 4 (October): 653–665.

Box, G. E. P., and G. Jenkins, 1970. *Time Series, Forecasting and Control*. Holden Day, San Francisco.

Crowder, M. J., 1976. Maximum likelihood estimation for dependent observations. *Journal of the Royal Statistical Society* B 38:45–53.

Engle, R. F., 1978. Testing price equations for stability across spectral frequency bands. *Econometrica*, 46, pp. 869–881.

Engle, R. F., 1982. Autoregressive conditional heteroscedasticity with estimates of the variance of United Kingdom inflation. *Econometrica* 50:987–1008.

Engle, Robert F., C. W. J. Granger, and Dennis Kraft, 1982. Combining competing forecasts of inflation using a bivariate ARCH model. *Journal of Economic Dynamics and Control*, forthcoming.

Engle, Robert F., and Dennis F. Kraft, 1983. Multiperiod forecast error variances of inflation estimated from ARCH Models. *Applied Time Series Analysis of Economic Data*, A. Zellner, ed., U.S. Department of Commerce, Bureau of the Census. Government Printing Office, Washington, D.C., pp. 293–302.

Gordon, Robert J., 1975. The impact of aggregate demand on prices. *Brookings Papers on Economic Activity*. The Brookings Institution, Washington, D.C., pp. 613–662.

Granger, C. W. J., 1980. Testing for causality: a personal viewpoint. *Journal of Economic Dynamics and Control* 2(4):329–352.

Granger, C. W. J., and P. Newbold, 1977. *Forecasting Economic Time Series.* Academic Press, New York.

Guthrie, Robert S., 1981. The relationship between wholesale and consumer prices. *Southern Economic Journal* 47 (April): 1046–1055.

Jenkins, G., 1979. *Modelling and Forecasting Time Series.* GJP Publications, Jersey, U.K.

Pagan, A. R., A. D. Hall, and P. K. Trivedi, 1981. Assessing the variability of inflation. Working Paper 049. Australia National University.

Popkin, Joel, 1974. Consumer and wholesale prices in a model of price behavior by stage of processing. *Review of Economics and Statistics* 56:486–501.

2 Recursive Stability Analysis: The Demand for Money during the German Hyperinflation

Jean-Marie Dufour

2.1 Introduction

An important way of assessing the reliability of an econometric model is to check whether it is stable over time. Frequently one does not have a precise idea or does not wish to make a specific hypothesis on the possible timing or the type of instability that may be involved. In such situations the investigator does not usually wish to use a test designed against a very precise alternative (e.g., Chow 1960, Quandt 1960, Farley and Hinich 1970, Cooley and Prescott 1976, Singh et al. 1976, Dufour 1982b) but would prefer an exploratory method.

By an exploratory method, we mean a procedure aimed at being sensitive to a wide variety of instability patterns and capable of yielding information on the type and timing of structural change. Such information can then be used either as a basis for splitting the sample into subperiods warranting separate estimation or as an input in the search of possible misspecifications (omitted variables, incorrect functional form, etc.). This is akin to the "analysis of residuals" in regression (Anscombe 1961, Anscombe and Tukey 1963, Belsley, Kuh, and Welsch 1980), "diagnostic checking" in time-series analysis (Box and Jenkins 1969, ch. 5), and in general, data analysis (Tukey 1962, 1977). The exploratory method should be viewed as part of the *routine* validation of a model estimated from ordered data. On the other hand, since the alternative is purposely left vague, one can usually devise more powerful tests against specific alternatives.

An intuitively attractive procedure of this type consists of estimating the model recursively and examining a number of resulting statistics. This approach was first formalized by Brown, Durbin, and Evans (1975); a systematization as well as a number of extensions were provided by Dufour (1979, 1982a). The main purpose of this chapter is to present a detailed illustration of recursive stability analysis. It additionally provides some evidence on the stability of the demand for money during the German hyperinflation.

One of the interesting features of recursive stability analysis, emphasized in Dufour (1982a), is that it allows the investigator to get a large number of different diagnostics at low cost. Though we will not compute here all the statistics considered in Dufour (1982a), we will emphasize the following items: (1) how the one- and several-steps-ahead recursive residuals can be cross-checked to analyze the timing of structural change, (2) how forward and backward recursive residuals can be compared and graphed together, (3) how the recursive estimates obtained by forward and backward estimation can be cross-checked with one another and with the recursive residuals, (4) how a number of simple and intuitive tests, besides the Cusum tests originally proposed by Brown et al. (1975), can be used to assess the statistical significance of the descriptive evidence. Further we will introduce a simple scaling of the recursive residuals, apparently not discussed previously, and will find that this operation enhances considerably the basic features of the recursive residuals.

The demand for money is certainly an econometric relationship for which the issue of stability over time has a considerable incidence on the conception of macroeconomic policy, and for this reason the problem has been widely disputed.[1] Furthermore situations of hyperinflation, because of the great variance in the data, constitute an especially propitious ground for testing the idea of a stable demand for money and for exploring alternative specifications. Here, we study the stability of two specifications of the demand for money during the German hyperinflation. The latter were previously considered by Frenkel (1977). They are relatively simple and will allow us to examine in detail several aspects of the procedures we wish to illustrate.

In section 2.2 we present the money demand equations that will be analyzed. In section 2.3 we describe the methodology used and define the main statistics considered. In section 2.4 we present the empirical results. Finally, in section 2.5 we summarize the findings and make some concluding remarks.

2.2 Model

In a well-known article on the demand for money during the German hyperinflation, Frenkel (1977) suggests using the forward premium on foreign exchange as a direct measure of expected inflation.[2] This choice is justified by the interest parity condition, evidence on the efficiency of foreign exchange markets during the period, and the argument that currency depreciation was overwhelmingly due to domestic inflation.[3] Frenkel then considers two functional forms of the demand for money. The first one is semilogarithmic:

$$\log\left(\frac{M_t}{P_t}\right) = \gamma - \eta\pi_t^* + u_t, \tag{2.1}$$

where M_t denotes the nominal money stock (at time t), P_t is the price level, π_t^* is the measure of anticipated rate of inflation and u_t is a random disturbance. The second form is double logarithmic:

$$\log\left(\frac{M_t}{P_t}\right) = \gamma' - \eta'\log(\pi_t^*) + v_t, \tag{2.2}$$

where v_t is a random disturbance. The data used are monthly (February 1921 to August 1923).[4] To be more precise, M_t is an index of the quantity of authorized bank notes in circulation and P_t is the cost of living index (current).[5] Expected inflation is measured by

$$\pi_t^* = 100\log\left(\frac{F_t}{S_t}\right) + 1, \tag{2.3}$$

where F_t and S_t are the forward and spot exchange rates between the German mark and the pound sterling (RM/£).[6]

Frenkel estimated the two forms (2.1) and (2.2) with a correction for autocorrelation (Cochrane-Orcutt algorithm). The results are (for the period February 1921 to August 1923)[7]

$$\log\left(\frac{M_t}{P_t}\right) = \underset{(0.560)}{4.980} - \underset{(0.270)}{1.651}\left(\frac{\pi_t^*}{100}\right), \quad \underset{(.046)}{\hat{\rho} = .967,} \tag{2.4}$$

$$SS = 0.334, \quad SE = 0.109, \quad DW = 1.66, \quad R^2 = .970,$$

$$\tilde{R}^2 = .563;$$

$$\log\left(\frac{M_t}{P_t}\right) = \underset{(0.057)}{6.197} - \underset{(0.028)}{0.358}\log(\pi_t^*), \quad \underset{(0.158)}{\hat{\rho} = 0.501,} \tag{2.5}$$

$$SS = 0.501, \quad SE = 0.134, \quad DW = 1.99, \quad R^2 = .955,$$

$$\tilde{R}^2 = .344.$$

We also reestimated both these equations using a fine grid search (Hildreth-Lu technique, by steps of 0.001).[8] For the double-logarithmic model we obtained essentially the same equation; for the semilogarithmic model we obtained

$$\log\left(\frac{M_t}{P_t}\right) = 3.248 - 1.622\left(\frac{\pi_t^*}{100}\right), \quad \hat{\rho} = 0.986, \tag{2.6}$$
$$\phantom{\log\left(\frac{M_t}{P_t}\right) = }(1.442)\ \ (0.267) \phantom{\left(\frac{\pi_t^*}{100}\right),\ \ } (0.030)$$

$$SS = 0.332, \quad SE = 0.109, \quad DW = 1.69, \quad R^2 = .970,$$
$$\tilde{R}^2 = .568.$$

We see that the estimate of ρ is very close to 1 (even more than originally obtained by Frenkel). This strongly suggests that the model should be in first difference form:[9]

$$\Delta\log\left(\frac{M_t}{P_t}\right) = \alpha - \eta\left(\frac{\Delta\pi_t^*}{100}\right) + \varepsilon_t. \tag{2.7}$$

When the latter model is estimated, one gets[10]

$$\Delta\log\left(\frac{M_t}{P_t}\right) = -0.0394 - 1.608\left(\frac{\Delta\pi_t^*}{100}\right) \tag{2.8}$$
$$\phantom{\Delta\log\left(\frac{M_t}{P_t}\right) = }(0.0202)\ \ (0.267)$$

$$SS = 0.333, \quad SE = 0.109, \quad DW = 1.70, \quad R^2 = .564.$$

In order to discriminate between the two functional forms (2.1) and (2.2), Frenkel used the Box-Cox procedure of considering the regression

$$\log\left(\frac{M_t}{P_t}\right) = \beta_0 + \beta_1 \frac{\pi_t^{*\lambda} - 1}{\lambda} + u_t. \tag{2.9}$$

When $\lambda = 1$, this relationship reduces to the semilogarithmic functional form; when $\lambda = 0$, it gives the double-logarithmic functional form. Equation (2.9) was estimated by the method of maximum likelihood (along with an autocorrelation coefficient ρ for u_t'; the likelihood ratio test for $\lambda = 1$ indicated that the semilogarithmic is the appropriate functional form. Nevertheless, as Frenkel notes, the estimated value of ρ is considerably lower for the double-logarithmic form than for the semilogarithmic one, so that an appreciably larger fraction of the fit of the first functional form is "attributed to the economic variables rather than to the autocorrelation coefficient." For this reason the author reports both sets of results. Frenkel also indicates that he split the sample into two phases and allowed different coefficients for the last nine months of the period. Using this Chow-type test, he did not find evidence of instability for both functional forms. As Frenkel himself points out, given the large variation in the data and the fact that the two hypotheses of constant elasticity and constant semielasticity are mutually inconsistent, this is somewhat surprising.

Let us recall that the German "hyperinflation" can be roughly dated (Cagan 1956, p. 26) as covering the period August 1922 to November 1923. Cagan, however, excluded from his sample the last four months of the hyperinflation (August to November 1923) because they did not "fit the regressions." Yet, if we look at the series of inflation rates over the period February 1921 to August 1923 (see appendix 2A), we see that deflation was actually taking place during the first four months (February to May 1921). The following fourteen months (June 1921 to July 1922) were a period of "moderate hyperinflation (with an average of 10 percent per month), and the period August 1922 to August 1923 corresponds to the "severe hyperinflation" (with an average of 104 percent per month).

As a test against parameter instability, the Chow test is aimed at detecting a very specific type of instability—a one-step shift at a given known time. Its power may indeed be very poor against other types of instability. We will thus reexamine the stability of the two functional forms described earlier using an "exploratory" methodology designed to be sensitive to a wider set of instability patterns. We now proceed to describe the basic principles of the methodology used.

2.3 Methodology

In this section we will sketch the main features of recursive stability analysis and define the main statistics used. For a detailed description and more complete references, the reader is referred to Dufour (1982a).

Let us consider the following standard regression model:

$$y_t = \mathbf{x}_t' \boldsymbol{\beta} + u_t, \quad t = 1, \ldots, T, \tag{2.10}$$

where y_t is an observation on the dependent variable, $\mathbf{x}_t$ is a $K \times 1$ column vector of nonstochastic regressors, $\boldsymbol{\beta}$ is a $K \times 1$ vector of regression coefficients, u_t is a disturbance term that follows a normal distribution with mean zero and variance σ^2. Assume also that the disturbances $u_1, \ldots, u_T$ are independent.

We wish to investigate the constancy of the regression coefficient $\boldsymbol{\beta}$ over different observations. In other words, we consider the alternative model

$$y_t = \mathbf{x}_t' \boldsymbol{\beta}_t + u_t, \quad t = 1, \ldots, T, \tag{2.11}$$

and wish to test the null hypothesis $H_0 : \boldsymbol{\beta}_1 = \cdots = \boldsymbol{\beta}_T \equiv \boldsymbol{\beta}$.

When the data have a natural order (e.g., time), a simple way to investigate the stability of the regression coefficients is to estimate the model recursively. Using the first K observations in the sample to get an initial estimate of $\boldsymbol{\beta}$, we gradually enlarge the sample, adding one observation at a time, and reestimate $\boldsymbol{\beta}$ at each step. We get in this way the sequence of estimates[11]

$$\mathbf{b}_r = (X_r'X_r)^{-1}X_r'\mathbf{Y}_r, \quad r = K, \dots, T, \tag{2.12}$$

where

$$X_r' = [\mathbf{x}_1, \dots, \mathbf{x}_r], \quad \mathbf{Y}_r = (y_1, \dots, y_r)'.$$

A computationally efficient algorithm allows us to compute this sequence (see Brown et al. 1975, p. 152). It is intuitively clear that the examination of the sequence of estimates can provide information on possible instabilities of the regression coefficients. We see also that two different permutations of the data usually yield different sequences of estimates. However, when the data are ordered (e.g., by time), it appears that the most easily interpretable results will be obtained by putting the data either in their original time order or in the reverse order. In the first case one gets "forward recursive estimates," and in the second case, "backward recursive estimates." In our analysis we will examine and compare the behaviors of these sequences of estimates, taking note especially of trends and discontinuities.

Recursive estimates constitute a descriptive device assessing the influence of different observations in a sequential updating process. However, elements of a sequence of recursive estimates are strongly correlated even under the null hypothesis of stability, and the analysis of their behavior remains delicate from a statistical point of view.[12] Consequently it is important to have statistics that are easier to interpret. For this purpose we look at the associated sequences of prediction errors. Namely we consider the sequences of prediction errors

$$v_{kr} = y_r - \mathbf{x}_r'\mathbf{b}_{r-k}, \quad r = K + k, \dots, T, \tag{2.13}$$

where $1 \le k \le T - 1$. Since these have different variances, it is convenient to standardize them and compute

$$w_{kr} = \frac{v_{kr}}{d_{kr}}, \quad r = K + k, \dots, T, \tag{2.14}$$

where $d_{kr} = [1 + \mathbf{x}_r'(X_{r-k}'X_{r-k})^{-1}\mathbf{x}_r]^{1/2}$. We call the sequence $w_{kr}, r = K + k,$

..., T, "k-steps ahead recursive residuals"—or simply "k-step recursive residuals." Depending on whether the sample is in forward or backward order, we get "forward" or "backward recursive residuals." It is easy to verify that under the null hypothesis of stability,

$$E(w_{kr}) = 0, \quad E(w_{kr}^2) = \sigma^2.$$

Further, when $k = 1$, one has

$$E(w_{1r}w_{1s}) = 0, \quad r \neq s,$$

so that the sequence w_{1r}, $r = K + 1, \ldots, T$, is a normal white noise. For $k \geq 2$, the sequence w_{kr}, $r = K + k, \ldots, T$, is dependent but only up to lag $k - 1$ (see Dufour 1982a, pp. 41–44).

It is not difficult to determine how relatively simple forms of structural change will affect the behavior of prediction errors (or recursive residuals). For example, a sudden shift in coefficients at some point t_0 in the sample will, under wide circumstances, lead to an increase in the size of prediction errors and/or a tendency either to overpredict or underpredict the dependent variable (for $t \geq t_0$), a systematic drift in one or several coefficients will often lead to a systematic tendency to over- or underpredict, and so on. Thus we will first use the sequences of standardized prediction errors to perform an exploratory analysis and search for patterns indicative of possible structural shifts. For this purpose it is especially useful to look at several "clues." The simple statistical properties of the one-step recursive residuals (forward or backward) designate them as the basic instrument of analysis for that search. However, we will find instructive to compare these with the k-step recursive residuals ($k \geq 2$): since the latter are forecasts using estimates from a sample further away in time, they may exhibit better-defined and more recognizable patterns; they can also help identify possible breakpoints. Similarly we will find of interest to compare forward and backward recursive residuals; for example, the backward residuals can be especially revealing in the early part of the period (for, initially, forward recursive residuals are not even defined), whereas the forward recursive residuals will usually have more power near the end of the sample.

When interpreting and comparing various sets of residuals, it is always useful to recall that all recursive residuals have the same standard error σ (under the null hypothesis). Interpretation will generally be easier if we scale the residuals with an estimate of σ. As the most natural estimate is the one obtained from the full sample (i.e., the standard error of the regression), we will compute

$$\tilde{w}_{kr} = \frac{w_{kr}}{\hat{\sigma}}, \quad r = K + k, \ldots, T, \tag{2.15}$$

where

$$\hat{\sigma}^2 = \frac{(\mathbf{Y}_T - X_T \mathbf{b}_T)'(\mathbf{Y}_T - X_T \mathbf{b}_T)}{(T - K)}.$$

This procedure can also help display the recursive residuals, for in most practical situations, it will bring all residuals in a convenient scale—not too close to zero and well inside the interval $(-10, -10)$.[13]

Though the first purpose of the instruments we defined is exploratory, it is important to assess the statistical significance of what is observed. Because one-step recursive residuals (forward and backward) have such simple statistical properties, we will mainly use these for this assessment. Roughly speaking, we expect that two main types of effects will result from structural shifts: tendencies either to over- or underpredict the dependent variable and discontinuities in the size of the prediction errors. Consequently we will compute a number of simple statistics aimed at being sensitive to these characteristics. Statistics especially sensitive to the sign of prediction errors include the Cusum test originally suggested by Brown et al. (1975), a Student t test and the corresponding Wilcoxon signed-rank test, runs tests based on the number of runs and the length of longest run, and serial dependence tests. Statistics sensitive to discontinuities in the size of prediction errors include the Cusum of squares test suggested by Brown et al. (1975) and heteroscedasticity tests. We will now define these succinctly.

If we let $w_t \equiv w_{1t}, t = K + 1, \ldots, T$, the Cusum test is based on considering the cumulative sums

$$W_r = \frac{1}{\hat{\sigma}} \sum_{j=K+1}^{r} w_j, \quad r = K + 1, \ldots, T, \tag{2.16}$$

where $\hat{\sigma}^2 = S_T/(T - K)$ and $S_T = \sum_{t=K+1}^{T} w_t^2$. The null hypothesis H_0 is rejected at level α if $C \equiv \max_{K+1 \leq r \leq T} |\tilde{W}_r| \geq c_\alpha$, where

$$\tilde{W}_r = \frac{W_r}{\{\sqrt{T - K} + 2[(r - K)/\sqrt{T - K}]\}} \tag{2.17}$$

and c_α depends on the level of the test ($c_{0.01} = 1.143, c_{0.05} = 0.948, c_{0.10} = 0.850$). In other words, H_0 is rejected if the graph of W_r crosses either one of two straight lines determined by the level of the test. The t test is based on the standard Student's t statistic to test the hypothesis that the recursive residuals have zero mean against a systematic tendency to over- or under-predict. It is based on the statistic

$$\tilde{t} = \frac{\sqrt{T - K}\,\bar{w}}{s_w}, \tag{2.18}$$

where

$$\bar{w} = \sum_{t=K+1}^{T} \frac{w_t}{T - K}, \quad s_w^2 = \sum_{t=K+1}^{T} \frac{(w_t - \bar{w})^2}{T - K - 1}; \tag{2.19}$$

under the null hypothesis $\tilde{t}$ follows a Student's t distribution with $T - K - 1$ degrees of freedom. The Wilcoxon signed-rank test is based on the statistic

$$S = \sum_{t=K+1}^{T} u(w_t) R_t^+, \tag{2.20}$$

where

$$u(z) = 1, \quad \text{if } z \geq 0,$$
$$\quad\quad = 0, \quad \text{if } z < 0, \tag{2.21}$$

$$R_t^+ = \sum_{i=K+1}^{T} u(|w_t| - |w_i|).$$

We may view it as a robust alternative to the t test; its distribution (for $T \leq 50$) has been extensively tabulated by Wilcoxon et al. (1973, pp. 171–259). For $T > 50$, one can use the standardized form $S' = [S - E(S)]/\sigma(S)$, where $E(S) = n(n + 1)/4$, $\sigma(S) = [n(n + 1)(2n + 1)/24]^{1/2}$, and $n = T - K$. Under H_0, S' is approximately $N(0, 1)$.

An intuitively attractive way of looking at the sequence of the recursive residuals consists of observing runs of overpredictions (or underpredictions), as defined by the sequence $u(w_t)$, $t = K + 1, \ldots, T$. Two simple tests are then obtained by considering the number of runs R in this sequence or by observing the length of the longest run in the sequence. The distribution of the number of runs R is obtained by noting that $R - 1$ follows a binomial distribution $Bi(T - K - 1, \frac{1}{2})$; a small number of runs suggests that the model has tendency to overpredict or underpredict. Besides, an especially long run of negative or positive errors of prediction suggests the presence of a shift. The probability of getting at least one run of a given length or greater may be computed from formulas (135) to (138) in Dufour (1982a).

In a large number of cases structural change leads to situations where the means of the cross products $Z_{kt} \equiv w_t w_{t+k}$, $t = K + 1, \ldots, T - k$ (where $1 \leq k \leq T - K - 1$) differ from zero (see Dufour 1982a, pp. 52–55). This suggests testing whether Z_{kt} has mean zero: we can do this by using "serial dependence tests" *not corrected for the mean* (for such tests are more accurately viewed in this case as location tests rather than serial dependence tests). We will consider two types of statistics for doing this: the modified von Neumann ratio

$$VR = \frac{(n - 1)^{-1} \sum_{t=K+1}^{T-1} (w_{t+1} - w_t)^2}{n^{-1} \sum_{t=K+1}^{T} w_t^2}, \tag{2.22}$$

where $n = T - K$, and rank Wilcoxon-type serial dependence tests based on statistics of the form

$$S_k = \sum_{t=K+1}^{T-k} u(Z_{kt}) R_{kt}^+, \quad k = 1, 2, \ldots, \tag{2.23}$$

where $R_{kt}^+ = \sum_{i=K+1}^{T-k} u(|Z_{kt}| - |Z_{ki}|)$. VR provides an exact parametric test of the null hypothesis $E(w_t w_{t+1}) = 0$, $t = K + 1, \ldots, T - 1$; for a table, see Theil (1971, pp. 728–729). Each statistic S_k is distributed like the Wilcoxon signed-rank statistic to test the zero median hypothesis; it gives an exact test of the null hypothesis $E(w_t w_{t+k}) = 0$, $t = K + 1, \ldots, T - k$, where $k \geq 1$ (see Dufour 1981). Further, under H_0, $E(S_k) = n_k(n_k + 1)/4$, and $\sigma(S_k) = [n_k(n_k + 1)(2n_k + 1)/24]^{1/2}$, where $n_k = T - K - k$.

The Cusum of squares test is based on considering the statistic

$$s_r = \frac{\sum_{j=K+1}^{r} w_j^2}{\sum_{j=K+1}^{T} w_j^2}, \quad r = K + 1, \ldots, T. \tag{2.24}$$

The null hypothesis is rejected at level α if

$$S \equiv \max_{1 \leq j \leq T-K-1} \left| s_{K+j} - \frac{j}{T - K} \right| \geq d_\alpha, \tag{2.25}$$

where d_α is obtained by entering table 1 of Durbin (1969) at $\alpha/2$ and $n = (1/2)(T - K) - 1$ (if $T - K$ is even), or by interpolating linearly between

$n = (1/2)(T - K) - (3/2)$ and $n = (1/2)(T - K) - (1/2)$ (if $T - K$ is odd). Finally, when an investigator has a more precise idea of a possible breaking point, a simpler test consists of dividing correspondingly the residuals in two subsets I_1 and I_2, with m_1 and m_2 elements, and of computing a test statistic for heteroscedasticity:

$$\bar{R} = \left(\frac{m_1}{m_2}\right)\left(\frac{\sum_{t \in I_2} w_t^2}{\sum_{t \in I_1} w_t^2}\right). \tag{2.26}$$

Under H_0, $\bar{R}$ follows an F distribution with (m_2, m_1) degrees of freedom; in a two-sided test, H_0 is rejected at level α if $\bar{R} \geq F_{\alpha/2}$ or $\bar{R} \leq F_{1-(\alpha/2)}$, where $P[F(m_2, m_1) \geq F_\alpha] = \alpha$.

Whenever possible we will report the marginal significance level (p value) of each statistic. Of course a test significant at a very low level provides stronger evidence against the null hypothesis.

2.4   Recursive Stability Analysis of Money Demand

We will now apply recursive stability analysis to study the stability over time of the semilog and the double-log models described in section 2.2. Since the correction for autocorrelation used by Frenkel may be an ad hoc solution to an instability problem, we will first study the stability of those two models without such a correction (estimation by ordinary least squares); then we will "correct" the models by transforming them, and we will reexamine their stability. In total, we will thus describe the results of four different recursive stability analyses.

For each model considered we will report both the forward and the backward recursive estimates of each coefficient as well as the k-step recursive residuals for $k = 1, 2, 3, 4,$ and 8. Recursive estimates for each coefficient and recursive residuals for $k = 1$ and 4, will also be plotted. To facilitate comparison between forward and backward series, we will print and plot the backward estimates and the backward residuals in forward order. Since the backward series are based on "future" observations, they are best interpreted if they are read in reverse order from the one in which they are printed or graphed: new observations are added as we move either up (in tables) or toward the left (in graphs).[14]

We give the test statistics for all the models in table 2.1.[15] To compute these, we used both forward and backward one-step recursive residuals. For the heteroscedasticity tests we selected August 1922 as point of division

Table 2.1
Test statistics based on one-step ahead recursive residuals

Model	Semilog (OLS)		Double-log (OLS)		Semilog (differenced)		Double-log ($\hat{\rho} = 0.501$)	
Direction of recursions	Forward	Backward	Forward	Backward	Forward	Backward	Forward	Backward
Number of residuals	29	29	29	29	28	28	28	28
Global location tests								
Cusum (C)	0.3260 (≥ 0.10)	1.339 (≤ 0.01)	1.275 (≤ 0.01)	0.631 (≥ 0.10)	0.3795 (≥ 0.10)	0.8494 (≥ 0.10)	1.003 (0.01, 0.05)	0.6612 (≥ 0.10)
τ	0.9772 (0.3368)	5.927 (2×10^{-6})	−3.326 (0.0025)	0.241 (0.8113)	−0.1938 (0.8478)	0.4749 (0.6387)	−2.721 (0.0113)	1.7865 (0.0853)
Wilcoxon[a]	209 (−0.184) (0.8648)	402 (3.989) (0.00007)	78 (−3.016) (0.0018)	255 (0.811) (0.4294)	187 (−0.364) (0.7282)	244 (0.934) (0.3620)	90 (−2.573) (0.0088)	287 (1.913) (0.0564)
Runs tests[b]								
Number of runs	7 (0.0019)	3 (15×10^{-7})	8 (0.0063)	10 (0.0436)	15 (0.6494)	11 (0.1239)	12 (0.2210)	12 (0.2210)
Longest run	14 (0.0010)	21 (5×10^{-6})	16 (0.00023)	11 (0.0096)	4 (0.8815)	8 (0.0844)	10 (0.0195)	7 (0.1715)
Serial dependence tests								
Von Neumann (modified)	1.476 (≥ 0.10)	0.0745 (0.002)	0.7174 (≤ 0.002)	0.7437 (≤ 0.002)	2.203 (≥ 0.10)	1.664 (≥ 0.10)	1.661 (≥ 0.10)	1.757 (≥ 0.10)
Wilcoxon:[a] $k = 1$	312 (2.482) (0.0118)	398 (4.444) (9×10^{-6})	325 (2.778) (0.0044)	335 (3.006) (0.0019)	176 (−0.312) (0.7676)	232 (0.103) (0.3126)	237 (1.153) (0.2584)	226 (0.890) (0.3864)
$k = 2$	193 (0.096) (0.9340)	361 (4.132) (0.00002)	268 (1.898) (0.0584)	282 (2.234) (0.0246)	194 (0.470) (0.6528)	186 (0.267) (0.8028)	207 (0.800) (0.4374)	222 (1.118) (0.2472)
$k = 3$	182 (0.165) (0.8810)	328 (3.873) (0.0001)	271 (2.426) (0.0140)	234 (1.486) (0.1428)	175 (0.336) (0.7510)	205 (1.144) (0.2634)	219 (1.520) (0.1336)	234 (1.924) (0.0550)
$k = 4$	215 (1.413) (0.1644)	294 (3.538) (0.0002)	244 (2.193) (0.0274)	175 (0.336) (0.7510)	132 (−0.514) (0.6236)	151 (0.029) (0.9888)	183 (0.943) (0.3596)	165 (0.429) (0.6480)

Table 2.1 (continued)

Model	Semilog (OLS)		Double-log (OLS)		Semilog (differenced)		Double-log ($\hat{\rho} = 0.501$)	
Direction of recursions	Forward	Backward	Forward	Backward	Forward	Backward	Forward	Backward
Number of residuals	29	29	29	29	28	28	28	28
Cusum of squares (S)	0.5074	0.2952	0.308	0.205	0.4329	0.4628	0.2853	0.2370
	(≤ 0.01)	(0.05, 0.10)	(0.01, 0.05)	(≥ 0.20)	(≤ 0.01)	(≤ 0.01)	(0.05, 0.10)	(0.10, 0.20)
Heteroscedasticity tests	24.827	0.150	1.257	1.098	6.460	7.901	2.742	2.374
	(8×10^{-8})	(0.0027)	(0.6561)	(0.8305)	(0.0010)	(0.0002)	(0.0649)	(0.1063)
Local t tests								
Beginning to July 1922	-4.246	29.209	-4.322	1.071	-2.195	0.998	-4.529	3.529
	(0.0006)	(3.8×10^{-12})	(0.0005)	(0.2983)	(0.0443)	(0.3323)	(0.0004)	(0.0026)
August 1922 to end	1.796	-0.011	-1.092	-0.907	0.599	0.081	-0.989	0.009
	(0.0958)	(0.9914)	(0.2947)	(0.3838)	(0.5595)	(0.9369)	(0.3407)	(0.9930)

Note: All the tests, except the runs tests, are two-sided test. Marginal significance levels (p values) are given in parenthesis under the test statistics; an interval of p values, such as (0.01, 0.05), indicates that the true p value is inside the interval (between 0.01 and 0.05).
[a] Standardized values of the Wilcoxon statistics are reported in parenthesis beside each statistic. Most p values are computed from the non-standardized Wilcoxon statistics using the Wilcoxon set al. (1973) table. In a few cases where the table was incomplete the normal approximation was used.
[b] There are one-sided tests: for example, $P[R \leq 7] = 0.0019$ and $P[L \geq 14] = 0.00104$, where R = number of runs (of $+$'s or $-$'s) and L = length of the longest run.

between the two subperiods: this is the month when according to Cagan (1956, p. 26), "hyperinflation" begins. Further we will compute t statistics to test whether the residuals have zero mean in each of these two subperiods (i.e., in the period ending in July 1922 and the one starting in August 1922). Wherever possible we will report the p values of the test statistics. This will allow the reader to adopt his own level of significance.[16] In discussing the results, we will, however, use the traditional 5 percent level as the basic benchmark for judging the statistical significance of the results.

   If we estimate the semilog and double-log models by ordinary least squares (February 1921 to August 1923), we get the following results:

$$\log\left(\frac{M_t}{P_t}\right) = 6.224 - 4.319\left(\frac{\pi_t^*}{100}\right), \qquad (2.27)$$
$$\phantom{\log\left(\frac{M_t}{P_t}\right) = }(0.0784)\,(0.572)$$

$$SS = 3.915, \quad SE = 0.367, \quad DW = 0.399, \quad R^2 = .662;$$

$$\log\left(\frac{M_t}{P_t}\right) = 6.186 - 0.362\log(\pi_t^*), \qquad (2.28)$$
$$\phantom{\log\left(\frac{M_t}{P_t}\right) = }(0.0324)\,(0.0179)$$

$$SS = 0.7690, \quad SE = 0.163, \quad DW = 0.909, \quad R^2 = .934.$$

Note that the fit produced by the double-log model is much better than the one obtained with the semilog model.

   Recursive estimates for the semilog model (estimated by ordinary least squares) are listed in table 2.2A and plotted in figure 2.1.[17] The most striking features are the discontinuity in the forward estimates of γ and $-\eta$ between August and October 1922 and the trend from April 1921 to July 1922. Similarly the backward estimates show two opposite trends separated by November 1922. The recursive residuals for the same model are listed in tables 2.3A and 2.3C (respectively unscaled and scaled) and plotted in figure 2.2 (for $k = 1, 4$). From the forward one-step recursive residuals we identify easily two periods with very different patterns: April 1921 to July 1922 and August 1922 to August 1923. They differ in two ways. First, the average size of the residuals is much greater in the second period than in the first one. This contrast is especially visible if we look at the scaled residuals: eight (among thirteen) residuals in the second period are nearly twice as large in absolute value as the largest residual in the first period; the most "outlying" residual is July 1923. Second, there is a tendency to overpredict in the first period (indicated by negative residuals) and, to a

Table 2.2
Recursive estimates for models estimated by ordinary least squares

Month	Forward γ	Forward $-\eta$	Backward γ	Backward $-\eta$	Forward γ'	Forward $-\eta'$	Backward γ'	Backward $-\eta'$
A. Semilog model					**B. Double-log model**			
2102			6.2240	−4.3191			6.1859	−0.3616
2103	6.9674	−251.9231	6.2083	−4.2583	5.8068	−0.4134	6.2041	−0.3716
2104	6.5284	15.6349	6.1904	−4.1889	6.6208	0.0369	6.2277	−0.3847
2105	6.5246	17.7694	6.1694	−4.1087	6.6324	0.0435	6.2329	−0.3872
2106	6.5389	11.3813	6.1455	−4.0174	6.6187	0.0350	6.2349	−0.3881
2107	6.5679	0.2161	6.1188	−3.9170	6.5774	0.0077	6.2272	−0.3848
2108	6.5723	−3.3804	6.0917	−3.8162	6.5521	−0.0066	6.2147	−0.3799
2109	6.5750	−4.3393	6.0639	−3.7117	6.5458	−0.0110	6.2120	−0.3788
2110	6.5847	−7.5464	6.0297	−3.5846	6.5299	−0.0221	6.1942	−0.3718
2111	6.6078	−14.2100	5.9935	−3.4505	6.4996	−0.0451	6.1750	−0.3645
2112	6.6114	−15.8662	5.9576	−3.3184	6.4886	−0.0523	6.1548	−0.3569
2201	6.6200	−18.7707	5.9128	−3.1522	6.4722	−0.0638	6.1321	−0.3480
2202	6.6512	−27.1246	5.8641	−2.9719	6.4344	−0.0935	6.1044	−0.3374
2203	6.6928	−36.7723	5.8206	−2.8114	6.3917	−0.1307	6.0859	−0.3304
2204	6.7339	−46.3258	5.7767	−2.6508	6.3464	−0.1701	6.0677	−0.3237
2205	6.7662	53.5367	5.7347	−2.4973	6.3087	−0.2038	6.0671	−0.3235
2206	6.7826	−56.8788	5.6849	−2.3151	6.2828	−0.2289	6.0705	−0.3247
2207	6.7946	59.0329	5.6158	−2.0635	6.2493	−0.2659	6.0495	−0.3171
2208	6.6101	−31.1974	5.5491	−1.8226	6.2306	−0.2927	6.0591	−0.3205
2209	6.5497	−23.0120	5.4860	−1.6068	6.2085	−0.3279	5.9720	−0.2910
2210	6.4228	−9.6459	5.4586	−1.5182	6.2111	−0.3229	5.9517	−0.2845
2211	6.4265	−10.0882	5.4356	−1.4719	6.1982	−0.3468	5.9150	−0.2777
2212	6.4225	−10.8438	5.4588	−1.5256	6.1863	−0.3643	5.9400	−0.2837
2301	6.4014	−9.3381	5.4975	−1.6377	6.1870	−0.3628	6.0927	−0.3298

2302	6.3768	−8.0217	5.5072	−1.6550	6.1833	−0.3723	6.0881	−0.3291
2303	6.3581	−8.1751	5.5477	−1.6616	6.1760	−0.3798	6.0807	−0.3171
2304	6.3580	−8.1864	5.6685	−1.9847	6.1794	−0.3737	6.7566	−0.5188
2305	6.3574	−8.0442	5.6960	−2.0510	6.1833	−0.3659	6.9817	−0.5814
2306	6.3443	−7.3835	5.6930	−2.0440	6.1867	−0.3560	7.3365	−0.6779
2307	6.2283	−4.4680	4.8071	−0.0965	6.1866	−0.3574	4.9227	−0.0419
2308	6.2240	−4.3191			6.1859	−0.3616		

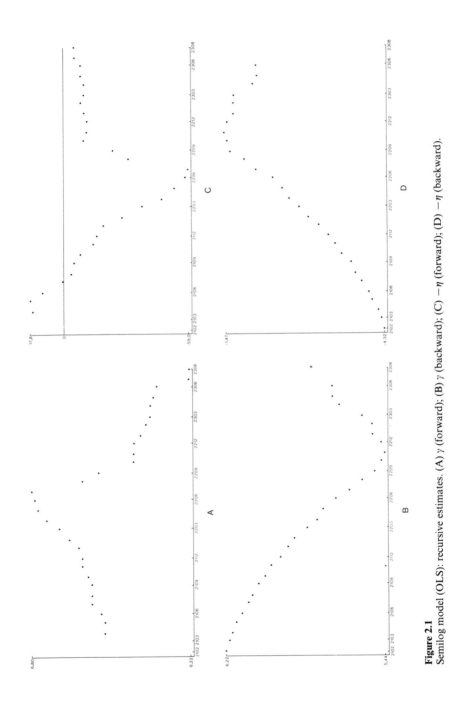

Figure 2.1
Semilog model (OLS): recursive estimates. (A) γ (forward); (B) γ (backward); (C) $-\eta$ (forward); (D) $-\eta$ (backward).

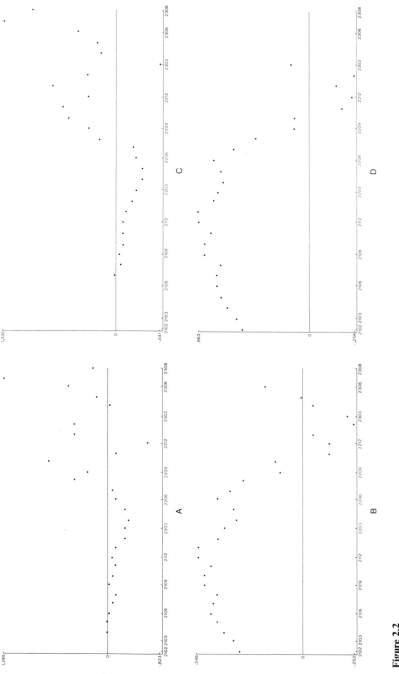

Figure 2.2
Semilog model (OLS): recursive residuals. (A) Forward one-step ahead; (B) backward one-step ahead; (C) forward four-steps ahead; (D) backward four-steps ahead.

lesser degree, a tendency to underpredict in the second period. Moreover we note that the k-step recursive residuals for $k \geq 2$ have basically the same characteristics. Statistically the contrast in the size of prediction errors is well pointed out by the Cusum of squares and heteroscedasticity tests (both significant at levels much lower than 0.01; see table 2.1). The tendency to overpredict is shown in a simple way by observing a run of fourteen consecutive negative one-step residuals from June 1921 to July 1922. The probability, under the null hypothesis, of obtaining at least one run of this length or greater is 0.001. Global location tests are not significant (at level 0.05), whereas the local t statistic for April 1921 to July 1922 has a very low p value: this again underscores the contrasting behavior of predictions between the two subperiods (overprediction followed by underprediction). We can note also some "serial dependence" at lag 1.

Turning now to backward recursive residuals, we note again two main features. First, we see a discontinuity of sign in October to November 1922 (for $k = 1, 2, 3, 4$): underprediction in the earlier period (positive residuals) and overprediction afterwards.[18] Second, the two subperiods identified earlier (April 1921 to July 1922, August 1922 to August 1923) differ again by the average size of the residuals. But the "large" residuals (for all k) are now concentrated in the first period. Statistically the backward one-step residuals deviate from what we expect under the null hypothesis even more strongly than the forward residuals. The tendency to underpredict the dependent variable in the earlier part of the sample is underscored by a run of twenty-one consecutive positive residuals from February 1921 to October 1922: the probability of obtaining at least one run of this length or greater is 0.000005. The total number of runs is less than four (an event with probability 0.0000015). Location and serial dependence tests are significant at levels much lower than 0.01. Finally, the discontinuity in the size of the residuals near August 1922 is pointed out by the heteroscedasticity test (significant at level 0.03).

The foregoing results strongly reject the hypothesis that the semilog model (estimated by OLS) is appropriate; they suggest the presence of an important structural break between August and November 1922 and (to a lesser degree) of a gradual shift before August 1922.

Consider now the double-log model estimated by ordinary least squares (tables 2.2B, 2.3B, 2.3D; figures 2.3, 2.4). Forward recursive estimates of γ' and $-\eta'$ show a trend till September (or November) 1922 and then stabilize; further, backward recursive estimates have a discontinuity in Novem-

Table 2.3
Recursive residuals for models estimated by ordinary least squares

Month	Forward residuals					Backward residuals				
	$k=1$	2	3	4	8	1	2	3	4	8
A. Semilog model										
2102						0.3384	0.3553	0.3752	0.3979	0.5064
2103						0.3679	0.3877	0.4104	0.4356	0.5524
2104	0.0098					0.4133	0.4363	0.4613	0.4866	0.6099
2105	0.0042	0.0100				0.4501	0.4750	0.5002	0.5259	0.6637
2106	-0.0153	-0.0081	0.0096			0.4779	0.5030	0.5285	0.5600	0.7090
2107	-0.0454	-0.0412	-0.0260	0.0092		0.4621	0.4876	0.5189	0.5518	0.7055
2108	-0.0598	-0.0741	-0.0648	-0.0438		0.4429	0.4746	0.5078	0.5404	0.7004
2109	-0.0086	-0.0241	-0.0474	-0.0424		0.5164	0.5493	0.5816	0.6218	0.7741
2110	-0.0388	-0.0391	-0.0538	-0.0704		0.5112	0.5436	0.5838	0.6272	0.7766
2111	-0.0819	-0.0902	-0.0852	-0.0987	0.0085	0.4748	0.5150	0.5585	0.5965	0.7643
2112	-0.0500	-0.0682	-0.0761	-0.0742	-0.0495	0.5442	0.5878	0.6259	0.6634	0.8431
2201	-0.0756	-0.0824	-0.1017	-0.1087	-0.0870	0.5464	0.5846	0.6223	0.6570	0.8466
2202	-0.1767	-0.1875	-0.1934	-0.2095	-0.1786	0.4481	0.4864	0.5218	0.5632	0.7282
2203	-0.1789	-0.2153	-0.2264	-0.2319	-0.2263	0.4112	0.4470	0.4888	0.5460	0.6709
2204	-0.2298	-0.2668	-0.3007	-0.3099	-0.2808	0.3523	0.3948	0.4529	0.5063	0.5550
2205	-0.1919	-0.2357	-0.2742	-0.3091	-0.3176	0.3713	0.4296	0.4832	0.5312	0.4847
2206	-0.0864	-0.1254	-0.1762	-0.2209	-0.2843	0.4500	0.5033	0.5508	0.5650	0.4869
2207	-0.0460	-0.0681	-0.1176	-0.1797	-0.2890	0.3755	0.4245	0.4407	0.4564	0.3553
2208	0.4244	0.3430	0.2814	0.1931	-0.0779	0.3231	0.3404	0.3566	0.3331	0.1411
2209	0.2804	0.5085	0.4078	0.3381	-0.0219	0.1278	0.1454	0.1254	0.0934	-0.0501
2210	0.7328	0.6542	0.6854	0.5546	0.1500	0.1470	0.1309	0.1072	0.0993	-0.0160
2211	-0.0964	0.5641	0.5588	0.6406	0.2244	-0.1181	-0.1393	-0.1444	-0.1786	0.0970
2212	-0.4647	-0.4740	0.1748	0.3265	0.2578	-0.1268	-0.1323	-0.1657	-0.2345	
2301	0.4146	0.3103	0.2284	0.7535	0.4741	-0.0432	-0.0789	-0.1359	-0.1410	
2302	0.4417	0.5886	0.4636	0.3431	0.5672	-0.2531	-0.2920	-0.2913	-0.2562	
2303	-0.6232	-0.5684	-0.4976	-0.5410	0.4854	-0.2243	-0.2191	-0.1701	0.1098	
2304	-0.0134	-0.0478	0.0689	0.1963	0.6107	-0.0393	-0.0303	0.1659		
2305	0.1487	0.1463	0.1095	0.2385	0.7379	0.0023	0.1793			
2306	0.4971	0.5144	0.5070	0.4639	0.4760	0.1981				
2307	1.2853	1.3781	1.3695	1.3303	1.1046					
2308	0.1784	0.8527	0.9673	0.9751	1.0497					

Table 2.3 (continued)

	Forward residuals					Backward residuals				
Month	k = 1	2	3	4	8	1	2	3	4	8
B. Double-log model										
2102						-0.3039	-0.3453	-0.3520	-0.3528	-0.2790
2103						-0.3441	-0.3508	-0.3516	-0.3366	-0.2456
2104	0.0101					-0.0780	-0.0804	-0.0694	-0.0522	0.0268
2105	0.0057	0.0103				-0.0281	-0.0176	-0.0012	0.0024	0.1018
2106	-0.0095	-0.0036	0.0100			0.1059	0.1205	0.1230	0.1434	0.2392
2107	-0.0456	-0.0418	-0.0273	0.0091		0.1692	0.1713	0.1900	0.2097	0.2933
2108	-0.0620	-0.0751	-0.0676	-0.0482		0.0299	0.0509	0.0731	0.0960	0.1849
2109	-0.0138	-0.0297	-0.0482	-0.0437		0.1976	0.2171	0.2372	0.2591	0.3042
2110	-0.0452	-0.0472	-0.0621	-0.0765		0.1922	0.2123	0.2342	0.2601	0.2656
2111	-0.0977	-0.1060	-0.1049	-0.1181	0.0075	0.1902	0.2114	0.2366	0.2515	0.2459
2112	-0.0551	-0.0733	-0.0816	-0.0822	-0.0626	0.1754	0.2025	0.2186	0.2328	0.1815
2201	-0.0853	-0.0925	-0.1111	-0.1187	-0.1112	0.1877	0.2037	0.2179	0.2126	0.2117
2202	-0.2002	-0.2109	-0.2170	-0.2338	-0.2265	0.1100	0.1255	0.1229	0.1150	0.1482
2203	-0.2324	-0.2623	-0.2728	-0.2782	-0.2879	0.0940	0.0924	0.0860	0.0976	0.1494
2204	-0.2907	-0.3245	-0.3531	-0.3624	-0.3592	0.0028	-0.0002	0.0168	0.0080	0.0751
2205	-0.2691	-0.3081	-0.3426	-0.3716	-0.3932	-0.0108	0.0067	-0.0009	0.0553	-0.0181
2206	-0.1962	-0.2321	-0.2741	-0.3113	-0.3691	0.0484	0.0365	0.0884	0.0926	0.0117
2207	-0.2502	-0.2780	-0.3179	-0.3641	-0.4461	-0.0150	0.0396	0.0479	0.0693	-0.0237
2208	-0.1207	-0.1780	-0.2165	-0.2697	-0.4254	0.1299	0.1322	0.1533	0.1375	-0.1927
2209	-0.1871	-0.2193	-0.2787	-0.3174	-0.5158	0.0291	0.0506	0.0372	-0.0256	-0.2658
2210	0.0288	-0.0527	-0.1017	-0.1732	-0.4022	0.1907	0.1804	0.1476	0.1489	-0.1034
2211	-0.2219	-0.1911	-0.2513	-0.2788	-0.4983	-0.0817	-0.1155	-0.1117	-0.1312	0.0536
2212	-0.2650	-0.3101	-0.2796	-0.3292	-0.4942	-0.1813	-0.1768	-0.1893	-0.3616	
2301	0.0189	-0.0338	-0.0982	-0.0762	-0.2998	0.0200	-0.0044	-0.1041	-0.1384	
2302	-0.1393	-0.1308	-0.1835	-0.2441	-0.3564	-0.1772	-0.2200	-0.2406	-0.2544	
2303	-0.2446	-0.2616	-0.2551	-0.2917	-0.3704	-0.3773	-0.3760	-0.3163	0.0445	
2304	0.1506	0.1260	0.0993	0.1010	-0.0759	-0.1129	-0.1434	0.0925		
2305	0.2004	0.2169	0.1910	0.1617	0.0498	-0.0897	0.1077			
2306	0.2494	0.2723	0.2896	0.2610	0.0904	0.1421				
2307	-0.0305	0.0081	0.0383	0.0617	-0.0636					
2308	-0.1145	-0.1179	-0.0806	-0.0511	-0.0810					

C. Semilog model: residuals scaled by $\hat{\sigma} = 0.367$[a]

2102						0.9219	0.9681	1.0223	1.0841	1.3799
2103						1.0024	1.0565	1.1183	1.1870	1.5052
2104	0.0268					1.1276	1.1889	1.2571	1.3260	1.6619
2105	0.0114	0.0271				1.2263	1.2943	1.3631	1.4329	1.8085
2106	−0.0416	−0.0219	0.0262			1.3023	1.3706	1.4401	1.5258	1.9320
2107	−0.1236	−0.1124	−0.0708	0.0250		1.2592	1.3285	1.4140	1.5037	1.9222
2108	−0.1629	−0.2020	−0.1765	−0.1194		1.2069	1.2931	1.3836	1.4726	1.9084
2109	−0.0233	−0.0655	−0.1291	−0.1155		1.4070	1.4967	1.5843	1.6942	2.1092
2110	−0.1056	−0.1066	−0.1465	−0.1917		1.3928	1.4811	1.5908	1.7090	2.1160
2111	−0.2231	−0.2457	−0.2322	−0.2691	0.0233	1.2936	1.4034	1.5218	1.6254	2.0825
2112	−0.1363	−0.1858	−0.2073	−0.2022	−0.1348	1.4828	1.6016	1.7054	1.8077	2.2973
2201	−0.2060	−0.2246	−0.2772	−0.2961	−0.2371	1.4888	1.5928	1.6955	1.7903	2.3069
2202	−0.4815	−0.5110	−0.5270	−0.5708	−0.4866	1.2211	1.3253	1.4219	1.5346	1.9841
2203	−0.4875	−0.5868	−0.6170	−0.6318	−0.6166	1.1205	1.2179	1.3317	1.4877	1.8281
2204	−0.6261	−0.7271	−0.8194	−0.8444	−0.7650	0.9600	1.0757	1.2341	1.3797	1.5121
2205	−0.5229	−0.6422	−0.7473	−0.8423	−0.8655	1.0117	1.1705	1.3167	1.4474	1.3206
2206	−0.2353	−0.3417	−0.4801	−0.6019	−0.7747	1.2262	1.3713	1.5009	1.5394	1.3267
2207	−0.1253	−0.1856	−0.3204	−0.4895	−0.7874	1.0231	1.1568	1.2009	1.2437	0.9135
2208	1.1564	0.9347	0.7668	0.5261	−0.2123	0.8804	0.9275	0.9717	0.9077	0.3845
2209	0.7639	1.3855	1.1113	0.9213	−0.0595	0.3483	0.3962	0.3416	0.2544	−0.1364
2210	1.9966	1.7825	1.8676	1.5113	0.4086	0.4004	0.3567	0.2922	0.2705	−0.0436
2211	−0.2627	1.5371	1.5227	1.7454	0.6113	−0.3218	−0.3796	−0.3935	−0.4866	0.2643
2212	−1.2662	−1.2916	0.4764	0.8897	0.7024	−0.3454	−0.3605	−0.4515	−0.6391	
2301	1.1298	0.8455	0.6224	2.0531	1.2918	−0.1178	−0.2150	−0.3702	−0.3842	
2302	1.2036	1.6038	1.2632	0.9347	1.5456	−0.6897	−0.7956	−0.7937	−0.6982	
2303	−0.6981	−1.5488	−1.3558	−1.4741	1.3225	−0.6111	−0.5970	−0.4634	0.2992	
2304	−0.0365	−0.1301	0.1878	0.5350	1.6639	−0.1070	−0.0826	0.4521		
2305	0.4051	0.3986	0.2983	0.6499	2.0107	0.0064	0.4885			
2306	1.3546	1.4017	1.3813	1.2640	1.2969	0.5399				
2307	3.5023	3.7551	3.7316	3.6249	3.0097					
2308	0.4861	2.3233	2.6356	2.6570	2.8602					

Table 2.3 (continued)

D. Double-log model: residuals scaled by $\hat{\sigma} = 0.163$

Month	Forward residuals k = 1	2	3	4	8	Backward residuals 1	2	3	4	8
2102						-1.8647	-2.1185	-2.1594	-2.1644	-1.7118
2103						-2.1109	-2.1520	-2.1570	-2.0652	-1.5068
2104	0.0620					-0.4783	-0.4935	-0.4255	-0.3203	0.1644
2105	0.0350	0.0634				-0.1726	-0.1082	-0.0072	0.0145	0.6242
2106	-0.0582	-0.0219	0.0610			0.6499	0.7392	0.7546	0.8795	1.4676
2107	-0.2798	-0.2562	-0.1677	0.0556		1.0379	1.0509	1.1656	1.2863	1.7991
2108	-0.3801	-0.4606	-0.4147	-0.2958		0.1833	0.3124	0.4483	0.5888	1.1344
2109	-0.0849	-0.1821	-0.2956	-0.2679		1.2123	1.3317	1.4553	1.5896	1.8661
2110	-0.2771	-0.2898	-0.3810	-0.4696		1.1790	1.3023	1.4366	1.5959	1.6295
2111	-0.5992	-0.6504	-0.6435	-0.7244	0.0457	1.1668	1.2970	1.4518	1.5431	1.5088
2112	-0.3380	-0.4499	-0.5007	-0.5042	-0.3838	1.0761	1.2425	1.3411	1.4280	1.1137
2201	-0.5231	-0.5672	-0.6817	-0.7282	-0.6820	1.1514	1.2496	1.3368	1.3043	1.2990
2202	-1.2284	-1.2936	-1.3310	-1.4341	-1.3894	0.6749	0.7699	0.7541	0.7053	0.9090
2203	-1.4260	-1.6093	-1.6737	-1.7069	-1.7661	0.5768	0.5668	0.5278	0.5985	0.9163
2204	-1.7834	-1.9910	-2.1663	-2.2230	-2.2037	0.0172	-0.0014	0.1029	0.0488	0.4604
2205	-1.6510	-1.8902	-2.1021	-2.2798	-2.4124	-0.0664	0.0409	-0.0057	0.3390	-0.1107
2206	-1.2039	-1.4239	-1.6815	-1.9096	-2.2645	0.2971	0.2242	0.5423	0.5680	0.0716
2207	-1.5350	-1.7056	-1.9503	-2.2336	-2.7367	-0.0922	0.2432	0.2938	0.4251	-0.1455
2208	-0.7407	-1.0921	-1.3283	-1.6546	-2.6097	0.7968	0.8108	0.9406	0.8438	-1.1820
2209	-1.1480	-1.3453	-1.7098	-1.9472	-3.1643	0.1783	0.3102	0.2279	-0.1573	-1.6307
2210	0.1769	-0.3234	-0.6241	-1.0628	-2.4674	1.1699	1.1069	0.9053	0.9135	-0.6345
2211	-1.3611	-1.1721	-1.5418	-1.7103	-3.0569	-0.5009	-0.7084	-0.6853	-0.8050	0.3287
2212	-1.6260	-1.9025	-1.7155	-2.0193	-3.0322	-1.1122	-1.0844	-1.1613	-2.2183	
2301	0.1160	-0.2076	-0.6025	-0.4677	-1.8393	0.1224	-0.0271	-0.6388	-0.8492	
2302	-0.8548	-0.8022	-1.1260	-1.4977	-2.1864	-1.0874	-1.3496	-1.4761	-1.5607	
2303	-1.5005	-1.6049	-1.5651	-1.7897	-2.2723	-2.3145	-2.3066	-1.9407	0.2732	
2304	0.9237	0.7729	0.6090	0.6198	-0.4657	-0.6923	-0.8800	0.5677		
2305	1.2291	1.3306	1.1715	0.9923	0.3053	-0.5503	0.6606			
2306	1.5298	1.6703	1.7769	1.6011	0.5543	0.8720				
2307	-0.1872	0.0495	0.2349	0.3785	-0.3899					
2308	-0.7022	-0.7233	-0.4947	-0.3137	-0.4969					

a. Scaled recursive residuals are obtained by dividing the recursive residuals by $\hat{\sigma}$; $\hat{\sigma}^2$ is the (unbiased) estimate of the standard error of the disturbances based on full sample.

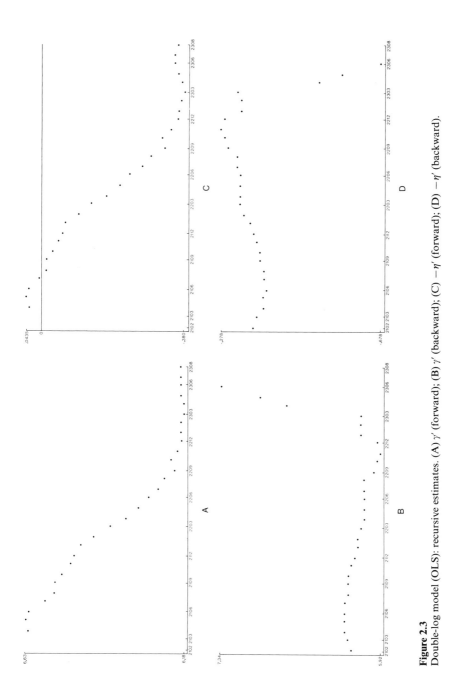

Figure 2.3
Double-log model (OLS): recursive estimates. (A) γ' (forward); (B) γ' (backward); (C) $-\eta'$ (forward); (D) $-\eta'$ (backward).

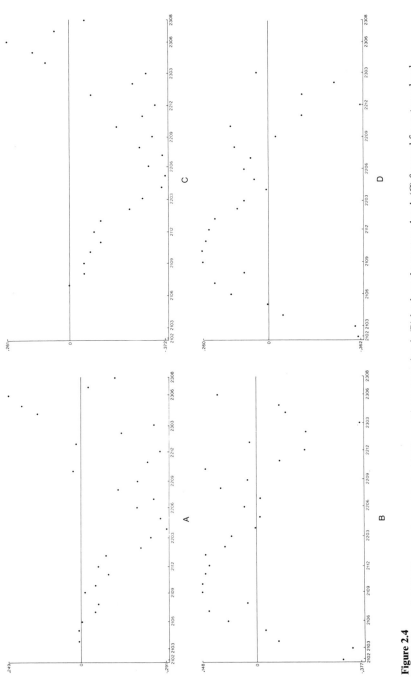

Figure 2.4
Double-log model (OLS): recursive residuals. (A) Forward one-step ahead; (B) backward one-step ahead; (C) forward four-steps ahead; (D) backward four-steps ahead.

ber 1922.[19] Forward recursive residuals (with various lags) indicate that the model tends to overpredict in the earlier part of the sample, and backward residuals show the opposite behavior. We see also a discontinuity in the size of the residuals in January to February 1922. From the forward one-step recursive residuals we notice a run of sixteen consecutive overpredictions: the probability of obtaining at least one run of this length or greater is 0.00023 under H_0, location tests ($\tilde{t}$, signed-rank, Cusum) as well as serial dependence tests (except at lag 2) are significant at levels lower than 0.05, and so on. On the other hand, backward recursive residuals show a tendency to underpredict before October 1922 (except in February to March 1921) and a discontinuity in the size of prediction errors in January to February 1922. Though the location and Cusum of squares tests are not significant at standard levels, the longest run and serial dependence tests (at lag 1) remain significant at levels lower than 0.01.

These results reject the hypothesis that the double-log (estimated by OLS) is appropriate; further they suggest the presence of relatively important discontinuities in February 1922 and near October 1922.

In view of the fact that the two models were "corrected for serial correlation" by assuming that the errors follow an $AR(1)$ process, we will now perform a stability analysis with "corrected" models. For the semilog model we consider the model in first-difference form with a constant term (equation 2.7). For the double-log model we consider the transformed equation

$$\log\left(\frac{M_t}{P_t}\right) - \hat{\rho} \log\left(\frac{M_{t-1}}{P_{t-1}}\right) = \gamma'(1 - \hat{\rho}) - \eta'[\log(\pi_t^*) - \hat{\rho}\log(\pi_{t-1}^*)] + u_t^*,$$

(2.29)

where $\hat{\rho} = .50146$ is the value of ρ obtained by using the Cochrane-Orcutt algorithm with the full sample.[20]

For the semilog model (equation 2.7), recursive estimates appear more erratic than before: however, a discontinuity near October 1922 remains visible from both forward and backward estimates (see table 2.4A, figure 2.5). Forward and backward recursive residuals look more "random" than previously (see tables 2.5A and 2.5C, and figure 2.6): the location, runs, and serial dependence tests all have high p values, except the t statistic over the period May 1921 to July 1922 which still suggests some tendency to overpredict in the forward recursions. On the other hand, we notice again the greater size of the recursive residuals in the period that starts in July

Table 2.4
Recursive estimates for models corrected for serial correlation

A. Semilog model (differenced)

Month	Forward α	Forward −η	Backward α	Backward −η
2103			−0.0394	−1.6076
2104	0.0133	3.8018	−0.0412	−1.6036
2105	0.0123	4.2002	−0.0435	−1.5992
2106	0.0125	−2.1662	−0.0457	−1.5947
2107	0.0130	−14.0014	−0.0475	−1.5913
2108	−0.0110	5.9928	−0.0476	−1.5912
2109	−0.0089	10.0390	−0.0478	−1.5906
2110	−0.0142	11.4622	−0.0517	−1.5833
2111	−0.0205	8.9075	−0.0522	−1.5821
2112	−0.0086	−0.6321	−0.0512	−1.5842
2201	−0.0118	−0.7971	−0.0556	−1.5741
2202	−0.0208	−4.5917	−0.0562	−1.5728
2203	−0.0237	−7.0075	−0.0511	−1.5831
2204	−0.0307	−4.1890	−0.0493	−1.5867
2205	−0.0303	−4.2446	−0.0459	−1.5938
2206	−0.0278	−2.7126	−0.0474	−1.5908
2207	−0.0262	−13.8734	−0.0525	−1.5804
2208	−0.0309	−6.6287	−0.0454	−1.5938
2209	−0.0290	−9.5932	−0.0393	−1.5980
2210	−0.0466	−1.6703	−0.0211	−1.6107
2211	−0.0609	−1.0129	−0.0237	−1.6214
2212	−0.0547	−1.5356	0.0054	−1.6908
2301	−0.0532	−0.8299	0.0053	−1.6903
2302	−0.0567	−1.2775	−0.0080	−1.7366
2303	−0.0465	−1.9894	0.0200	−1.6927
2304	−0.0363	−1.7048	−0.0038	−1.5352
2305	−0.0334	−1.6828	−0.0623	−1.5152
2306	−0.0312	−1.6127	−0.1021	−1.4512
2307	−0.0311	−1.7681	−0.1715	−1.4094
2308	−0.0394	−1.6076		

B. Double-log model ($\hat{\rho} = .501$)

Month	Forward γ'	Forward −η'	Backward γ'	Backward −η'
2103			6.1972	−0.3575
2104	6.6070	0.0180	6.2191	−0.3680
2105	6.6139	0.0200	6.2049	−0.3633
2106	6.6019	0.0122	6.1992	−0.3610
2107	6.5576	−0.0198	6.1801	−0.3547
2108	6.5477	−0.0075	6.1614	−0.3490
2109	6.5559	−0.0009	6.1652	−0.3504
2110	6.5359	−0.0134	6.1321	−0.3402
2111	6.4963	−0.0472	6.1094	−0.3326
2112	6.4935	−0.0467	6.0864	−0.3255
2201	6.4739	−0.0605	6.0566	−0.3151
2202	6.4204	−0.1094	6.0214	−0.3035
2203	6.3753	−0.1581	6.0081	−0.2992
2204	6.3301	−0.1987	5.9854	−0.2922
2205	6.2984	−0.2312	5.9891	−0.2934
2206	6.2817	−0.2518	5.9727	−0.2882
2207	6.2429	−0.3138	5.9024	−0.2665
2208	6.2462	−0.3059	5.8857	−0.2615
2209	6.2255	−0.3568	5.8179	−0.2461
2210	6.2357	−0.3171	5.8308	−0.2490
2211	6.2173	−0.3556	5.8456	−0.2654
2212	6.2030	−0.3684	5.9185	−0.2784
2301	6.2062	−0.3474	6.0433	−0.3104
2302	6.2018	−0.3694	6.0522	−0.3243
2303	6.1849	−0.3682	6.0639	−0.3097
2304	6.1906	−0.3469	7.2827	−0.6435
2305	6.1933	−0.3405	7.0403	−0.5945
2306	6.1948	−0.3316	6.9533	−0.5744
2307	6.1990	−0.3513	6.1304	−0.4063
2308	6.1972	−0.3575		

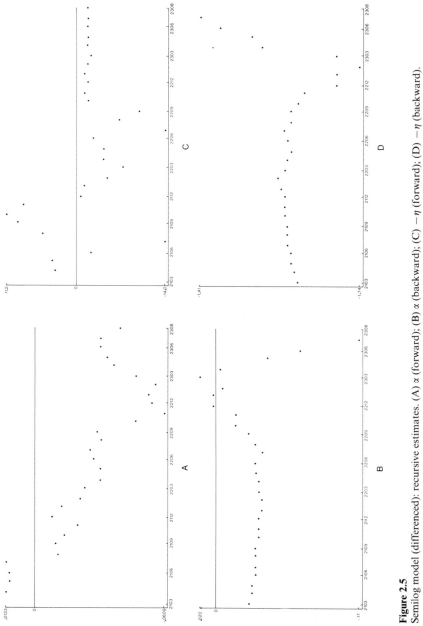

Figure 2.5
Semilog model (differenced): recursive estimates. (A) α (forward); (B) α (backward); (C) $-\eta$ (forward); (D) $-\eta$ (backward).

Table 2.5
Recursive residuals for models corrected for serial correlation

Month	Forward residuals					Backward residuals				
	$k=1$	2	3	4	8	1	2	3	4	8
A. Semilog model (differenced)										
2103						0.0533	0.0555	0.0576	0.0593	0.0638
2104						0.0648	0.0668	0.0685	0.0685	0.0718
2105	−0.0018					0.0577	0.0594	0.0595	0.0596	0.0670
2106	−0.0163	−0.0164				0.0459	0.0459	0.0461	0.0499	0.0540
2107	−0.0477	−0.0500	−0.0496			0.0019	0.0021	0.0059	0.0064	0.0053
2108	−0.0376	−0.0269	−0.0206	−0.0196		0.0054	0.0092	0.0098	0.0087	0.0068
2109	0.0307	0.0404	0.0213	0.0107		0.0889	0.0893	0.0882	0.0924	0.0825
2110	−0.0317	−0.0286	−0.0416	−0.0438		0.0120	0.0109	0.0152	0.0158	0.0071
2111	−0.0689	−0.0720	−0.0646	−0.0664		−0.0218	−0.0175	−0.0168	−0.0218	−0.0202
2112	0.0549	0.0530	0.0464	0.0429	0.0123	0.0864	0.0869	0.0818	0.0799	0.0754
2201	−0.0344	−0.0283	−0.0355	−0.0393	−0.0517	0.0117	0.0067	0.0050	0.0017	−0.0046
2202	−0.1269	−0.1295	−0.1271	−0.1345	−0.1395	−0.0908	−0.0924	−0.0954	−0.0938	−0.1178
2203	−0.0530	−0.0658	−0.0687	−0.0692	−0.0700	−0.0306	−0.0337	−0.0323	−0.0272	−0.0543
2204	−0.0731	−0.0756	−0.0839	−0.0866	−0.0810	−0.0526	−0.0511	−0.0460	−0.0528	−0.1000
2205	0.0062	0.0005	−0.0032	−0.0134	−0.0199	0.0212	0.0261	0.0192	0.0133	−0.0288
2206	0.0523	0.0525	0.0485	0.0432	0.0204	0.0712	0.0641	0.0581	0.0405	0.0275
2207	−0.0928	−0.0864	−0.0861	−0.0851	−0.1204	−0.0916	−0.0971	−0.1142	−0.1113	−0.1482
2208	0.0348	−0.0148	−0.0079	−0.0080	−0.0262	−0.0740	−0.0909	−0.0880	−0.1139	−0.1031
2209	−0.0796	0.0050	−0.0408	−0.0337	−0.0498	−0.2051	−0.2017	−0.2270	−0.2253	−0.1551
2210	0.2032	0.0985	0.0592	0.0062	0.0130	0.0297	0.0077	0.0077	0.0236	0.0828
2211	−0.2093	−0.2873	−0.2228	−0.1161	−0.0760	−0.2590	−0.2565	−0.2434	−0.2663	−0.0732
2212	0.0835	0.0436	−0.1518	−0.0693	−0.0070	0.0009	0.0110	−0.0126	0.0155	
2301	0.1086	0.0716	0.1034	0.2272	0.0162	0.1115	0.0808	0.0884	0.1372	
2302	−0.1685	−0.1198	−0.1371	−0.1152	−0.0064	−0.1893	−0.1744	−0.1196	−0.0847	
2303	0.1363	0.1751	0.0871	0.1171	−0.0531	0.0908	0.1357	0.1657	0.2088	
2304	0.2839	0.2504	0.2211	0.2444	0.1711	0.2562	0.2789	0.3171		
2305	0.0800	0.0952	0.0917	0.0795	0.1842	0.1217	0.1695			
2306	0.0731	0.0770	0.1024	0.0704	0.0738	0.1614				
2307	−0.0473	−0.0320	−0.0261	0.0323	−0.0633					
2308	−0.1720	−0.1427	−0.1481	−0.1481	−0.0802					

B. Double-log model ($\hat{\rho} = 0.501$)

2103						-0.1529	-0.1417	-0.1362	-0.1214	-0.0680
2104						0.1222	0.1250	0.1350	0.1447	0.1814
2105	0.0057					0.0408	0.0524	0.0634	0.0606	0.1225
2106	-0.0079	-0.0052				0.1431	0.1525	0.1498	0.1665	0.2180
2107	-0.0423	-0.0408	-0.0358			0.1367	0.1342	0.1502	0.1608	0.2044
2108	-0.0515	-0.0569	-0.0571	-0.0515		-0.0201	0.0000	0.0139	0.0275	0.0836
2109	0.0111	0.0067	-0.0103	-0.0128		0.2040	0.2141	0.2242	0.2367	0.2558
2110	-0.0451	-0.0410	-0.0466	-0.0582		0.1189	0.1301	0.1442	0.1607	0.1713
2111	-0.0845	-0.0915	-0.0841	-0.0881		0.1168	0.1302	0.1458	0.1505	0.1809
2112	-0.0147	-0.0236	-0.0292	-0.0269	-0.0386	0.1140	0.1320	0.1374	0.1471	0.1672
2201	-0.0638	-0.0649	-0.0786	-0.0851	-0.0867	0.1285	0.1336	0.1428	0.1381	0.1883
2202	-0.1650	-0.1721	-0.1727	-0.1861	-0.1853	0.0439	0.0539	0.0512	0.0571	0.1052
2203	-0.1405	-0.1651	-0.1727	-0.1733	-0.1822	0.0673	0.0645	0.0699	0.0960	0.1104
2204	-0.1880	-0.2061	-0.2276	-0.2341	-0.2362	-0.0086	-0.0011	0.0287	0.0339	0.0196
2205	-0.1362	-0.1571	-0.1769	-0.2001	-0.2254	0.0312	0.0592	0.0628	0.0882	0.0005
2206	-0.0719	-0.0889	-0.1124	-0.1353	-0.1848	0.1060	0.1073	0.1317	0.1246	0.0399
2207	-0.1560	-0.1661	-0.1856	-0.2125	-0.2734	0.0209	0.0452	0.0399	0.0377	-0.0387
2208	0.0121	-0.0413	-0.0581	-0.0861	-0.2032	0.1515	0.1471	0.1556	0.1329	-0.1179
2209	-0.1408	-0.1115	-0.1579	-0.1710	-0.2946	-0.0265	-0.0173	-0.0384	-0.0636	-0.1865
2210	0.1126	0.0356	0.0351	-0.0267	-0.1514	0.1718	0.1590	0.1540	0.1711	0.1554
2211	-0.2624	-0.1997	-0.2383	-0.1894	-0.2996	-0.1672	-0.1870	-0.1755	-0.1951	-0.0671
2212	-0.1896	-0.2217	-0.1844	-0.2166	-0.2583	-0.1199	-0.1155	-0.1285	-0.3155	
2301	0.1211	0.0943	0.0265	0.0783	-0.0671	0.1262	0.0950	0.0981	0.1243	
2302	-0.1802	-0.1413	-0.1649	-0.2225	-0.1889	-0.1787	-0.2113	-0.1735	-0.1547	
2303	-0.1987	-0.2050	-0.1991	-0.2083	-0.2180	-0.3167	-0.2522	-0.1832	-0.0451	
2304	0.2366	0.2304	0.1935	0.2175	0.0880	0.1554	0.1488	0.2253		
2305	0.0942	0.1235	0.1170	0.0855	0.0760	0.0215	0.1221			
2306	0.1166	0.1268	0.1604	0.1544	0.0542	0.1880				
2307	-0.1898	-0.1673	-0.1508	-0.1015	-0.1271					
2308	-0.1194	-0.1467	-0.1310	-0.1191	-0.0860					

Table 2.5 (continued)

C. Semilog model (differenced): residuals scaled by $\hat{\sigma} = 0.109$

Month	Forward residuals					Backward residuals				
	$k=1$	2	3	4	8	1	2	3	4	8
2103						0.4889	0.5095	0.5287	0.5443	0.5850
2104						0.5941	0.6131	0.6286	0.6288	0.6588
2105	−0.0163					0.5296	0.5452	0.5454	0.5471	0.6144
2106	−0.1499	−0.1505				0.4211	0.4215	0.4231	0.4576	0.4958
2107	−0.4373	−0.4588	−0.4548			0.0170	0.0190	0.0539	0.0587	0.0484
2108	−0.3450	−0.2472	−0.1894	−0.1800		0.0495	0.0846	0.0895	0.0799	0.0624
2109	0.2813	0.3709	0.1951	0.0984		0.8156	0.8196	0.8095	0.8476	0.7567
2110	−0.2905	−0.2624	−0.3820	−0.4017		0.1099	0.1004	0.1395	0.1450	0.0655
2111	−0.6324	−0.6602	−0.5930	−0.6094		−0.1995	−0.1601	−0.1543	−0.1995	−0.1852
2112	0.5034	0.4864	0.4253	0.3933	0.1128	0.7927	0.7972	0.7503	0.7328	0.6915
2201	−0.3159	−0.2596	−0.3254	−0.3606	−0.4745	0.1074	0.0617	0.0454	0.0156	−0.0424
2202	−1.1638	−1.1880	−1.1663	−1.2339	−1.2801	−0.8326	−0.8474	−0.8755	−0.8608	−1.0804
2203	−0.4860	−0.6035	−0.6302	−0.6345	−0.6424	−0.2803	−0.3095	−0.2961	−0.2497	−0.4981
2204	−0.6704	−0.6937	−0.7696	−0.7944	−0.7434	−0.4828	−0.4690	−0.4220	−0.4839	−0.9176
2205	0.0564	0.0041	−0.0297	−0.1226	−0.1825	0.1944	0.2396	0.1760	0.1223	−0.2644
2206	0.4794	0.4819	0.4451	0.3960	0.1868	0.6529	0.5881	0.5332	0.3717	0.2522
2207	−0.8517	−0.7925	−0.7895	−0.7806	−1.1044	−0.8407	−0.8912	−1.0473	−1.0212	−1.3599
2208	0.3194	−0.1354	−0.0725	−0.0736	−0.2404	−0.6789	−0.8343	−0.8071	−1.0447	−0.9455
2209	−0.7300	0.0459	−0.3743	−0.3094	−0.4570	−1.8814	−1.8500	−2.0823	−2.0667	−1.4229
2210	1.8641	0.9040	0.5430	0.0567	0.1195	0.2724	0.0706	0.0710	0.2168	0.7593
2211	−1.9202	−2.6358	−2.0442	−1.0651	−0.6971	−2.3757	−2.3528	−2.2326	−2.4434	−0.6712
2212	0.7656	0.3999	−1.3926	−0.6360	−0.0643	0.0079	0.1005	−0.1159	0.1420	
2301	0.9962	0.6568	0.9485	2.0843	0.1488	1.0230	0.7411	0.8111	1.2584	
2302	−1.5461	−1.0994	−1.2579	−1.0566	−0.0586	−1.7363	−1.6004	−1.0974	−0.7767	
2303	1.2502	1.6064	0.7995	1.0741	−0.4871	0.8333	1.2453	1.5203	1.9151	
2304	2.6042	2.2975	2.0280	2.2426	1.5699	2.3508	2.5588	2.9087		
2305	0.7335	0.8734	0.8410	0.7297	1.6896	1.1167	1.5551			
2306	0.6703	0.7063	0.9390	0.6462	0.6773	1.4807				
2307	−0.4342	−0.2933	−0.2391	0.2965	−0.5806					
2308	−1.5784	−1.3090	−1.3587	−1.3584	−0.7357					

D. Double-log model ($\hat{\rho} = 0.501$): residuals scaled by $\hat{\sigma} = 0.134$

2103						−1.1413	−1.0573	−1.0164	−0.9062	−0.5073
2104						0.9118	0.9329	1.0075	1.0795	1.3534
2105	0.0424					0.3047	0.3908	0.4734	0.4525	0.9140
2106	−0.0586	−0.0384				1.0678	1.1382	1.1177	1.2422	1.6267
2107	−0.3155	−0.3047	−0.2673			1.0202	1.0016	1.1212	1.2003	1.5253
2108	−0.3842	−0.4244	−0.4258	−0.3846		−0.1497	0.0003	0.1038	0.2055	0.6239
2109	0.0825	0.0498	−0.0768	−0.0958		1.5225	1.5980	1.6734	1.7666	1.9093
2110	−0.3366	−0.3058	−0.3475	−0.4344		0.8875	0.9709	1.0764	1.1991	1.2786
2111	−0.6305	−0.6827	−0.6275	−0.6576		0.8719	0.9714	1.0877	1.1232	1.3502
2112	−0.1093	−0.1761	−0.2181	−0.2007	−0.2881	0.8508	0.9849	1.0250	1.0976	1.2475
2201	−0.4763	−0.4844	−0.5862	−0.6353	−0.6466	0.9587	0.9969	1.0654	1.0303	1.4055
2202	−1.2310	−1.2842	−1.2888	−1.3885	−1.3831	0.3278	0.4023	0.3822	0.4258	0.7850
2203	−1.0483	−1.2318	−1.2885	−1.2931	−1.3596	0.5022	0.4815	0.5213	0.7166	0.8235
2204	−1.4029	−1.5377	−1.6981	−1.7472	−1.7630	−0.0643	−0.0085	0.2141	0.2528	0.1463
2205	−1.0160	−1.1724	−1.3203	−1.4933	−1.6823	0.2326	0.4416	0.4683	0.6584	0.0039
2206	−0.5365	−0.6631	−0.8390	−1.0096	−1.3793	0.7910	0.8008	0.9825	0.9296	0.2974
2207	−1.1643	−1.2396	−1.3852	−1.5857	−2.0404	0.1558	0.3375	0.2978	0.2811	−0.2884
2208	0.0903	−0.3079	−0.4332	−0.6428	−1.5160	1.1308	1.0975	1.1613	0.9919	−0.8799
2209	−1.0508	−0.8322	−1.1784	−1.2759	−2.1985	−0.1981	−0.1294	−0.2863	−0.4747	−1.3916
2210	0.8402	0.2654	0.2621	−0.1995	−1.1295	1.2817	1.1864	1.1490	1.2767	1.1594
2211	−1.9585	−1.4899	−1.7784	−1.4132	−2.2359	−1.2480	−1.3958	−1.3093	−1.4560	−0.5010
2212	−1.4146	−1.6543	−1.3763	−1.6165	−1.9275	−0.8944	−0.8621	−0.9589	−2.3546	
2301	0.9037	0.7034	0.1978	0.5840	−0.5010	0.9415	0.7088	0.7319	0.9273	
2302	−1.3448	−1.0543	−1.2308	−1.6605	−1.4096	−1.3334	−1.5768	−1.2945	−1.1546	
2303	−1.4826	−1.5302	−1.4858	−1.5546	−1.6266	−2.3634	−1.8818	−1.3672	−0.3363	
2304	1.7660	1.7194	1.4441	1.6234	0.6564	1.1597	1.1101	1.6816		
2305	0.7027	0.9217	0.8734	0.6381	0.5670	0.1603	0.9110			
2306	0.8699	0.9463	1.1973	1.1524	0.4048	1.4027				
2307	−1.4162	−1.2484	−1.1250	−0.7575	−0.9484					
2308	−0.8910	−1.0947	−0.9774	−0.8885	−0.6415					

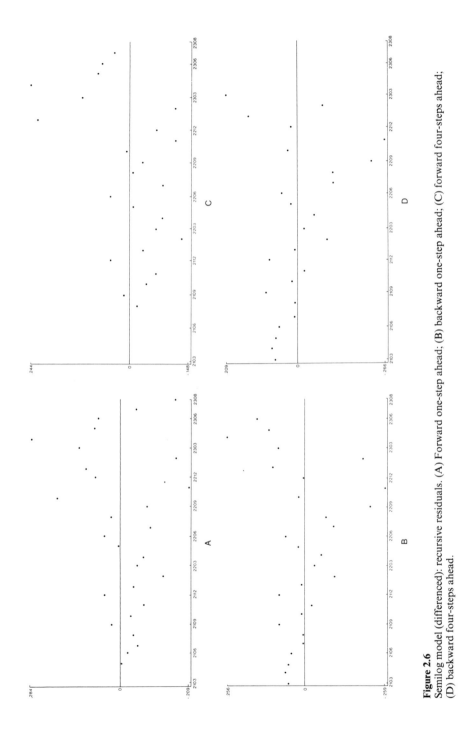

Figure 2.6
Semilog model (differenced): recursive residuals. (A) Forward one-step ahead; (B) backward one-step ahead; (C) forward four-steps ahead;
(D) backward four-steps ahead.

1922 and even more so after October 1922 (see table 2.5C). In the earlier period the only possibly outlying point is February 1922. The difference in average size is underscored by the Cusum of squares and heteroscedasticity tests which are significant at very low levels (for both forward and backward one-step recursive residuals). Thus, though the results for this model look "cleaner" than for the original model, they suggest the presence of a discontinuity between July and November 1922 and the possibility of an outlying observation in February 1922.

For the double-log model (equation 2.29), the results are qualitatively quite similar to those obtained without transformation. Recursive estimates (table 2.4B, figure 2.7) show basically the same pattern and suggest again a discontinuity near September 1922. Forward recursive residuals (tables 2.5B and 2.5D, figure 2.8) show overpredictions in the early part of the sample (e.g., before August 1922), backward residuals show underpredictions over the same period, and both sets have a discontinuity in size in February 1922. Though most of the test statistics are less significant than those obtained from the OLS recursions, the global location tests and the longest run test (based on forward one-step residuals) are significant at levels lower than 0.02; further the local t tests (beginning July 1922) have p values of 0.0004 (forward recursions) and 0.0029 (backward recursions). Thus this model still shows several signs indicating it is not satisfactory; in particular, the results suggest the presence of relatively important discontinuities in February 1922 and between August and November 1922.

2.5 Conclusion

Our main findings may be summarized as follows. The double-log model shows signs of instability both before and after the correction for serial correlation selected by Frenkel is applied. The results obtained in both cases are similar, though the "corrected" model appears somewhat "cleaner." Forward recursions indicate a tendency to overpredict demand for money before October 1922, whereas backward recursions yield underpredictions over the same period. We identified February 1922 and the neighborhood of October 1922 as relatively important discontinuity points. Backward recursions also indicate that the two first observations (February to March 1921) may be troublesome for this model.

For the untransformed semilog model recursive residuals exhibit a great contrast between the two periods separated by July to August 1922. In the

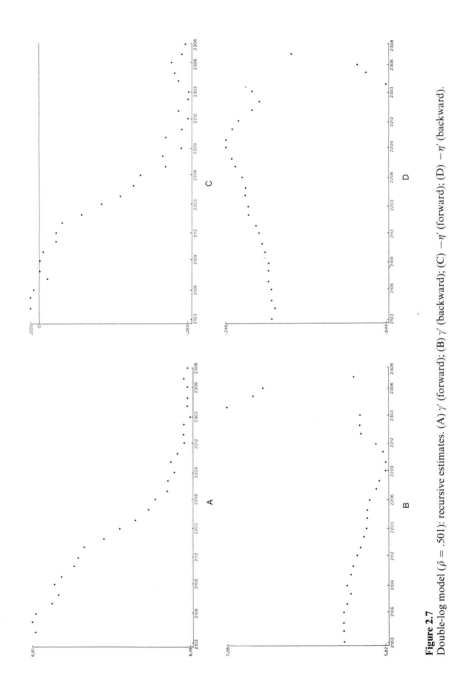

Figure 2.7
Double-log model ($\hat{\rho} = .501$): recursive estimates. (A) γ' (forward); (B) γ' (backward); (C) $-\eta'$ (forward); (D) $-\eta'$ (backward).

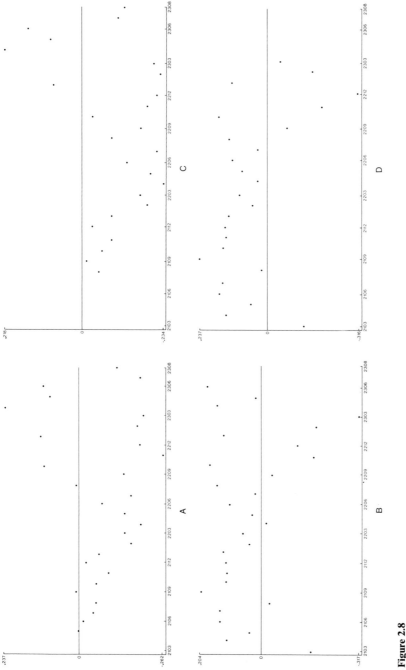

Figure 2.8
Double-log model ($\hat{\rho} = .501$): recursive residuals. (A) Forward one-step ahead; (B) backward one-step ahead; (C) forward four-steps ahead; (D) backward four-steps ahead.

early period forward recursions overpredict demand for money and backward recursions underpredict it. Further the average size of the forward recursive residuals is much larger in the second period than in the first one, but the opposite holds for the backward recursive residuals. Results suggest the presence of a relatively important shift between August and November 1922 and (to a lesser degree) of a gradual shift before August 1922. Finally, when the semilog model is differenced, recursive residuals look more "random." However, we note again an important "heteroscedasticity": the large residuals, from both forward and backward recursions, are concentrated in the second part of the sample, except for February 1922. Results suggest a relatively important discontinuity between July and November 1922, and the possibility of an outlying point in February 1922.

These results suggest that none of the specifications studied is satisfactory. Though there is generally no reason to expect that different models will exhibit instability at precisely the same dates, we saw that all the specifications considered showed signs of perturbations in the neighborhood of August 1922. This month is the beginning of the "severe hyperinflation" as dated by Cagan. We also found that February 1922 and February to March 1921 may be troublesome points.

The fact that a model shows signs of instability does not mean it is not a "good" approximation in a relative sense. Nevertheless, it would certainly be of interest to remove the problems noticed. We hope that the information gathered here may be useful for both appreciating the model and improving the specification.[21] The purpose of this chapter was not to propose an alternative specification that could be deemed "stable" but simply to illustrate a diagnostic method.

We end with some comments on the method. Applying recursive stability analysis both allowed us to detect instability in the four models considered and brought useful insights on the timing of the structural change. We saw that comparing various sets of k-step recursive residuals between each other and with the recursive estimates could contribute appreciably to the analysis. We saw also that scaling the recursive residuals made them much more intelligible. Finally, we found that most of the test statistics computed worked well as ways of assessing the statistical significance of the results of the recursive estimations; among these, the longest run, heteroscedasticity, Cusum of squares, and various location tests were especially intuitive and illuminating.

Table 2.6
Data

Month	LFOR	LSPO	LMON	LCOL	FPRE	INF
2101	5.41780	5.42490	13.5768	7.07240	0.289600	
2102	5.47650	5.48480	13.5923	7.04490	0.166700	−2.71253
2103	5.49690	5.50530	13.5975	7.03700	0.161500	−0.786888
2104	5.56160	5.56830	13.6075	7.02730	0.329900	−0.965311
2105	5.49080	5.49720	13.6138	7.02110	0.368500	−0.618082
2106	5.61560	5.62040	13.6518	7.06220	0.520300	4.19563
2107	5.66660	5.66990	13.6724	7.13090	0.673300	7.11148
2108	5.78190	5.78690	13.6971	7.19520	0.505700	6.64123
2109	6.09280	6.09580	13.7636	7.22550	0.693900	3.07637
2110	6.64100	6.64380	13.8136	7.31590	0.720600	9.46120
2111	6.91700	6.91870	13.9041	7.48160	0.830300	18.0219
2112	6.64310	6.64640	14.0222	7.56420	0.674800	8.61073
2201	6.75190	6.75460	14.0341	7.62120	0.733200	5.86558
2202	6.92880	6.93050	14.0703	7.80340	0.832200	19.9854
2203	7.16900	7.16930	14.1555	7.97140	0.961500	18.2937
2204	7.09800	7.09840	14.2260	8.14210	0.958600	18.6135
2205	7.13570	7.13570	14.3013	8.24350	1.00000	10.6719
2206	7.43940	7.43840	14.4075	8.33010	1.10500	9.04604
2207	7.96710	7.96310	14.5248	8.59270	1.39700	30.0306
2208	8.80780	8.78510	14.7432	8.95740	3.26910	44.0082
2209	8.90920	8.86780	15.0172	9.49690	5.13860	71.5149
2210	10.0965	9.97110	15.3938	10.0018	13.5315	65.6820
2211	10.5640	10.4549	15.8561	10.7057	11.9058	102.162
2212	10.4688	10.4103	16.3768	11.1347	6.84950	53.5721
2301	12.0519	11.8982	16.8186	11.6292	16.3736	63.9678
2302	11.7764	11.5617	17.3858	12.4848	22.4674	135.279
2303	11.5712	11.5229	17.8334	12.5616	5.83180	7.98261
2304	11.9676	11.8636	18.0077	12.5961	11.4050	3.51020
2305	12.8088	12.6854	18.2760	12.8521	13.3420	29.1753
2306	13.8353	13.6530	18.9153	13.5476	19.2321	100.471
2307	15.8769	15.3841	19.8999	15.1413	50.2807	392.193
2308	17.9051	17.5429	22.6575	17.8863	37.2167	1456.46

2.6 Appendix: Data

The data used in this paper are identical to those used by Frenkel (1977). They were kindly made available to us by him. The symbols are defined as follows:

LFOR = logarithm of one-month forward rate,
LSPO = logarithm of spot exchange rate,
LMON = logarithm of money supply,
LCOL = logarithm of cost of living index,
FPRE = forward premium on foreign exchange.

The data on money and prices come from Graham (1930) and Tinbergen (1934), and the data on exchange rates were obtained from Einzig (1937). As pointed out to us by Frenkel, "the spot and the forward exchange rates are end of month," obtained by (linear) interpolation from the series given by Einzig. "Einzig reports the difference between the spot and the forward rates; this was subtracted from the corresponding spot rate so as to generate the forward rate." The forward premium on foreign exchange is defined as

$$FPRE_t = (LFOR_t - LSPO_t)100 + 1.$$

"The addition of 1 was done so as to ensure that FPRE > 0. This was necessary since some of the regressions used the logarithm of FPRE. For the semilogarithmic regressions, the added 1 is only affecting the constant term." The inflation rates given in the appendix table were computed as

$$INF_t = \frac{100(COL_t - COL_{t-1})}{COL_{t-1}},$$

where

$$COL_t = \exp(LCOL_t).$$

Notes

The author wishes to thank Arnold Zellner, Jacob Frenkel, Nicholas Kiefer, Robert E. Lucas, Jr., Houston Stokes, Leonard Dudley, and the members of the University of Chicago Econometrics and Statistics Colloquium for several helpful comments. This work was supported by Grants from the Social Sciences and Humanities Research Council of Canada, Foundation FCAC of the Government of Quebec and the Center for Computational Research in Economics and Management Science at MIT. The author thanks also Sophie Mahseredjian and Hélène Nadeau for their devoted research assistance.

1. See Boorman (1980, pp. 353–356), Laidler (1977, pp. 34–35), and Judd and Scadding (1982).

2. Alternative methods of modeling price expectation require more specific assumptions on the formation of expectations. In this context the main methods used are adaptive expectations (Cagan 1956, Bisignano 1975, Khan 1975, 1977, Jacobs 1975, 1977, Cagan and Kincaid 1977) and rational expectations (Sargent and Wallace 1973, Sargent 1977, Evans 1978, Salemi and Sargent 1979, Burmeister and Wall 1982, Goodfriend 1982).

3. For further discussion of the use of this variable, see Abel et al. (1979), Frenkel (1979, 1980), Salemi (1980), Flood and Garber (1980), Krasker (1980), McCulloch (1980), Dufour (1981), Allen and McCrickard (1982).

4. The data on money and prices come from Graham (1930) and Tinbergen (1934).

5. Frenkel (1977) also considered the wholesale price index but found that the cost of living index is preferable. We will go along with this conclusion and use only the consumer price index.

6. The exchange rate data come from Einzig (1937). The 1 is added to $\pi_t = 100 \log(F_t/S_t)$ because the latter may take negative values (at the beginning of the period), a feature that poses a problem for the double-logarithmic model. This choice was also justified by estimating the latter model with $\pi_t^* = \pi_t + k$: a value of k approximately equal to 1 was obtained (using nonlinear least squares). For the semilogarithmic model, adding 1 to π_t simply modifies the constant term.

7. Standard errors are given in parenthesis; $\hat{\rho}$ is the final estimated value of the autoregressive coefficient; SS is the sum of squared residuals, SE is the standard error of the regression, DW is the Durbin-Watson statistic, R^2 is the coefficient of determination (based on the original dependent variable), and $\bar{R}^2$ is the coefficient of determination based on the transformed dependent variable. Standard errors are conditional standard errors as produced by the Cochrane-Orcutt iterative technique (e.g., as implemented in the TSP3.5 package).

8. Note that we also duplicated exactly Frenkel's results.

9. To make the model somewhat more general, we will not set the constant at zero (as complete differencing would suggest).

10. It is of interest to note here that a random walk process on the errors is one of two conditions, given by Sargent and Wallace (1973) and Sargent (1977), under which the adaptive expectations scheme suggested by Cagan is "rational"; the second condition is that economic agents expect that the rate of money creation will be constant in the future. Khan (1975) also found a value of ρ very close to 1 in estimating a semilogarithmic demand for money equation with Cagan's original adaptive expectations scheme.

11. We assume here that rank $(X_r) = K$, $r = K, \ldots, T$.

12. One can show easily that recursive estimates follow a "heteroscedastic random walk"; see Dufour (1982a, eq. 24). Thus the observation of a "trend" must be interpreted with great care.

13. Though scaled recursive residuals are similar to t statistics, one can check easily that they do not generally follow Student t distributions. It would certainly be of interest to study their distribution and use it to perform tests on individual observations. Note also that $\hat{\sigma}^2$ tends to overestimate σ^2 when structural change is present (see Dufour 1982a, pp. 60–61): clearly this can make a number of important residuals look "small" and should be discounted when interpreting the results.

14. Most computations were performed using a FORTRAN program called RECSTA on a CDC Cyber computer. The program is available from the author on request.

15. Previous applications of the CUSUM tests appear in Brown et al. (1975), Khan (1974, 1978), Heller and Khan (1979), Cameron (1979), Riddell (1979), Hwang (1980).

16. These can also be used in simultaneous testing to combine the various tests used, such as using Bonferroni inequality (see Miller 1966, 1977).

17. Because they are too far from the other estimates, the recursive estimates based on two observations only were dropped from figures 2.1 and 2.3.

18. It is important to recall here that these residuals are determined using coefficients based on "future" observations.

19. In interpreting recursive estimates, one must always keep in mind that the variance of recursive estimates is "large" at the beginning of the recursive estimation process and relatively small toward the end; hence sometimes weird values occur at the beginning, and there is the impression of relative stability near the end of the sample.

20. Recursive residuals obtained in this way will not enjoy exactly their theoretical properties (for the true value of ρ is unknown). However, if $\hat{\rho}$ is a consistent estimate of ρ, we can still expect it will fall in the neighborhood of the true value of ρ and thus provide approximately valid test statistics. But this is not guaranteed. In view of this difficulty, we performed some sensitivity analysis by considering models transformed by different values of ρ inside a grid in the neighborhood of ρ: for the semilog model, $\rho = 0.5\ (0.1)\ 0.90$ and $0.95\ (0.01)\ 0.99$; for the double-log model, $\rho = 0.1\ (0.1)\ 0.9$ and $0.45\ (0.01)\ 0.55$. In all cases we obtained essentially the same conclusions or results that looked "more unstable." The limits of these grids exceed two standard errors of $\hat{\rho}$, as given by the Cochrane-Orcutt procedure. For further discussion of this problem, see Dufour (1982a, sec. 2.5).

21. Some alternative possible specifications may be found in Frenkel (1977, 1979), Abel et al. (1979), and Allen and McCrickard (1982). However, a careful study of their stability remains to be done.

References

Abel, A., R. Dornbusch, J. Huizinga, and A. Marcus, 1979. Money demand during hyperinflation. *Journal of Monetary Economics* 5:97–104.

Allen, S. D., and D. L. McCrickard, 1982. Variability of the inflation rate and the forward premium in a money demand function: the case of the German hyperinflation. *Economic Inquiry* 20:619–632.

Anscombe, P. J., 1961. Examination of residuals. *Proceedings of the 4th Berkeley Symposium on Mathematical Statistics and Probability* 1:1–36.

Anscombe, P. J., and J. W. Tukey, 1963. The examination and analysis of residuals. *Technometrics* 5:141–160.

Belsley, D. A., E. Kuh, and R. E. Welsch, 1980. *Regression Diagnostics: Identifying Influential Data and Sources of Collinearity.* Wiley, New York.

Bisignano, J., 1975. Cagan's real money demand with alternative error structures: Bayesian analysis for four countries. *International Economic Review* 16:487–502.

Boorman, J. T., 1980. The evidence on the demand for money: theoretical formulations and emperical results. In *Current Issues in Monetary Theory and policy*, 2nd ed., T. M. Havrilesky and J. T. Boorman, eds. AHM Pub. Corp., Arlington Heights, Illinois, pp. 315–360.

Box, G. E. P., and G. M. Jenkins, 1969. *Time Series Analysis, Forecasting and Control.* Holden-Day, San Francisco.

Brown, R. L., J. Durbin, and J. M. Evans, 1975. Techniques for testing the constancy of regression relationships over time (with discussion). *Journal of the Royal Statistical Society, Series B* 37:149–192.

Burmeister, E., and K. D. Wall, 1982. Kalman filtering estimation of unobserved rational expectations with an application to the German hyperinflation. *Journal of Econometrics* 20:255–284.

Cagan, P., 1956. The monetary dynamics of hyperinflation. In *Studies in the Quantity Theory of Moeny*, M. Friedman, ed. The University of Chicago Press, Chicago, pp. 25–117.

Cagan, P., and G. Kincaid, 1977. Jacobs' estimates of the hyperinflation model: comment. *Economic Inquiry* 15:111–118.

Chow, C., 1960. Tests of equality between sets of coefficients in two linear regressions. *Econometrica* 28:591–605.

Cooley, T. F., and E. C. Prescott, 1976. Estimation in the presence of stochastic parameter variations. *Econometrica* 44:167–184.

Cameron, N., 1979. The stability of Canadian demand for money functions 1954–75. *Canadian Journal of Economics* 12:258–281.

Dufour, J.-M., 1979. Methods for specification errors analysis with macroeconomic applications. Ph.D. dissertation, University of Chicago, Chicago.

Dufour, J.-M., 1981. Rank tests for serial dependence. *Journal of Time Series Analysis* 2:117–128.

Dufour, J.-M., 1982a. Recursive stability analysis of linear regression relationships: an exploratory methodology. *Journal of Econometrics* 19:31–76.

Dufour, J.-M., 1982b. Generalized Chow tests for structural change: a coordinate-free approach. *International Economic Review* 23:565–575.

Durbin, J., 1969. Tests for serial correlation in regression analysis based on the periodogram of least squares residuals. *Biometrika* 56:1–15.

Einzig, P., 1937. *The Theory of Forward Exchange Rate.* Macmillan, London.

Evans, P., 1978. Time-series analysis and the German hyperinflation. *International Economic Review* 19:195–209.

Farley, J. U., and M. Hinich, 1970. Testing for a shifting slope coefficient in a linear model. *Journal of the American Statistical Association* 65:1320–1329.

Flood, R. P., and P. M. Garber, 1980. A pitfall in estimation of models with rational expectations. *Journal of Monetary Economics* 6:433–435.

Frenkel, J. A., 1975. Inflation and the formation of expectations. *Journal of Monetary Economics* 1:403–421.

Frenkel, J., 1977. The forward exchange rate, expectations, and the demand for money: the German hyperinflation. *American Economic Review* 67:653–670.

Frenkel, J. A., 1979. Further evidence on expectations and the demand for money during the German hyperinflation. *Journal of Monetary Economics* 8:81–96.

Frenkel, J. A., 1980. The forward exchange rate, expectations, and the demand for money— the German hyperinflation: reply. *American Economic Review* 70:771–775.

Goodfriend, M. S., 1982. An alternate method of estimating the Cagan money demand function in hyperinflation under rational expectations. *Journal of Monetary Economics* 9:43–57.

Graham, F., 1930. *Exchange, Prices and Production in Hyper-Inflation: Germany, 1920–23.* Princeton University Press, Princeton, N.J.

Heller, H. R., and M. S. Khan, 1979. The demand for money and the term structure of interest rates. *Journal of Political Economy* 87:109–129.

Hwang, H. -S., 1980. A test of a disequilibrium model. *Journal of Econometrics* 12:319–334.

Jacobs, R. L., 1975. A difficulty with monetarist models of hyperinflation. *Economic Inquiry* 13:337–360.

Jacobs, R. L., 1977. Hyperinflation and the supply of money. *Journal of Money, Credit and Banking* 9:287–303.

Judd, J. P., and J. L. Scadding, 1982. The search for a stable money demand function: a survey of the post-1973 literature. *Journal of Economic Literature* 20 (September):993–1023.

Khan, M. S., 1974. The stability of the demand for money function of the United States. *Journal of Political Economy* 82:1205–1219.

Khan, M., 1975. The monetary dynamics of hyperinflation: a note. *Journal of Monetary Economics* 1:355–362.

Khan, M., 1977. The variability of expectations in hyperinflations. *Journal of Political Economy* 85:817–827.

Khan, M. S., 1978. The relative stability of velocity and the investment multiplier. *Journal of Monetary Economics* 4:103–119.

Krasker, W. A., 1980. The "Peso problem" in testing the efficiency of forward exchange markets. *Journal of Monetary Economics* 6:269–276.

McCulloch, J. H., 1980. Forward exchange rate determination in efficient markets with purchasing power parity with log-normal uncertainty, with empirical reference to the German hyperinflation. Working Paper no. 64. Department of Economics and the Mershen Center, Ohio State University, Columbus.

Miller, R., 1966. *Simultaneous Statistical Inference.* McGraw-Hill, New York.

Miller, R., 1977. Developments in multiple comparisons 1966–1976. *Journal of the American Statistical Association* 72:779–788.

Quandt, R. E., 1960. Tests of the hypothesis that a linear regression obeys two separate regimes. *Journal of the American Statistical Association* 55:324–330.

Riddell, W. C., 1969. The empirical foundations of the Phillips curve: evidence from Canadian wage contract data. *Econometrica* 47:1–24.

Salemi, M. K., 1980. The forward exchange rate, expectations and the demand for money—the German hyperinflation: comment. *American Economic Review* 70:763–770.

Salemi, M. K., and T. J. Sargent, 1979. The demand for money during hyperinflation under rational expectations. *International Economic Review* 20:741–758.

Sargent, T. J., 1977. The demand for money during hyperinflation under rational expectations: I. *International Economic Review* 18:59–82.

Sargent, T. J., and N. Wallace, 1973. Rational expectations and the dynamics of hyperinflation. *International Economic Review* 14:328–350.

Singh, B., A. L. Nagar, N. K. Choudhry, and B. Raj, 1976. On the estimation of structural change: a generalization of the random coefficients regression model. *International Economic Review* 17:340–361.

Stern, R. M., C. F. Baum, and M. N. Greene, 1979. Evidence on structural change in the demand for aggregate U.S. imports and exports. *Journal of Political Economy* 87:179–192.

Theil, H., 1971. *Principles of Econometrics.* North-Holland, Amsterdam.

Tinbergen, J., 1934. *International Abstracts of Economic Statistics, 1919–1930.* International Conference of Economic Services, London.

Tukey, J. W., 1962. The future of data analysis. *Annals of Mathematical Statistics* 33:1–67.

Tukey, J. W., 1977. *Exploratory Data Analysis.* Addison-Wesley, Reading, Mass.

Wilcoxon, F., S. K. Katti, and R. A. Wilcox, 1973. Critical values and probability levels for the Wilcoxon rank sum test and the Wilcoxon signed rank test. In *Selected Tables in Mathematical Statistics*, Vol. 1. The Institute of Mathematical Statistics and American Mathematical Society, Providence (Rhode Island), pp. 171–259.

3 A Bayesian Analysis of the Determinants of Inflation

Edward E. Leamer

3.1 Introduction

The persistence of inflation despite unanimous public opposition reveals that either a secret cabal of policymakers controls our economy for its own purposes or, for want of ability or knowledge, the determinants of inflation are beyond our control. Persual of the business sections of the newspapers leads me to believe that lack of knowledge is the culprit.

Keynesians, monetarists, pragmatists, gradualists, antimonetarists, supply-siders, microfoundationists, classicists, rational expecters, random walkers, and so on and on—the macroeconomics landscape is littered with economists carrying different banners and offering different advice. I adopt at the outset the hopeful attitude that empirical evidence, properly employed, could move these disparate sects in the direction of a consensus. I assume that the Bayesian subjective probability model characterizes properly formed opinions. Differences in opinions are then due either to differences in observations or to differences in subjective prior probabilities. Since macroeconomists have access to more or less the same macro data, we must point to differing priors as the source of the disparate opinions.

At a minimum I intend to demonstrate whether or not different priors about the causes of inflation can lead to different inferences from the U.S. post-World War II macro data. But I begin with a more ambitious task in mind. I suspect that much of the source of differing opinions, even after having observed the macro data set, is not due to dogmatically held priors but rather to improper processing of the available data. Empirical economists have not had Bayesian training and the way they use their priors is to search for a model that yields estimates more or less consistent with prior opinion. It is hard to imagine that this would change anyone's mind. Here I will show, for example, how strongly a Keynesian must believe in the irrelevance of monetary policy to conclude, after having seen the data, that money does not matter. If this is a very dogmatically held belief, most of us will draw a different inference from the data set. If the data are reasonably convincing, a consensus may emerge. Thus the ideal outcome of this work would be a decisive statement of the usefulness of empirical evidence for studying this macroeconomics issue.

In order to perform this analysis, it is necessary to write down a general macromodel with a parameterization so broad that special parameter values imply models of the Keynesian type, of the monetarist type, and so forth. Then prior distributions for these parameters must be selected to represent the opinions of each of the sects. This is not an easy task.

Theoretical and empirical models of inflation rest implicitly or explicitly on assumptions about market-clearing processes and about the formation of expectations: coordination and information, to use Leijonhufvud's (1981) title. One viewpoint, which is associated with the name of Keynes, is that price increases are preceded by realized excess demands that give rise to unintended reductions of inventories of goods or laborers. Fiscal and monetary policy can affect the rate of inflation only by first affecting the level of excess demand. In terms of mathematical symbols we could write such a system as

$$\Delta \log P = \beta_0 + \beta_1 X, \tag{3.1}$$

$$X = \gamma_0 + \gamma_1 F + \gamma_2 M, \tag{3.2}$$

where $\Delta \log P$ is the rate of inflation, F is the fiscal policy, M is money, and X is the level of excess demand. Equation (3.2) summarizes the IS-LM system, and equation (3.1) can be thought to combine a Phillips curve with a price markup rule.

At a theoretical level this Keynesian model leaves much to be desired. The period for which this model is thought to apply is left unspecified. Expectations seem to be myopic. The failure of markets to clear has no stated dynamic implications—that is, notional demands are unaffected by coordination failures. Supply is taken as fixed.

The extreme opposite viewpoint is that markets clear instantaneously and that changes in inventories of goods or labor reflect changes in expectations about the future path of prices and wages. A static version of this viewpoint is summarized by the quantity equation $MV = PQ$. If Q and V are fixed, we would then have a monetarist model of inflation,

$$\Delta \log P = \beta_0 + \beta_1 \Delta \log M, \tag{3.3}$$

with $\beta_0 = 0$ and $\beta_1 = 1$.

This monetarist model also leaves much to be desired. There are no dynamics in the model, no uncertainty, no reason for inventories of goods or labor.

Given the obvious shortcomings of these two models as characterizations of dynamic processes, it may seem surprising that they serve as foundations for the empirical work on the determinants of inflation. Nevertheless, most studies use one of these two frameworks with a few lagged variables thrown in. These lagged variables are justified as reflecting expectation formation, but it is fair to say that the dynamic empirical models that result do not have a solid theoretical foundation, or at least not a fully articulated one. Since neither my experience nor my desires allow me to specify a complete model of inflation, I will, with a queasy feeling, follow the path of my predecessors and "dynamize" the model in an ad hoc fashion. The resulting empirical work, though lacking a theoretical foundation, should still appeal to some macroeconomists, who seem to not need one.

The approach that I take is to combine these two models into the composite model

$$\Delta\log P = \beta_0 + \beta_1 X + \beta_2 \Delta\log M, \tag{3.4}$$

$$X = \gamma_0 + \gamma_1 F + \gamma_2 M, \tag{3.5}$$

and to characterize the difference between the Keynesian and the monetarist viewpoints in terms of the choice of prior distributions for the parameters in this general model. A Keynesian expects to see β_2 small, whereas a monetarist expects to see β_1, γ_1, and γ_2 small. Keynesians and monetarists are also distinguished by their attitudes toward the dynamics in the system, with the Keynesians generally expecting a relatively sluggish response. In addition a distinction is drawn between classical and Friedmaniac attitudes toward the dynamics in the excess demand equation (3.5). Though both expect no long-run effect of money ($\gamma_2 = 0$), a Friedmaniac allows short-run effects.

The priors I will be defining will leave most readers uncomfortable. In practice, the only prior distribution that does not cause discomfort is the diffuse prior, but the use of a diffuse prior for the analysis of economic data is either a delusion or a deceit. To combat the feeling of discomfort that you properly will feel, I report a global sensitivity analysis. A sensibly inclusive family of priors in the neighborhood of the hypothesized prior is selected, and the corresponding family of inferences is identified. If all the inferences in this set are essentially the same, we may conclude that inferences from these data are "resilient," that is, insensitive to the choice of prior. If this set includes substantially different inferences, the conclusions from these data are judged to be "fragile" and unworthy of attention.

Those of you who are not reading this chapter for its methodological contribution but for the light it sheds on the debate over the inflation/ unemployment trade-offs may now terminate reading, since I regret to inform you that virtually all the inferences I report are fragile. A monetarist can find convincing evidence that money growth affects inflation, though a Keynesian remains unconvinced. Both do agree that if unemployment slows inflation, the effect is small. Otherwise, this data set is not particularly useful. Neither Keynesians nor monetarists will find their personal beliefs greatly influenced by it. Nor does it produce anything approaching a consensus.

3.2 A General Model of Inflation

The model I will use to illustrate how priors play a role in inferring the determinants of inflation consists of the two equations described in tables 3.3 and 3.4. Variables are defined in table 3.1 The first difference operator Δ_i and the averaging operator A_i are defined in table 3.2. The inflation equation expresses the rate of inflation in terms of six variables, each with its own distributed lag. The first set of explanatory variables are lagged inflation rates. These variables allow "momentum" in the inflation process, possibly due to the formation of expectations. Inflation rates up to three years earlier are allowed to affect the current rate. A general distributed lag of this length would require thirteen variables, one for each quarter. Computer limitations force an economy of parameterization on any empirical exercise. In this case the number of explanatory variables is limited to at most twenty-five. Accordingly the distributed lag process is characterized in terms of four variables: inflation rates over the past quarter, the past year, the past two years, and the past three years.

The second set of variables in the inflation equation are growth rates of money, with timing similar to the lagged inflation rates. The third set of variables are unemployment rates. The Phillips curve is traditionally expressed in terms of the inverse of the unemployment rate, a form that is also adopted here. This variable is multiplied by 25 to make the derivative of the inflation rate with respect to U evaluated at $U = 5$ equal to the coefficient. This facilitates the formation of prior information, since the size of the coefficient on $25U^{-1}$ is the approximate answer to the question: How much would the inflation rate increase if the unemployment rate fell from 5 to 4 percent?

Table 3.1
Variable definitions (all data seasonally adjusted)

Symbol	Description	Source
P	Fixed weight GNP deflator (1972 = 100)	Gordon data set
M	Money: M1B 1959–80 spliced to M1, 1947–58 (splice factor = 0.9845722	Federal Reserve System data base via San Francisco Federal Bank librarian
U	Unemployment percentage (0–100) (survey of week including 12th day of month, average over quarter)	Gordon data set
D	Federal government deficit in billions	Dept. of Commerce, BEA, Business Condition Digest
Y	GNP in billions of dollars	
E	Crude oil price per barrel (34° ex Ras al Tanurah)	*Petroleum Economist*
C_1	Price control "on" dummy equal to 2/3 from 1971 third quarter to 1972 fourth quarter (C_1 sums to 4)	Gordon data set
C_2	Price control "off" dummy equal to 1 from 1974 second quarter to 1975 first quarter (C_2 sums to 4)	Gordon data set
G	Federal government purchases of goods and services (billions of dollars)	Business Condition Digest
A	G − taxes + transfers + gross private domestic investment − capital consumption allowances + net exports (billions) [Friedman − Meiselman definition]	Dept. of Commerce, NIPA's Survey of Current Business
F	Civilian Labor Force in millions	Dept. of Commerce, BLS, Business Condition Digest

Table 3.2
Notation

$x = \log X$

$L^n x_t = x_{t-n}$

$\Delta_n x_t = 400(x_t - x_{t-n})/n$

    $=$ average growth at annual rates of X over the previous n quarters

$A_n x = (x_t + x_{t-1} + \cdots + x_{t-n+1})/n$

    $=$ average value of x over current and $n-1$ preceding quarters

Table 3.3
Inflation equation

	$\Delta_1 p =$
Intercept	β_0
Lagged Inflation	$+ \beta_1 L\Delta_1 p + \beta_2 L\Delta_4 p + \beta_3 L\Delta_8 p + \beta_4 L\Delta_{12} p$
Money	$+ \beta_5 \Delta_1 m + \beta_6 \Delta_4 m + \beta_7 \Delta_8 m + \beta_8 \Delta_{12} m$
Unemployment	$+ \beta_9 25U^{-1} + \beta_{10} A_4 25U^{-1} + \beta_{11} A_8 25U^{-1} + \beta_{12} A_{12} 25U^{-1}$
Deficit/GNP	$+ \beta_{13} 100D/Y + \beta_{14} A_4 (100D/Y) + \beta_{15} A_8 (100D/Y)$ $+ \beta_{16} A_{12} (100D/Y)$
Oil price	$+ \beta_{17} \Delta_1 e + \beta_{18} \Delta_4 e + \beta_{19} \Delta_8 e + \beta_{20} \Delta_{12} e$
Price controls	$+ \beta_{21} C_1 + \beta_{22} C_2$

Table 3.4
Unemployment equation

	$25U^{-1} =$
Intercept	γ_0
Lagged unemployment	$+ \gamma_1 L(25U^{-1}) + \gamma_2 LA_4 (25U^{-1}) + \gamma_3 LA_8 (25U^{-1})$ $+ \gamma_4 LA_{12}(25U^{-1})$
Money	$+ \gamma_5 m + \gamma_6 \Delta_1 m + \gamma_7 \Delta_4 m + \gamma_8 \Delta_8 m + \gamma_9 \Delta_{12} m$
Prices	$+ \gamma_{10} Lp + \gamma_{11} L\Delta_1 p + \gamma_{12} L\Delta_4 p + \gamma_{13} L\Delta_8 p$ $+ \gamma_{14} L\Delta_{12} p$
Real government	$+ \gamma_{15} (G/LP) + \gamma_{16} A_4 (G/LP) + \gamma_{17} A_8 (G/LP)$ $+ \gamma_{18} A_{12}(G/LP)$
Real autonomous expenditures	$+ \gamma_{19} (A/LP) + \gamma_{20} A_4 (A/LP) + \gamma_{21} A_8 (A/LP)$ $+ \gamma_{22} A_{12}(A/LP)$
Labor force	$+ \gamma_{23} F$

The fourth variable is the government deficit scaled by GNP. Monetarists do not believe the deficit has a direct impact on the inflation rate. This opinion is well expressed by Meiselman (1981) who, in a report titled "Are Tax Cuts Inflationary," writes: "Inflation occurs when the quantity of money expands faster than output.... Changes in tax rates, or other provisions of the tax code, will affect inflation if these changes alter output.... If a deficit is financed by selling government bonds to the Federal Reserve, the resulting increase in the supply of money reduces the value of money, which is to say, inflation results." Since the level of money is controlled for in equation (3.4), the only route for deficits to affect prices is through their impact on output, and the effect will be small according to this monetarist prescription. The Keynesian contrary opinion is not often fully articulated because prices remain in the wings of the Keynesian drama. One view, built on hazy notions of inflexible prices, allows fiscal policy to affect inflation only through the route of excess demand, which is captured by the unemployment variable. Another viewpoint is that fiscal policy affects the level of aggregate demand which in turn influences both the level of prices and the unemployment rate. My reading of the editorial pages of newspapers makes me believe that most editorial writers are uncertain of the link between deficits and inflation. This view persists even though prominent Keynesians such as Heller (1979) find otherwise: "Even a cursory inspection of the data on deficits and inflation shows little relation between the two." It is probably fair to say that Heller expected to see a link, whereas Meiselman (1981) did not. The fact that they both came to the same conclusion from an examination of the data is a very hopeful sign for those who think data can be useful.

The possibility that deficits generate inflation by first affecting the money supply suggests that we should add to our model a third equation describing the determinants of money.[1] It is logically possible to continue to add equations in this way until inflation is traced back to the big bang. The decision to terminate these linkages with money taken as given reflects the belief that money can be controlled or, to put it differently, that the reaction function can be altered. The interpretation of the coefficients in our two-equation model is rendered difficult if these parameters depend on the money supply reaction function, as is suggested by the rational-expectations logic of Lucas (1972) and Lucas and Sargent (1978). In that event an attempt to control inflation by restricting money growth must take into account the effects of the new policy rule on the parameters. In this article, I will ignore this problem and adopt the out-of-fashion attitude that the parameters are invariant to the money rule. Moreover money is treated as if it were exogenous.

The next variable is the price of oil. It would come as a great surprise to me if anyone estimated an inflation equation before 1974 with oil prices as an explanatory variable. The coincidence of the formation of OPEC and the inflation of the 1970s has changed that completely, and energy prices have found their way into the Keynesian price markup equations such as those of Frye and Gordon (1980). Quantity theorists would expect to the contrary that increases in the price of imported oil would modestly lower real GNP (oil imports were less than 1 percent of GNP) and consequently modestly increase the price level. Otherwise, an increase in the price of oil, if the demand for oil is inelastic, would leave less income to spend on other commodities generally and would lower their prices. Okun (1981, p. 3) argues, however: "No professional economist will ever against insist (as some did early in 1974) that a major rise in the price of oil cannot raise the price level since it merely pushes other prices down," and he generalizes "that the same truth applies to hikes in indirect taxes, from price supports and minimum wages."

The last two variables measure the effect of the Nixon price controls. These variables are taken from Frye and Gordon (1980) and are designed to select the period over which the controls were removed (1974.1 to 1975.1). Each sums to four so that the estimated coefficients indicate the cumulative effect of the controls program on the price level.[2]

To make the two equation system linear, the unemployment equation is expressed in terms of $25U^{-1}$ which greatly facilitates policy analysis. The unemployment rate is allowed to depend on past unemployment rates, on the current labor force, and on distributed lags in money, prices, government, and autonomous expenditures. In writing this equation, I have tried to understand the IS-LM model. A version of that model seems to take prices and wages as fixed in the short run (a quarter?). Aggregate demand is then determined by monetary and fiscal policy as well as by the "autonomous" component: investment plus net exports. If this aggregate demand does not match aggregate supply, measured by the labor force, then unemployment results. The unemployment equation accordingly includes current values of money, prices, government expenditure, autonomous expenditure, and the labor force.

Also included in the unemployment equation are distributed lags of money and prices. The acceleration hypothesis, cited by Frisch (p. 1298), is that only changes in the rate of growth of money have real effects. This viewpoint, which is most often associated with the name of Milton Friedman, is consistent with the proposition of Lucas (1972, 1973) and Barro (1977) that only "unexpected" money has real effects, if expectations are formed by extrapolating past money growth experience into the future. Barro's (1977) econometric model of unemployment is similar to the one used here, although he estimates a two-equation system, the second equation determining expectations of money growth and the first expressing unemployment as a function of unanticipated money movements.

Prior for the Inflation Equation

A monetarist and a Keynesian prior for the inflation equation are described in table 3.5. If the monetarist prior means were imposed exactly, the inflation equation would be $\Delta_1 p = \alpha + \Delta_1 m$: money growth in the quarter causes an equal increase in the price level. If the Keynesian prior means were imposed exactly, the inflation equation would become $\Delta_1 p = \alpha + 75U^{-1}$: an increase in the unemployment rate from 5 to 6 percent would reduce inflation by 2.5 percent $[75 \times (6^{-1} - 5^{-1})]$.

The standard errors on these prior means reflect the level of uncertainty that is likely to be attached to these beliefs. For example, the monetarist prior allows some one-quarter momentum in prices, since the coefficient on lagged price can vary from zero by as much as 0.4, in the sense that an *a priori* 95 percent interval for β_1 is $(-0.4, 0.4)$. This means that as much as 40 percent of last quarter's inflation can be carried over into this quarter. The corresponding figures for annual, biannual, and triannual carry-over are 20, 10, and 5 percent. If these figures seem high, remember the most likely estimates are zero, and these numbers indicate extremes beyond which the coefficients are not expected to go.

The monetarist prior allows some momentum but insists that the system has a short memory in the sense that the coefficients are expected to decline (geometrically) as the lag length increases. The Keynesian prior allows more momentum and less memory loss (at an arithmetic pace).

A monetarist prior constraint $\sum_1^8 \beta_1 = 1$ expresses the idea that in the long run, prices are proportional to money. A constant money growth rate at x percent in the long run produces inflation at the rate of x times $(\beta_5 + \beta_6 + \beta_7 + \beta_8)/(1 - \beta_1 - \beta_2 - \beta_3 - \beta_4)$, which, when set to one, generates the constraint $\sum_1^8 \beta_i = 1$. The standard error on this linear combination

Table 3.5
Probable values of coefficients, inflation equation: two times prior standard errors (means in parentheses if not zero)

Coefficients		Monetarist prior	Keynesian prior
Prices	β_1	0.4	0.5
	β_2	0.2	0.4
	β_3	0.1	0.3
	β_4	0.05	0.2
Money	β_5	a	0.1
	β_6	0.4	0.08
	β_7	0.2	0.06
	β_8	0.1	0.04
	$\sum_1^8 \beta_i$	(1.0)0.2	a
Unemployment	β_9	0.4	a
	β_{10}	0.2	0.10
	β_{11}	0.1	0.08
	β_{12}	0.05	0.06
	$\sum_9^{12} \beta_i + 3\sum_1^4 \beta_i$	a	(3.0)3.0
Deficit	β_{13}	1.0	10.0
	β_{14}	0.5	8.0
	β_{15}	0.25	6.0
	β_{16}	0.125	4.0
Oil prices	β_{17}	0.05	a
	β_{18}	0.025	0.1
	β_{19}	0.0125	0.08
	β_{20}	0.00625	0.06
	$\sum_{17}^{20} \beta_i + 0.1\sum_1^4 \beta_i$	a	(0.1)0.1
Controls	β_{21}	∞	∞
	$\beta_{21} + \beta_{22}$	1	(−5.0)5.0
	β_{22}	∞	∞

a. Implicit in other prior constraints.

is difficult to select because, for example, the opinion that $\theta_1/(1 - \theta_2)$ is close to one is not equivalent to the opinion that $\theta_1 + \theta_2$ is close to one. The former opinion can be expressed by the statement that $[\theta_1(1 - \theta_2)^{-1} - 1]^2$ is small, or equivalently that $(\theta_1 + \theta_2 - 1)^2/(1 - \theta_2)^2$ is small. This could be well approximated by the statement that $(\theta_1 + \theta_2 - 1)^2$ is small if θ_2 is close to zero. Thus the prior that $\sum_1^4 \beta_i$ is small allows us to treat the statement that $\sum_1^8 \beta_i$ is within 0.2 of 1 as an approximation to the statement that the long-run multiplier $\sum_5^8 \beta_i/(1 - \sum_1^4 \beta_i)$ is within 0.2 of 1.

In addition to the long-run proportionality between money and prices, the monetarist prior embodies the idea that money is likely to have a rapid impact on prices, since the lagged effects, β_6, β_7, and β_8, all have zero means with declining standard errors. The Keynesian prior, on the other hand, has zero means for all the money variables, with small standard errors that decline relatively slowly with time, thereby reflecting the Keynesian belief that money does not have much of a direct effect on price, and also the belief that the system may be sluggish.

The unemployment variable is treated oppositely with the Keynesian expecting an effect but the monetarist expecting none. The Keynesian prior for the sum $\sum_9^{12} \beta_i + 3 \sum_1^4 \beta_i$ is located at 3, which would mean that an increase in unemployment from 5 to 6 percent would reduce the rate of inflation by $3 \times 25 \times (6^{-1} - 5^{-1}) = 2.5$ percent per annum in the long run. The fairly large standard error on this sum allows this effect to be as small as zero or as large as 5 percent. The Keynesian expects the current unemployment rate to be the conveyor of information about excess demand in the labor market, which drives price changes, and consequently means for the lagged unemployment coefficients are set to 0 with declining standard errors. The monetarist prior has means for all the unemployment coefficients equal to zero with rapidly declining standard errors.

The federal deficit is treated as a doubtful direct cause of inflation by both the monetarist and the Keynesian. If a deficit coefficient were equal to one, a rise in the federal deficit from 0.1 to 0.2 percent of GNP would raise the rate of inflation by 0.1 percent, a very small number. This is the upper limit of the monetarist's range of prior estimates. The Keynesian is ten times as uncertain because he thinks fiscal policy determines excess demand which may not be fully captured by the unemployment variable.

A Keynesian using a markup model of prices expects to see increases in the cost of oil passed onto the consumer in higher prices. With oil inputs making up about 10 percent of costs, every percentage increase in oil prices would raise final goods prices by 0.1 percent. The sum $\sum_{17}^{20} \beta_i + 0.1 \sum_1^4 \beta_i$ accordingly has mean 0.1 and a large standard error of $0.1/2$. The time it takes to pass these costs along is not expected to be a quarter, and the lagged coefficients on oil prices are given large standard errors. The monetarist, in contrast, is fairly certain that oil price increases do not lead to inflation if they are not "monetized" by expanding money.

The net effect of the price controls $\beta_{21} + \beta_{22}$ is expected by the monetarist to be zero with a small standard error but is expected by the Keynesian to be minus five with a relatively large standard error.

The Choice of Prior: Unemployment Equation

The formation of a prior for the unemployment equation is more difficult than the inflation equation because neither the monetarist nor the Keynesian model offers much advice about the magnitudes of the coefficients. I adopt the same convention as in the inflation equation that the monetarist expects less momentum and more rapid memory loss than the Keynesian, and I take the prior standard errors on the lagged unemployment rates to be the same as the prior standard errors on lagged inflation rates in the inflation equation.

The Keynesian prior otherwise is built on an IS-LM model of aggregate demand which takes prices as fixed for a period (a quarter) at the level of the previous quarter and generates aggregate demand as a function of the exogenously given levels of money, government expenditures, and autonomous expenditures (investment plus net exports). These expenditure components are deflated by the previous quarter's prices, which means that I am taking as predetermined (independent of current prices) the nominal government and autonomous expenditures. The priors for the coefficients of these two expenditure variables imply that each extra $5,000 in expenditure is expected to generate one extra job in the long run.[3] The relatively large standard errors and their slow rate of decay reflect the Keynesian's uncertainty about the precise timing of the job-creating effect of these expenditure variables.

The money variable in the unemployment equation is in logarithmic form, and the Keynesian chooses a prior mean for γ_5 such that a 1 percent rise in money would lower unemployment from 5.0 to 4.9 percent. A similar drop in prices in the previous period would have the same beneficial effect on unemployment. (Here I am thinking of the money demand function.) The growth rate variables for money and prices are all treated as doubtful. The coefficient for the labor variable in the Keynesian prior is selected under the assumption that the level of employment is decided by IS-LM analysis independent of the number of job seekers. Unemployment is then just the gap between the number seeking jobs and the number the economy can employ.[4]

Monetarists can be divided into classicists, who think money has no effect on unemployment, and Friedmaniacs, who expect no long-run effects but allow short-run effects. For the Friedmaniacs the sum of the coefficients (the long-run effects) are constrained rather tightly to zero but otherwise the prior is uninformative. The classicist treats all variables as doubtful, with zero prior means. For example, the expenditure variables are thought to affect the allocation of the work force among government, consumer goods, and investment goods but not to have an impact on measured unemployment. Likewise a large labor force lowers the real wage but leaves unaffected the number of individuals (optimally) searching for a new job. Money influences the price level, not the unemployment rate.

A Bayesian Sensitivity Analysis

Most readers of the previous section on the choice of priors will find themselves amused or irritated by the notion of characterizing precise Keynesian or monetarist priors. It is the incredulity that invariably greets any particular prior probability distribution that in the past has prevented Bayesian analysis from being used routinely. On the other hand, there is little doubt that data analysts, particularly macroeconomists, use prior information as a guide for the selection of variables. There has to be a reason why a formal Bayesian analysis is not used in practice when judgment is so often used and so often reported as the reason for selecting one set of estimates over another. The reason, I believe, is that researchers are unable to form complete prior distributions. The description in the previous section involves so many twists and turns, so many partly arbitrary decisions, that you have to feel uncomfortable with the final product. You ought to be uncomfortable as well with the usual ad hoc regression selection procedures, but many people are blissfully ignorant and act as if the equation they select were really the only one that matters anyway.

A sensitivity analysis can be used to combat the arbitrariness associated with the choice of prior distribution. Two forms of sensitivity analysis are used here to study the effect of a change in the prior variance matrix. For the first form of sensitivity analysis, estimates are formed using priors that are either more diffuse or more concentrated than the priors defined in tables 3.5 and 3.6. The prior is altered by multiplying the prior covariance matrix V_0 by a scale factor σ_1^2 that takes on several values between zero and infinity. In the second form of sensitivity analysis the prior covariance matrix V is allowed to take on any value in an interval around V_0: $\lambda^{-2}V_0 \leq V \leq \lambda^2 V_0$, where λ is a scalar assuming several values exceeding one and where $A \leq B$ means $B - A$ is positive semidefinite. Corresponding to this interval of prior covariance matrices is an interval of Bayes estimates from which extreme values are selected to indicate the ambiguity in the estimates

Table 3.6
Probable values of coefficients, unemployment equation: two times prior standard errors (means in parentheses if not zero)

Coefficients		Keynesian	Classical	Friedmaniac
Unemployment	γ_1	0.5	0.4	0.4
	γ_2	0.4	0.2	0.2
	γ_3	0.3	0.1	0.1
	γ_4	0.2	0.05	0.05
Money	γ_5	(10)10	5	1.0
	γ_6	5	4	∞
	γ_7	4	2	∞
	γ_8	3	1	∞
	γ_9	2	0.5	∞
	$\sum_6^9 \gamma_i$	a	a	1.0
Prices	γ_{10}	$(-10)10$	5	1.0
	γ_{11}	5	4	∞
	γ_{12}	4	2	∞
	γ_{13}	3	1	∞
	γ_{14}	2	0.5	∞
	$\sum_{11}^{14} \gamma_i$	a	a	1.0
Government	γ_{15}	a	0.4	∞
	γ_{16}	1.0	0.2	∞
	γ_{17}	0.8	0.1	∞
	γ_{18}	0.6	0.05	∞
	$\sum_1^4 \gamma_i + \sum_{15}^{18} \gamma_i$	(1)1.0	a	∞
	$\sum_{15}^{18} \gamma_i$	a	a	0.1
Autonomous	γ_{19}	a	0.4	∞
	γ_{20}	1.0	0.2	∞
	γ_{21}	0.8	0.1	∞
	γ_{22}	0.6	0.05	∞
	$\sum_1^4 \gamma_i + \sum_{19}^{22} \gamma_i$	(1)1.0	a	∞
	$\sum_{19}^{22} \gamma_i$	a	a	0.1
Labor	γ_{23}	$(-1)1$	0.1	0.1

a. Implicit in other prior constraints.

associated with the ambiguity in the prior. The second form of sensitivity analysis is often preferred, since it is unlikely that the prior covariance matrix could be selected so that it is known up to a scale factor. For more details, see Leamer and Leonard (1983) or Leamer (1978, 1982).

3.3   Estimation Results

Estimates of the Inflation Equation

Estimates of the inflation equation using the monetarist and the Keynesian priors and data from 1954, quarter two, to 1980, quarter two, are reported in tables 3.7 and 3.8. The second column in these tables, headed by $\sigma_1 = 0$, contains least-squares estimates subject to the constraints in the prior because here the prior covariance matrix has been multiplied by the scalar $\sigma_1 = 0$. The monetarist prior constrains all coefficients to zero except the current money growth rate, with a coefficient of one, and the two dummies for the price controls, which are constrained to have coefficients that sum to zero. As you move to the right in these tables, the prior constraints are imposed with less and less confidence. The column headed by $\sigma_1 = 1$ contains estimates based on the priors defined in tables 3.5 and 3.6. The adjacent columns dilute or sharpen the prior by a factor of two. At the penultimate column the prior is fully diluted, and the estimates are just the unconstrained least-squares values. The corresponding t values are recorded in the last column. Also the row labeled "Confidence" is the confidence level attaching to the sample ellipsoid on which the corresponding estimate lies.

Examination of the unconstrained least-squares values in the column headed $\sigma_1 = \infty$ and the t values in the last column might lead you to the following conclusions:

1. The inflation process has a long memory and large momentum, where the momentum is measured by the sum of the coefficients on the lagged inflation terms and the memory is measured by the average lag of inflation behind its determinants. The three-year average rate of inflation has the largest and most significant coefficient of the lagged inflation rates. The same is true for the money growth coefficients.

2. The short-run impact of money growth on inflation is small, but the long-run coefficient $(0.06 + 0.43 - 0.68 + 0.88)/(1 + 0.19 - 0.11 + 0.06 - 0.80) = 2.05$ is large enough to embarrass even a monetarist.

Table 3.7
Estimates of inflation equation: monetarist prior

| | s^b | \multicolumn{6}{c}{σ_1 (prior standard error scale factor)} |
		0	0.5	1.0	2.0	∞	t^c
Confidence		1.0	0.999	0.996	0.937	0	
Intercept	∞	-0.24	1.07	1.36	1.21	0.96	1.0
$L\Delta_1 p$	0.4	0	0.29	0.20	0.07	-0.19	-1.8
$L\Delta_4 p$	0.2	0	0.11	0.20	0.28	0.11	0.4
$L\Delta_8 p$	0.1	0	0.03	0.06	0.10	-0.06	-0.2
$L\Delta_{12} p$	0.05	0	0.01	0.02	0.06	0.80	2.4
$\Delta_1 m$	a	1.0	0.20	0.11	0.08	0.06	0.8
$\Delta_4 m$	0.4	0	0.21	0.21	0.17	0.43	2.3
$\Delta_8 m$	0.2	0	0.08	0.13	0.16	-0.68	-1.6
$\Delta_{12} m$	0.1	0	0.03	0.05	0.12	0.88	2.3
$25U^{-1}$	0.4	0	-0.15	-0.25	-0.43	-1.05	-2.8
$A_4 25U^{-1}$	0.2	0	-0.01	0.02	0.14	0.96	1.4
$A_8 25U^{-1}$	0.1	0	0	0.01	0.05	0.47	0.5
$A_{12} 25U^{-1}$	0.05	0	0	0	0	-0.67	-1.1
$100D/Y$	1.0	0	-0.43	-0.65	-0.88	-1.15	-5.1
$A_4 100D/Y$	0.5	0	0.05	0.14	0.16	-0.64	-1.5
$A_8 100D/Y$	0.25	0	0.05	0.11	0.22	1.10	1.8
$A_{12} 100D/Y$	0.125	0	0.01	0.01	-0.02	-0.44	-0.9
$\Delta_1 e$	0.05	0	0.01	0.01	0	0.01	-0.8
$\Delta_4 e$	0.025	0	0.01	0.01	0.01	0.01	0.5
$\Delta_8 e$	0.0125	0	0	0.01	0.02	0.09	4.0
$\Delta_{12} e$	0.00625	0	0	0	0	-0.04	-1.3
C_1	—	-5.9	-2.59	-2.25	-2.2	-2.75	-2.2
C_2	—	5.9	2.24	2.24	1.8	-0.55	-0.4

a. Implicit in other prior constraints.
b. Twice the prior standard error.
c. Least-squares t values.

Table 3.8
Estimates of inflation equation: Keynesian prior

	s^b	σ_1 (prior standard error scale factor)				
		0	0.5	1.0	2.0	∞
Confidence		1.0	0.997	0.809	0.180	0
Intercept	∞	-12.2	0.98	0.64	0.45	0.96
$L\Delta_1 p$	0.5	0	0.17	0.04	-0.05	-0.19
$L\Delta_4 p$	0.4	0	0.27	0.30	0.19	0.11
$L\Delta_8 p$	0.3	0	0.16	0.26	0.32	-0.06
$L\Delta_{12} p$	0.2	0	0.09	0.18	0.35	0.80
$\Delta_1 m$	0.1	0	0.04	0.08	0.11	0.06
$\Delta_4 m$	0.08	0	0.02	0.05	0.12	0.43
$\Delta_8 m$	0.06	0	0.01	0.02	0.05	-0.68
$\Delta_{12} m$	0.04	0	0	0.01	0.03	0.88
$25U^{-1}$	a	3.0	-0.21	-0.49	-0.77	-1.05
$A_4 25U^{-1}$	0.10	0	0.20	0.46	0.69	0.96
$A_8 25U^{-1}$	0.08	0	0	0	0	-0.47
$A_{12} 25U^{-1}$	0.06	0	0	0	0.01	-0.67
$100D/Y$	10	0	0.18	-1.07	-1.11	-1.14
$A_4 100D/Y$	8	0	0.54	0.05	-0.19	-0.64
$A_8 100D/Y$	6	0	0.07	0.86	1.04	1.10
$A_{12} 100D/Y$	4	0	0	-0.16	-0.30	-0.44
$\Delta_1 e$	a	0.10	0	0	0	-0.01
$\Delta_4 e$	0.1	0	0.02	0.02	0.01	0.01
$\Delta_8 e$	0.08	0	0.04	0.06	0.07	0.09
$\Delta_{12} e$	0.06	0	-0.01	-0.03	-0.05	-0.04
C_1	∞	-8.09	-2.47	-2.53	-2.96	-2.75
C_2	∞	3.09	-0.97	-0.30	0.16	-0.55

a. Implicit in other prior constraints.
b. Two times the prior standard.

3. High levels of unemployment in the current quarter, rather than suppressing inflation, actually stimulate it. This is in conformity with the quantity equation, since higher levels of unemployment mean lower output and "fewer goods being chased by the given supply of dollars." Recall that a coefficient of 3, as expected by the Keynesian, would mean that an increase in unemployment from 5 to 6 percent would reduce the rate of inflation by 2.5 percent per annum. The least-squares estimate of -1.05 for the current quarter means that this increase in the unemployment rate by 1 percent would increase the rate of inflation by 0.8 percent. This initial impact is offset as time proceeds so that a two-year sustained high level of unemployment does reduce inflation, but in the long run the estimated effect of $25U^{-1}$ is the small (and statistically insignificant number) -0.85.

4. The deficit surprisingly has both short- and long-run negative effects on the inflation rate. The higher the deficit relative to GNP, the lower the inflation rate.

5. Energy prices do get passed onto other goods in general after a two-year period. The long-run coefficient is 0.15, which means that 15 percent of energy inflation is passed on.

6. The Nixon controls lowered the rate of inflation by 2.75 percent, and the removal of the controls did not cause a burst of pent-up price increases to offset this effect.

Some of these findings seem to conflict with monetarist opinions; others conflict with Keynesian opinions. But what seems apparent from estimates and t values may not actually be there if this data evidence is formally pooled with the prior information. The pooled estimates based on the priors presented earlier are indicated in the columns headed by $\sigma_1 = 1$. These estimates lead to the following conclusions:

1. In contrast to the least-squares results, the monetarist does not find the level of momentum to be high or the lag length long. Most of the action occurs within a year. The Keynesian, as expected, finds both higher momentum and longer lag length.

2. The monetarist estimate of the long-run money coefficient is 0.96, and the Keynesian estimate is 0.76. These are both much lower than the least-squares estimate of 2.03. The Keynesian prior in this case is rather sharply altered by the data.

3. Even a Keynesian with a tighter prior ($\sigma_1 = 0.5$) than the one we are using cannot find the Phillips curve that he expects.

4. Both the Keynesian and the monetarist find that the federal deficit

reduces inflation, although a Keynesian with a tighter prior ($\sigma_1 = 0.5$) does find that the deficit induces inflation.

5. Both the Keynesian and the monetarist conclude that energy price increases are passed on; the Keynesian long-run coefficient (0.17) is higher than his prior estimate of 0.1. Even the monetarist ends up with a surprisingly large long-run value of 0.045.

6. The short-run impact of the price control program is estimated to be about the same by the Keynesian and the monetarist, but the monetarist concludes that the removal of the controls completely offsets the temporary reduction in inflation.

The preceding discussion has to be regarded with a great deal of skepticism because it is all based on rather fanciful and unlikely priors. The unconstrained least-squares estimates use diffuse priors which would be implicitly rejected by researchers when they omit variables in the usual ad hoc fashion. The Bayes estimates sensibly omit variables in a "partial" way, but they are built on highly specialized and therefore unlikely prior notions. If a minor change in the prior leads to a major change in the inference, inference with this data set will have to be regarded as too fragile to be worth serious consideration.

One way to study the fragility of a Bayesian inference to identify a family of priors in the neighborhood of the hypothesized prior distribution. If all priors in a neighborhood of credible size lead to essentially the same conclusion, then the inference can be judged to be sturdy. If, on the other hand, it is necessary to employ an incredibly narrow set of priors to obtain a usefully narrow set of estimates, then inferences from these data are too fragile to be useful. The neighborhood I will study here takes the location of the prior as fixed but lets the prior variance V lie in an interval $\lambda^{-2} V_0 \leq V \leq \lambda^2 V_0$, where V_0 is the initial hypothesized variance matrix. For example, if $\lambda = 2$, prior standard errors are allowed to be either twice as large or half as small. Given my considerable uncomfortableness in selecting a prior, this seems like a reasonable interval of prior variance matrices.

Extreme estimates for the long-run coefficients using these neighborhoods of priors are reported in table 3.9. If $\lambda = 1$, the interval of covariance matrices is just a point, and the corresponding interval of Bayes estimates is a point. If $\lambda = 2$, there is only one interval of estimates that does not overlap the origin. Only the inference with the monetarist prior that money matters can be judged to be sturdy. In every other case the inference is

Table 3.9
Bounds for estimates of the long-run coefficients, inflation equation: prior
variance matrix bounded from above and below ($\lambda^{-2} V_0 \leq V \leq \lambda^2 V_0$)

		Monetarist bounds				Keynesian bounds		
	Mean	$\lambda = 1$	$\lambda = 2$	$\lambda = 4$	Mean	$\lambda = 1$	$\lambda = 2$	$\lambda = 4$
Money	1.0	1.0	1.5	2.2	0	0.8	1.8	3.0
		1.0	0.5	0		0.8	−0.3	−1.6
Unemployment^{-1}	0	−0.4	0.3	1.2	3.0	−0.2	0.9	2.5
		−0.4	−1.0	−1.7		−0.2	−1.3	−2.7
Deficit	0	−0.8	0.1	1.2	0	−1.5	1.1	4.3
		−0.8	−1.7	−3.0		−1.5	−3.7	−5.8
Oil prices	0	0.1	0.1	0.2	0.1	0.2	0.4	0.5
		0.1	−0.0	−0.1		0.2	−0.0	−0.3

fragile, in the sense that the sign of the estimate is indeterminate. (The
interval of estimates for energy prices at $\lambda = 2$ is almost strictly positive,
and a slightly narrower interval of priors would lead to a determinate sign.)

The prior means for these long-run effects are also reported in table 3.9.
Almost all of the intervals for $\lambda = 2$ include the corresponding prior mean.
Thus neither the Keynesian nor the monetarist need be convinced that his
prior estimate is wrong, since each can find a prior covariance matrix close
to the initial one which reproduces the prior mean as an estimate. The one
exception is that the Keynesian must conclude that the Phillips curve is not
as important as he expected since the maximum estimate of the coefficient
on unemployment is only 0.9 with the Keynesian prior and with $\lambda = 2$.

These bounds generally include not only the corresponding prior mean
but the mean of the other prior distributions as well. For example, the
Keynesian interval for money includes the monetarist prior mean of 1.0.
Thus the Keynesian is unable to convince himself that the monetarist is
incorrect about the role of money. The exceptions are that the monetarist is
convinced that the Keynesian is wrong about the effect of money and about
the effect of unemployment.

To sum up, most of the inferences that might be made from this macro
data set seem excessively fragile. The monetarist may come away from this
exercise with a relatively happy feeling because he regards his conclusion
that money matters to be resilient, as is his opinion that unemployment

does not have much impact on inflation. The Keynesian, in contrast, is unable to find a Phillips curve with nearly the effect he expects, nor is he able to rule out the substantial effect of money expected by the monetarist. The Keynesian is able to find (fragile) estimates of a considerable energy price markup. He is also able to find a Keynesian prior that leads to the conclusion that there is no effect of money on prices.[5]

Estimates of the Unemployment Equation

Estimates of the unemployment equation are reported in tables 3.10, 3.11, and 3.12. Examination of the unconstrained least-squares values in the column headed $\sigma_1 = \infty$ and the t values in the next column might lead you to the following conclusions:

1. The memory in the unemployment process is much shorter than the memory in the inflation process. The coefficient on the previous quarter's unemployment rate is virtually one. The annual and biannual averages have smaller effects, and the triannual average has no effect. The biannual money growth is by far the most important of the money variables. The inflation rates have mixed effects, with the triannual influence being essentially zero. Most of the effects of government expenditure and autonomous expenditure are felt in the first quarter.
2. High levels of money are associated with high levels of unemployment, though rapid growth over the past two years reduces unemployment.
3. High levels of prices (and lower real wages?) tend to reduce unemployment, as do high inflation rates.
4. The job-creating effect of government and autonomous expenditures in the current quarter is substantial but is partially offset over time.
5. The level of the labor force does not have an effect on the unemployment rate.

Bayesian estimates based on the classical prior are generally just scaled-down versions of the least-squares estimates, as might be expected since the classical prior treats all coefficients as if they were likely to be small. Estimates built on the Friedmaniac prior are somewhat different. Remember the Friedmaniac expects no long-run impact of any of the variables but allows an effect in the short-run (unexpected events being the cause of unemployment). The major difference between the Friedmaniac estimates and the classical estimates are the coefficients of the expenditure variables,

Table 3.10
Estimates of unemployment equation: classical prior

| | s^b | σ_1 (prior standard error scale factor) | | | | | t^c |
		0	0.5	1.0	2.0	∞	
Confidence		1.0	0.996	0.703	0.061	0	
Intercept		5.2	9.5	8.6	10.3	12.7	1.4
$L25U^{-1}$	0.4	0	0.74	0.92	1.02	1.05	11.4
LA_425U^{-1}	0.2	0	-0.01	-0.14	-0.30	-0.55	-3.6
LA_825U^{-1}	0.1	0	-0.01	-0.00	0.07	0.35	1.4
$LA_{12}25U^{-1}$	0.05	0	-0.01	-0.01	-0.01	-0.01	0
m	5	0	-1.89	-2.83	-5.36	-9.19	-1.8
$\Delta_1 m$	4	0	0.01	0.02	0.03	0.02	1.4
$\Delta_4 m$	2	0	0.10	0.08	0.06	0	0
$\Delta_8 m$	1	0	0.21	0.14	0.14	0.24	2.4
$\Delta_{12} m$	0.5	0	-0.06	-0.02	0.03	0	0
Lp	5	0	0.32	1.48	3.79	7.01	1.5
$L\Delta_1 p$	4	0	0.06	0.06	0.06	0.05	2.4
$L\Delta_4 p$	2	0	0.03	-0.06	-0.08	-0.09	-1.7
$L\Delta_8 p$	1	0	0.01	0.04	0.06	0.07	0.9
$L\Delta_{12} p$	0.5	0	0	0	0	0.02	0.2
G/LP	0.4	0	0.03	0.07	0.23	1.63	1.1
$A_4 G/LP$	0.2	0	0	0	0.01	-0.91	-0.3
$A_8 G/LP$	0.1	0	0	0	0	0.52	0.1
$A_{12} G/LP$	0.05	0	0	0	0	-0.84	-0.3
X/LP	0.4	0	0.08	0.27	0.66	2.06	3.5
$A_4 X/LP$	0.2	0	0.01	0.01	-0.01	-1.00	-0.8
$A_8 X/LP$	0.1	0	0	0	0	0.87	0.5
$A_{12} X/LP$	0.05	0	0.03	0	0	-0.70	-0.4
F	0.1	0	-0.01	-0.01	0	0.03	0.5

a. Implicit in other prior constraints.
b. Twice the prior standard error.
c. Least-squares t values.

Table 3.11
Estimates of unemployment equation: Friedmaniac prior

	s^b	σ_1 (prior standard error scale factor)				
		0	0.5	1.0	2.0	∞
Confidence		1.0	0.77	0.06	0.0006	0
Intercept		4.81	4.5	4.02	4.75	12.74
$L25U^{-1}$	0.4	0	0.68	0.86	0.99	1.05
$LA_4 25U^{-1}$	0.2	0	0.03	-0.09	-0.25	-0.55
$LA_8 25U^{-1}$	0.1	0	0.01	0.01	0.05	0.35
$LA_{12} 25U^{-1}$	0.05	0	0	0	0	-0.01
m	1	0	-0.12	-0.17	-0.33	-9.19
$\Delta_1 m$	∞	-0.07	0	0.02	0.02	0.02
$\Delta_4 m$	∞	0	0.03	0.03	0.01	0
$\Delta_8 m$	∞	0.06	0.17	0.13	0.12	0.24
$\Delta_{12} m$	∞	0.01	-0.04	-0.06	-0.04	0
Lp	1	0	-0.17	-0.25	-0.38	7.01
$L\Delta_1 p$	∞	-0.01	0.06	0.06	0.06	0.05
$L\Delta_4 p$	∞	0.17	-0.03	-0.05	-0.06	-0.09
$L\Delta_8 p$	∞	0.17	0.09	0.11	0.12	0.07
$L\Delta_{12} p$	∞	-0.33	-0.05	-0.06	-0.07	0.02
G/LP	∞	4.35	4.61	3.63	2.87	1.63
$A_4 G/LP$	∞	-6.93	-6.52	-5.78	-4.55	-0.91
$A_8 G/LP$	∞	32.71	6.74	6.17	5.34	0.52
$A_{12} X/LP$	∞	-30.12	-4.82	-4.01	-3.65	-0.84
X/LP	∞	1.39	2.03	2.12	2.06	2.06
$A_4 X/LP$	∞	5.06	-1.07	-1.74	-1.99	-1.00
$A_8 X/LP$	∞	-2.54	-0.14	0.55	0.85	0.87
$A_{12} X/LP$	∞	-3.9	-0.81	-0.92	-0.89	-0.70
F	0.1	0	-0.03	-0.02	-0.01	0.03

a. Implicit in other prior constraints.
b. Two times the prior standard error.

Table 3.12
Estimates of unemployment equation: Keynesian prior

	s^b	σ_1 (prior standard error scale factor)				
		0	0.5	1.0	2.0	∞
Confidence		1.0	0.975	0.031	0	0
Intercept		73.9	−3.9	5.12	10.3	12.74
$L25U^{-1}$	0.5	0	0.80	0.96	1.02	1.05
$LA_4 25U^{-1}$	0.4	0	−0.03	−0.24	−0.43	−0.55
$LA_8 25U^{-1}$	0.3	0	−0.01	0.12	0.27	0.35
$LA_{12} 25U^{-1}$	0.2	0	−0.07	−0.07	−0.07	−0.01
m	10	10.0	3.73	−1.56	−5.56	−9.19
$\Delta_1 m$	5	0	0.02	0.02	0.02	0.02
$\Delta_4 m$	4	0	0.05	0.03	0.01	0
$\Delta_8 m$	3	0	0.14	0.14	0.20	0.24
$\Delta_{12} m$	2	0	−0.10	−0.02	0	0
Lp	10	−10.0	−1.28	1.28	3.83	7.01
$L\Delta_1 p$	5	0	0.07	0.06	0.06	0.05
$L\Delta_4 p$	4	0	−0.02	−0.05	−0.07	−0.09
$L\Delta_8 p$	3	0	0.02	0.06	0.07	0.07
$L\Delta_{12} p$	2	0	0.02	0.01	0	0.02
G/LP	a	1.0	0.77	1.03	1.35	1.63
$A_4 G/LP$	1.0	0	−0.16	−0.27	−0.39	−0.91
$A_8 G/LP$	0.8	0	−0.17	−0.24	−0.31	0.52
$A_{12} G/LP$	0.6	0	−0.15	−0.24	−0.32	−0.84
X/LP	a	1.0	0.70	1.32	1.79	2.06
$A_4 X/LP$	1.0	0	−0.24	−0.57	−0.77	−1.00
$A_8 X/LP$	0.8	0	−0.13	−0.24	−0.18	0.87
$A_{12} X/LP$	0.6	0	−0.06	−0.10	−0.11	−0.70
F	1	−1.0	−0.12	−0.04	0.01	0.03

a. Implicit in other prior constraints.
b. Two times the prior standard error.

Table 3.13
Bounds for estimates of the long-run coefficients, unemployment equation: prior variance matrix bounded from above and below $(\lambda^{-2}V_0 \le V \le \lambda^2 V_0)$

	Classical prior				Friedmaniac				Keynesian prior		
	Mean	$\lambda=1$	$\lambda=2$	$\lambda=4$	Mean	$\lambda=1$	$\lambda=2$	$\lambda=4$	$\lambda=1$	$\lambda=2$	$\lambda=4$
Money	0	−12.4	28.7	85.7	10	−0.8	15.7	49.4	−6.5	60.9	149
		−12.4	−58.4	−123.4		−0.8	−17.6	−53.3	−6.5	−68.0	−144
Money growth	0	1.0	2.0	3.5	0	0.6	1.4	2.27	0.72	2.1	3.8
		1.0	0	−1.3		0.6	−0.3	−1.86	0.72	−0.7	−2.6
Prices	0	6.5	41.4	94.2	−10	−1.2	12.2	36.2	5.34	60.7	132.8
		6.5	−24.3	−71.7		−1.2	−14.5	−37.1	5.34	−50.6	−125.2
Inflation	0	0.17	0.5	1.0	0	0.18	0.7	1.25	0.29	1.0	2.1
		0.17	−0.2	−0.7		0.18	−0.3	−1.14	0.29	−0.5	−7.1
Government	0	0.3	6.5	14.5	1.0	0	1.8	6.06	1.21	9.5	19.5
		0.3	−5.4	−12.4		0	−1.8	−6.05	1.21	−7.0	−16.9
Autonomous	0	1.2	7.9	17.6	1.0	0.1	1.8	5.87	1.68	12.6	26.4
		1.2	−4.7	−13.3		0.1	−1.7	−5.61	1.68	−8.7	−21.7
Labor force	0	0	0.8	1.7	−1	−0.1	0.4	1.20	−0.15	0.6	1.4
		0	−0.8	−1.6		−0.1	−0.6	−1.31	−0.15	−1.0	−2.1

which in the Friedmaniac case allow for substantial unemployment induced by variability in expenditure over time. A prescription for low unemployment is higher levels of real expenditures in the current quarter than over the last year, and higher levels of real expenditure over the last two years than over the last three.

Bayesian estimates based on the Keynesian prior are rather similar to the estimates based on the classical prior. The Keynesian is surprised to find that high levels of money and low levels of prices cause unemployment, but his priors about the effect of current expenditure are confirmed, though the job-creating effect of these expenditure variables are largely offset in the long run.

Extreme estimates of the long-run effects formed from priors in the neighborhoods of these are reported in table 3.13. Almost all of the inferences about the signs of these effects are fragile in the sense that zero is included in the interval of estimates corresponding to the interval of priors $V_0/4 \leq V \leq 4V_0$. The exception is the conclusion by the classicist that high rates of money growth have job-creating effects. This conclusion is surprising to the classicist since his prior mean is zero. In all other cases the bounds at $\lambda = 2$ contain the corresponding prior mean. Moreover the intervals generally include the means of the other two prior distributions. The exceptions are that neither the classicist nor the Friedmaniac can find an estimate for the effect of the labor force which is as negative as the Keynesian expects. Thus there is little in this data set that can be regarded as convincing evidence to a Friedmaniac, a classicist, or a Keynesian.

3.4 Concluding Remarks

My intention was to show that macro inflation data speak clearly if they are processed in a conceptually clear manner. However, it turns out that ambiguities in the definition of prior information about the inflation process seem not to be substantially eliminated by the data evidence. In general, there are Keynesian priors that yield Keynesian results, but there are also Keynesian priors that yield monetarist results. The same can be said for monetarist priors. I suspect that evidence of a similar degree of fragility could be uncovered for many macroeconomic data analyses. Beyond the obvious fact, then, that data analyses are always to be treated skeptically, the following conclusion emerges: the theoretical honing of macromodels is likely to be a more productive activity than data mining with ill-defined priors.

Notes

Support from NSF Grant SES78-09479 is gratefully acknowledged. Thomas Wolfe provided able research assistance, advice, and constant discouragement. David Blair assisted on an earlier version of the empirical work. Much of the data was supplied to the MIT Center for Computational Research in Economics and Management Science by Robert Gordon for analysis by a group of statisticians and econometricians interested in model choice and model vailidity issues.

1. For example, see Barro (1978a, b) or Hamburger and Zwick (1981).

2. Suppose the inflation rate $p_t - p_{t-1} = (1 - L)p_t$ is generated by the process $(1 - L)p_t = \beta x$, where x_t is a dummy variable taking on the value n^{-1} in the first n periods and zero otherwise. Then $p_t = \beta x_t/(1 - L) = \beta(x_t + x_{t-1} + x_{t-2} + \cdots)$, and the effect of x on the future price level is $\beta n n^{-1} = \beta$.

3. If E represents the number employed and F the labor force, then $U^{-1} = F/100(F - E)$ and $\partial(25)U^{-1}/\partial E = (25)F/100(F - E)^2 = 25U^{-1}(F - E)$. Then if the derivative of E with respect to X is taken to be $1/5{,}000$, the derivative $\partial 25U^{-1}/\partial X = (\partial 25U^{-1}/\partial E)(\partial E/\partial X) = 25U^{-1}/5{,}000(F - E)$. If total unemployment $F - E$ were 100 million and U were 5 percent, then $\partial 25U^{-1}/\partial X = 10^{-11}$, which is the coefficient on X we would expect if X were measured in dollars. If X is measured in billions (10^9) and is deflated by a price index in the neighborhood of 100, the expected coefficient is $10^{-11} \times 10^{11} = 1.0$. The proposition that in the long run each \$5,000 in government expenditure generates one extra job is therefore approximated by the constraint $\sum_1^{18}\gamma_i/(1 - \sum_1^4\gamma_i) = 1$. As described before, the prior on this ratio is approximated by a prior on the sum $\sum_{15}^{18}\gamma_i + \sum_1^4\gamma_i$ with mean 1 and standard deviation $\frac{1}{2}$.

4. If unemployment is $U = 100(F - E)/F$, then $\partial 25^{-1}/\partial F = -25E/100(F - E)^2$. If employment were 10^8 and unemployment 5×10^6, then this derivative would be -10^{-6}, which would be the expected coefficient if F were measured in laborers. But if F is measured in millions of laborers, the expected coefficient becomes -1.

5. It should be pointed out that the prior covariance matrix that leads the Keynesian to the most substantial coefficient on energy price is not the same covariance matrix that implies the largest unemployment effect. For this reason the preceding discussion may be regarded to be slightly misleading. This suggests the interesting mathematical problem to find the covariance matrix in the interval $\lambda^{-2}V_0 \leq V \leq \lambda^2 V_0$ which implies a Bayes estimate closest to the prior means.

References

Anderson, L., and D. Karnosky, 1972. The appropriate time frame for controlling monetary aggregates: the St. Louis evidence. *Controlling Monetary Aggregates II: The Implementation.* Conference Series No. 9. Federal Reserve Bank of Boston, Boston, Mass., September.

Barro, R. J., 1978. Unanticipated money, output and the price level in the United States. *Journal of Political Economy* 86 (August): 549–580.

Barro, R. J., 1977. Unanticipated money growth and unemployment in the United States. *American Economic Review* 67 (March): 101–115.

Berman, P. I., 1978. *Inflation and the Money Supply in the United States, 1956–1977.* D. C. Heath, Lexington, Mass.

Frisch, H., 1977. Inflation theory, 1963–1975: a second generation "Survey." *Journal of Economic Literature* 15 (December): 1289–1317.

Frye, J., and R. J. Gordon, 1980. The variance and acceleration of inflation in the 1970's: alternative explanatory models and methods. Mimeo.

Gordon, R. J., 1981. Output fluctuations and gradual price adjustment. *Journal of Economic Literature* 19 (June): 493–530.

Gordon, R. J., 1976. Recent developments in the theory of inflation and unemployment. *Journal of Monetary Economics* 2 (April): 185–220.

Hamburger, M. J., and B. Zwick, 1981. Deficits, money and inflation. *Journal of Monetary Economics* 7: 141–150.

Heller, W. W., 1979. Balanced budget fallacies. *Wall Street Journal*, March 16, p. 22.

Laidler, D., and M. Parkin, 1975. Inflation: a survey. *The Economic Journal* 85 (December): 741–809.

Leamer, E. E., 1982. Sets of Posterior Means with Bounded Variance Priors. *Econometrica* 50 (May): 725–736.

Leamer, E. E., 1978. *Specification Searches*. Wiley, New York.

Leamer, E. E., and H. Leonard, 1983. Reporting the Fragility of Regression Estimates. *Review of Economics and Statistics* 65 (May): 306–317.

Leijonhufvud, A., 1981. *Information and Coordination*. Oxford University Press, New York.

Leijonhufvud, A., 1980. What Was the Matter with IS-LM? Working paper 186. Department of Economics, UCLA.

Lucas, R. E., Jr., 1981. Tobin and Monetarism: A Review Article. *Journal of Economic Literature* 19 (June): 558–567.

Lucas, R. E., Jr., 1973. Some International Evidence on Output-Inflation Trade Offs. *American Economic Review* 63 (June): 326–334.

Lucas, R. E., Jr., 1972. Expectations and the Neutrality of Money. *Journal of Economic Theory* 4 (April): 103–124.

Lucas, R. E., Jr., and T. J. Sargent, 1978. After Keynesian Macroeconomics. In *After the Phillips Curve: Persistence of High Inflation and High Unemployment*. Federal Reserve Bank of Boston Conference. Vol. 19. Federal Reserve Bank, Boston.

Meiselman, D. I., 1981. Are Tax Cuts Inflationary? *Manhattan Report on Economic Policy*, Vol. 1, pp. 1–3.

Okun, A., 1981. *Prices and Quantities*. The Brookings Institution, Washington, D.C.

Sargent, T. J., 1976a. The Observational Equivalence of Natural and Unnatural Rate Theories of Macroeconomics. *Journal of Political Economy* 84: 631–640.

Sargent, T. J., 1976b. A Classical Macroeconometric Model for the United States. *Journal of Political Economy* 84: 207–237.

Stein, J. L., 1981. Monetarist, Keynesian, and New Classical Economics. *American Economic Review* 71 (May): 139–149.

4 The Use of Outside Information in Econometric Forecasting

Mark N. Greene, E. Philip Howrey, and Saul H. Hymans

4.1 Introduction

Outside information is invariably used to produce timely econometric forecasts. When a quarterly econometric model is used, an important source of outside information is the monthly data that become available during the quarter. As monthly data on such variables as retail sales, the unemployment rate, interest rates, industrial production, personal consumption expenditures, and personal income are released, the quarterly forecast is revised to be consistent with this new information.

Outside information is typically used in an informal, ad hoc way to modify econometric forecasts. The purpose of the research described in this chapter is to investigate the properties of a scientifically sound approach to the use of outside information. In the following section the forecasting procedure is described. The methods are then applied to a small macroeconometric model to determine the maximum potential gain in forecast accuracy that can be expected from the use of outside information.

4.2 The Use of Outside Information

In this section we describe a procedure for utilizing outside information to improve the forecast accuracy of an econometric model. This procedure provides a rationale for using monthly data, for example, to update or modify quarterly econometric model forecasts. An attractive feature of this proposed method of sequential revision of quarterly forecasts is that it does not require modification of the quarterly forecasting model. Thus it is possible, at least in principle, to obtain improved forecasts simply by augmenting a quarterly forecasting model with an auxiliary outside-information system.

To provide the motivation for the proposed forecasting procedure, we consider first a simple, suboptimal method of using outside information to revise or improve a forecast. Suppose an econometric model produces an unbiased forecast of the gth endogenous variable, $\hat{Y}_g$, with a forecast error variance, $\hat{\sigma}_g^2$, and that outside information such as current monthly data can be used to obtain another unbiased forecast $\tilde{Y}_g$ with forecast error variance $\tilde{\sigma}_g^2$. By combining the two forecasts according to

$$\bar{Y}_g = \hat{k}\hat{Y}_g + \tilde{k}\tilde{Y}_g, \tag{4.1}$$

an improved forecast may be obtained. Indeed, it is trivial to verify that if the two forecast errors are uncorrelated, the forecast weights

$$\hat{k} = \frac{\hat{\sigma}_g^2}{(\hat{\sigma}_g^2 + \tilde{\sigma}_g^2)} \tag{4.2}$$

and

$$\hat{k} = \frac{\tilde{\sigma}_g^2}{(\hat{\sigma}_g^2 + \tilde{\sigma}_g^2)} = 1 - \tilde{k} \tag{4.3}$$

will yield a minimum variance (linear) unbiased forecast of Y_g with a prediction error variance equal to

$$\bar{\sigma}_g^2 = \frac{\hat{\sigma}_g^2 \tilde{\sigma}_g^2}{(\hat{\sigma}_g^2 + \tilde{\sigma}_g^2)}. \tag{4.4}$$

The way in which the forecast based on outside information is used to revise the model forecast is best seen by rewriting the combined forecast (using the above weights) as

$$\bar{Y}_g = \hat{Y}_g + \tilde{k}(\tilde{Y}_g - \hat{Y}_g). \tag{4.5}$$

This shows that the revised forecast $\bar{Y}_g$ is adjusted toward $\tilde{Y}_g$ by adding the fraction $\tilde{k}$ of the discrepancy between $\tilde{Y}_g$ and $\hat{Y}_g$ to the original model forecast. The proportional reduction in $\hat{\sigma}_g^2$ achieved by using the outside information is $\hat{\sigma}_g^2/(\hat{\sigma}_g^2 + \tilde{\sigma}_g^2)$. Thus the value of outside information clearly depends on the variances $\hat{\sigma}_g^2$ and $\tilde{\sigma}_g^2$.

The major shortcoming of this approach is that $\tilde{Y}_g$ affects only the forecast of Y_g. It would be preferable to recognize that $\tilde{Y}_g$ may contain information about other variables as well and thus to allow the outside information to modify the forecasts of all of the variables in the model. In order to develop this more general approach, we introduce explicitly a forecasting model and an auxiliary outside-information system. Predictions from these two systems are then combined to obtain an optimal forecast.

The structural form of a quarterly linear forecasting model is written as

$$CY(t) = AY(t - 1) + BX(t) + U(t), \quad t = 1, 2, \ldots, \tag{4.6}$$

where

$Y(t)$ = a $G*1$ vector of endogenous variables valued at time t,

$X(t)$ = a $K*1$ vector of exogenous variables valued at time t,

A, B, C = conformable matrices of structural parameters,

$U(t)$ = a $G*1$ vector of disturbances with mean zero and covariance matrix Σ_u.

The reduced form used for forecasting is written as

$$Y(t) = PY(t-1) + QX(t) + V(t), \tag{4.7}$$

where

$$D = C^{-1},$$

$$P = DA,$$

$$Q = DB,$$

$$V(t) = DU(t).$$

The one-quarter ahead forecast of $Y(t)$, given $Y(t-1)$ and $X(t)$, is

$$\hat{Y}(t) = PY(t-1) + QX(t) \tag{4.8}$$

so that

$$Y(t) = \hat{Y}(t) + V(t), \tag{4.9}$$

where

$V(t)$ = a $G*1$ vector of disturbances with mean zero and covariance matrix $\Sigma_v = D\Sigma_u D'$.

This last equation summarizes the stochastic relationship between the predicted and realized values of the endogenous variables implied by the forecasting model.[1]

We assume that some outside information is also available and refer specifically to monthly observations on some of the endogenous variables in the quarterly model to illustrate the approach. Let $y_g(t, i)$ denote the gth variable in Y for month i of quarter t. Then, assuming $Y_g(t)$ is a flow variable,

$$Y_g(t) = \sum_{i=1}^{3} y_g(t, i). \tag{4.10}$$

A forecast of $Y_g(t)$ based on data for the first month of any quarter is given by[2]

$$\tilde{Y}_g(t, 1) = \hat{\beta}_{g01} + \hat{\beta}_{g11} y_g(t, 1).$$ (4.11)

Similarly a forecast based on observations for the first two months of the quarter is denoted by

$$\tilde{Y}_g(t, 2) = \hat{\beta}_{g02} + \hat{\beta}_{g12} y_g(t, 1) + \hat{\beta}_{g22} y_g(t, 2).$$ (4.12)

Such forecasts can be made for all elements of Y for which monthly observations exist. Let $\tilde{Y}(t)$ denote the $H * 1$ vector of all such "outside information" forecasts, and let θ denote a "selection" matrix that picks out the $H \leq G$ elements of $Y(t)$ corresponding to $\tilde{Y}(t)$.[3] Then the outside-information system is summarized by

$$\tilde{Y}(t) = \theta Y(t) + W(t),$$ (4.13)

where

$W(t) =$ a $H * 1$ vector of disturbances with mean zero and covariance matrix Σ_w.

Collecting the results for the quarterly forecasting model and the outside-information system, we have (4.9) and (4.13) together.

By analogy with our earlier result we write the combined predictor as

$$\bar{Y}(t) = \hat{Y}(t) + K[\tilde{Y}(t) - \theta \hat{Y}(t)].$$ (4.14)

This combined forecast can be shown to have two desirable properties—namely under certain conditions, indicated shortly, it is the minimum variance linear unbiased predictor of $Y(t)$ and it also satisfies the identities of the econometric model.

The optimality of the combined predictor can be established using the following lemma.

LEMMA 4.1 Let x be a random vector with mean μ and covariance matrix Σ. Let x_1 denote the first n_1 elements of x, and let x_2 denote the remaining $n_2 > 0$ elements of x. Partition μ and Σ conformably, and suppose Σ_{22} is nonsingular. The predictor

$$\hat{x}_1 = \mu_1 + K(x_2 - \mu_2),$$

where

$$K = \Sigma_{12} \Sigma_{22}^{-1}$$

is the best linear unbiased predictor of x_1 given x_2.

Proof Consider the linear predictor $k_1 + k_2 x_2$. This predictor is (unconditionally) unbiased for x_1 if

$$E(x_1 - k_1 - k_2 x_2) = \mu_1 - k_1 - k_2 \mu_2 = 0.$$

Thus $k_1 = \mu_1 - k_2 \mu_2$, and unbiasedness requires that the forecast take the form $\tilde{x}_1 = \mu_1 + k_2(x_2 - \mu_2)$. If $k_2 = K + \delta$, the covariance matrix of $x_1 - \tilde{x}_1$ is

$$V \equiv E[(x_1 - \tilde{x}_1)(x_1 - \tilde{x}_1)']$$

$$= \Sigma_{11} - \Sigma_{12} \Sigma_{22}^{-1} \Sigma_{21} + \delta \Sigma_{22} \delta'.$$

It follows that the covariance matrix of $x_1 - \hat{x}_1$ is $\Sigma_{11} - \Sigma_{12} \Sigma_{22}^{-1} \Sigma_{21}$, and the prediction error covariance matrix of any other unbiased linear predictor exceeds this by a positive semidefinite matrix. □

We state the optimality of the predictor $\bar{Y}(t)$ in the following theorem.

THEOREM 4.1 Given the system

$$Y(t) = \hat{Y}(t) + V(t),$$

$$\tilde{Y}(t) = \theta Y(t) + W(t),$$

where $V(t) \sim (0, \Sigma_v)$, $W(t) \sim (0, \Sigma_w)$, and $V(t)$ and $W(t)$ are mutually as well as serially uncorrelated,[4] the best linear unbiased predictor of $Y(t)$, given $\tilde{Y}(t)$, is $\bar{Y}(t)$ in (4.14), with

$$K = \Sigma_v \theta'(\theta \Sigma_v \theta' + \Sigma_w)^{-1}, \tag{4.15}$$

and the prediction error covariance matrix of $\bar{Y}(t)$ is

$$\Omega = (I - K\theta)\Sigma_v. \tag{4.16}$$

Proof Write the system as

$$x_1 \equiv \hat{Y}(t) + V(t),$$

$$x_2 \equiv \theta Y(t) + W(t) = \theta \hat{Y}(t) + \theta V(t) + W(t),$$

so that

$$\mu_1 = E(x_1) = \hat{Y}(t),$$

$$\mu_2 = E(x_2) = \theta\hat{Y}(t),$$

$$\Sigma_{11} = E[(x_1 - \mu_1)(x_1 - \mu_1)'] = \Sigma_v,$$

$$\Sigma_{12} = E[(x_1 - \mu_1)(x_2 - \mu_2)'] = \Sigma_v\theta',$$

and

$$\Sigma_{22} = E[(x_2 - \mu_2)(x_2 - \mu_2)'] = \theta\Sigma_v\theta' + \Sigma_w.$$

The results of the theorem follow directly from lemma 4.1, provided Σ_{22} is nonsingular. $\square$

In order for the combined forecast to be reasonable, it should satisfy the identities of the structural model. The forecast $\hat{Y}(t)$ will automatically satisfy the identities, but there is no obvious reason for the outside-information forecast $\tilde{Y}(t)$ to satisfy them. Thus the following result is reassuring.

THEOREM 4.2 The optimal predictor $\bar{Y}(t)$ defined in Theorem 4.1 will satisfy any identities that appear in the structural form of the econometric model.

Proof The structural model is rewritten as

$$C_1 Y(t) = A_1 Y(t-1) + B_1 X(t) + U_1(t),$$

$$C_2 Y(t) = A_2 Y(t-1) + B_2 X(t),$$

so that the first G_1 equations are stochastic and the remaining $G_2 = G - G_1$ equations are identities. Let

$$\eta(t) = A_2 Y(t-1) + B_2 X(t).$$

The forecast $\bar{Y}(t)$ will satisfy the identities if and only if

$$C_2 \bar{Y}(t) = \eta(t).$$

Now

$$C_2 \bar{Y}(t) = C_2 \hat{Y}(t) + C_2 K[\tilde{Y}(t) - \theta\hat{Y}(t)].$$

Since $\hat{Y}(t)$ is a forecast obtained from the structural model, it necessarily satisfies the identities—that is,

$C_2 \hat{Y}(t) = \eta(t)$.

Moreover, since $C_2 K = C_2 \Sigma_v \theta'(\theta \Sigma_v \theta' + \Sigma_w)^{-1}$, it follows that $C_2 K = 0$. To see this, consider

$$C_2 \Sigma_v = C_2 D \Sigma_u D'$$

$$= C_2 \left[\frac{C_1}{C_2} \right]^{-1} \Sigma_u D'$$

$$= [0 : I] \left[\begin{array}{c|c} \Sigma_{11} & 0 \\ \hline 0 & 0 \end{array} \right] D'$$

$$= 0. \; \square$$

We conclude this discussion of the properties of the combined forecast by noting that, provided $V(t)$ and $W(t)$ are uncorrelated, the potential gain in precision associated with using outside information along with a given econometric model is maximized as $\Sigma_w \to 0$—that is as the quality of the outside information approaches that of a perfect forecast. According to (4.16) the reduction in the prediction error variance that accompanies the use of outside information is

$$\Delta = K \theta \Sigma_v$$

$$= \Sigma_v \theta'(\theta \Sigma_v \theta' + \Sigma_w)^{-1} \theta \Sigma_v,$$

a positive semidefinite matrix. As $\Sigma_w \to 0$, this approaches the value

$$\Delta^* = \Sigma_v \theta'(\theta \Sigma_v \theta')^{-1} \theta \Sigma_v.$$

Since the difference between Δ^* and Δ,

$$\Delta^* - \Delta = \Sigma_v \theta'[(\theta \Sigma_v \theta')^{-1} - (\theta \Sigma_v \theta' + \Sigma_w)^{-1}] \theta \Sigma_v,$$

is positive semidefinite, we conclude that the maximum contribution of outside information occurs at $\Sigma_w = 0$.[5]

The preceding results are based on a linear forecasting model. Since most econometric models are nonlinear, these techniques are not directly applicable. The usual procedure in the case of nonlinear models is to apply the results of the linear theory to a linear approximation to the nonlinear model.[6] Suppose, as is usually the case, that the structural model is a system of nonlinear equations of the form

$$F[Y(t), Y(t - 1), X(t)] = U(t). \tag{4.17}$$

The one-step ahead forecast, given $Y(t-1)$ and $X(t)$, is typically obtained by solving the system

$$F[\hat{Y}(t), Y(t-1), X(t)] = 0 \tag{4.18}$$

for $\hat{Y}(t)$. If $F[Y(t), Y(t-1), X(t)]$ is expanded in a Taylor series about the point $[\hat{Y}(t), Y(t-1), X(t)]$, the result is

$$F[Y(t), Y(t-1), X(t)] = F[\hat{Y}(t), Y(t-1), X(t)]$$

$$+ \left[\frac{\partial F}{\partial Y(t)}\right][Y(t) - \hat{Y}(t)] + R(t). \tag{4.19}$$

Defining $C_t = \partial F/\partial Y(t)$ and setting $F[\hat{Y}(t), Y(t-1), X(t)] = 0$, we have

$$U(t) = C_t[Y(t) - \hat{Y}(t)] + R(t), \tag{4.20}$$

or

$$Y(t) = \hat{Y}(t) + D_t U(t) - D_t R(t), \tag{4.21}$$

where

$$D_t = C_t^{-1}. \tag{4.22}$$

Assuming that $D_t R(t)$ is negligible, the forecasting model can be expressed as

$$Y(t) = \hat{Y}(t) + V(t), \tag{4.23}$$

where

$$V(t) = D_t U(t).$$

Thus with a nonlinear model the time-invariant covariance matrix Σ_v of the linear model is replaced by $\Sigma_v(t) = D_t \Sigma_u D_t'$. The combined forecast is now given by

$$\bar{Y}(t) = \hat{Y}(t) + K_t[\tilde{Y}(t) - \theta \hat{Y}(t)],$$

where K_t and D_t now vary with t.[7]

4.3 Some Empirical Results

The procedures introduced in the preceding section for utilizing outside information in econometric forecasting are applied to an empirical model in this section. The model, a simplified version of the Michigan Quarterly Econometric Model, is summarized first. This is followed by an analysis of static one-quarter ahead forecasts. Finally, the accuracy of dynamic forecasts is investigated.

A Simple Macroeconomic Forecasting Model

In order to investigate the magnitude of the potential improvement in forecast accuracy resulting from the availability of outside information, we constructed a thirteen-equation econometric model based on the Michigan Quarterly Econometric Model (MQEM) of the U.S. economy. The test model consists of simplified versions of the consumption, employment, and income sectors of MQEM. The model is closed with identities so that the resulting dynamic simultaneous equation system determines GNP, personal income, corporate profits, consumption, and the unemployment rate. We thus obtained a model of manageable size, yet characteristic of the macroeconometric models currently in regular use.

The definitions of the variables are shown in table 4.1, and the equations are listed in table 4.2. A simplified flow diagram of the model is shown in figure 4.1 to provide an overview of the structure of the model. The figure indicates that the three consumption functions are driven primarily by real disposable income. Gross national product is obtained by adding exogenous expenditure X_1 to aggregate consumption expenditure. Nominal personal income is obtained by first converting real GNP to nominal terms and then subtracting corporate profits and other net withdrawals X_2 from the income stream. Finally, personal taxes are subtracted from personal income to yield disposable income which in turn is converted to real disposable income. The unemployment rate is determined by GNP but has no contemporaneous feedback effects on the real variables in the model.

The parameter values shown in table 4.2 were obtained by the method of ordinary least squares for the period 1960.1 through 1969.4. Although the least squares estimator is not the preferred estimator, the parameter values so determined do not differ in any important ways from the two-stage least-squares estimates. In the experiments reported subsequently, the model was reestimated (but not respecified) each "year" before forecasts for the next year were generated. This successive reestimation helps to keep the model correctly calibrated over the period of the experiments and corresponds to the reestimation that operating models undergo periodically.

Despite the fact that this is an enormously simplified version of an

Table 4.1
Endogenous and exogenous variables in the experimental model

Endogenous	
CD72	Consumption: durables (billions of 1972 $s)
CN72	Consumption: nondurables (billions of 1972 $s)
CS72	Consumption: services (billions of 1972 $s)
GNP	Gross national product (billions of current $s)
GNP72	Gross national product (billions of 1972 $s)
RUM	Unemployment rate: male, 20 and over (%)
TW	Taxes withheld (billions of current $s)
YCP	Corporate profits (billions of current $s)
CD	Durable consumption (billions of current $s)
CN	Nondurable consumption (billions of current $s)
YD	Disposable income (billions of current $s)
$YD72$	Disposable income (billions of 1972 $s)
YP	Personal income (billions of current $s)

Exogenous	
DAS	Auto strike dummy
PC	Consumption deflator (1972 = 100)
PCD	Durable consumption deflator (1972 = 100)
PCN	Nondurable consumption deflator (1972 = 100)
RAAA	Corporate AAA interest rate (%)
TAXCHG	Tax revenue affects of statutory tax changes (billions of current $s)
TIME	Time trend
X_1	Investment, net exports, and government purchases (billions of 1972 $s)
X_2	Capital consumption allowance and indirect business taxes (billions of current $s)

operating econometric model, it does contain the basic features of the parent model. For this reason we feel it is a useful vehicle for investigating the contribution of outside information to forecast accuracy.

The Potential Value of Outside Information   The covariance matrix Σ_v of reduced-form disturbances provides a measure of the forecast error variance of ex post forecasts generated by the econometric model.[8] The availability of outside information offers the potential to reduce this prediction error variance. In this section we consider the limits on the potential improvement in forecast accuracy that could be achieved within the context of the experimental model described earlier.

Outside information is available on four of the thirteen endogenous variables in our model. Monthly observations on the unemployment rate and personal income are directly available. In addition monthly retail sales

Table 4.2
Equations in the experimental model

1. Personal income

$$YP \equiv GNP - YCP - X_2$$

2. Disposable income

$$YD \equiv YP - TW$$

3. Real disposable income

$$YD72 \equiv \frac{YD}{PC} * 100$$

4. Real GNP

$$GNP72 \equiv C72 + X1$$

5. Nominal GNP

$$GNP \equiv GNP72 * \frac{PC}{100}$$

6. Nominal nondurable consumption

$$CN \equiv CN72 * \frac{PCN}{100}$$

7. Nominal durable consumption

$$CD \equiv CD72 * \frac{PCD}{100}$$

8. Real nondurable consumption

$$CN72 = \underset{(57)}{51} + \underset{(0.06)}{0.12\,\Delta YD72} + \underset{(0.04)}{0.17\,YD72_{-1}}$$

$$- \underset{(59)}{15} \frac{PCN_{-1}}{PC_{-1}} - \underset{(109)}{58} \frac{\Delta PCN}{PC} + \underset{(0.14)}{0.42\,CN72_{-1}}$$

9. Real services consumption

$$CS72 = \underset{(6.90)}{7.44} - \underset{(0.02)}{0.01} \sum_{i=1}^{4} YD72_{-i} + \underset{(0.03)}{0.06\,\Delta YD72}$$

$$+ \underset{(0.16)}{0.19\,TIME} + \underset{(0.09)}{0.91\,CS72_{-1}}$$

Table 4.2 (continued)

---

10. Real durable consumption

$$CD72 = -6.74 + 0.18[YD72_{-1} - 0.65 \, YD72_{-2}]$$
$$(5.43) \quad (0.05) \qquad (0.14)$$

$$+ 0.12[RAAA_{-1} - 0.65 \, RAAA_{-2}] + 1.77 \, DAS - 0.63 \, DAS_{-1}$$
$$(1.26) \qquad 0.14) \qquad\qquad (0.52) \qquad (0.57)$$

$$- 2.10[RUM_{-1} - 0.65 \, RUM_{-1}] + 0.58 \, CD72_{-1}$$
$$(1.03) \qquad (0.14) \qquad\qquad (0.15)$$

11. Corporate profits

$$YCP = 3.40 + 0.45 \, \Delta GNP - 4.41 \, \Delta PC + 0.92 \, YCP_{-1}$$
$$(1.17) \quad (0.04) \qquad (1.08) \qquad (0.02)$$

12. Tax withholdings

$$\Delta TW = -0.02 + 0.17 \, \Delta YP + TAXCHG$$
$$(0.28) \quad (0.03)$$

13. Unemployment rate (Okun's law)

$$\Delta RUM = 0.25 - 14.8 \frac{GNP72}{GNP72_{-1}} - 15.8 \frac{GNP72_{-1}}{GNP72_{-2}} + 0.03 \, \Delta RUM_{-1}$$
$$(0.06) \quad (3.72) \qquad\quad (4.95) \qquad\qquad (0.13)$$

Note: Coefficients were estimated via OLS over the period 1960.1 to 1969.4. Estimated standard errors are shown in parentheses. Equations 1 through 7 are nonstochastic; equations 8 through 13 are stochastic.

data can be used to construct estimates of nominal purchases of consumer durables and nondurables.[9] As noted previously, the maximum gain in forecast accuracy is achieved when the outside information is exact. Thus we can investigate the maximum gain in forecast accuracy for our test model by assuming that the values of these four variables are known in advance.

The theoretical results are summarized in table 4.3 for three different sample periods. The first column in the table, M, contains the theoretical forecast standard errors (FSE) of one-quarter ahead ex post predictions of selected endogenous variables implied by the model as estimated over the period 1960.1 to 1969.4. Thus the entry 2.52 for GNP72 indicates that the approximate 95% error bounds for the predicted value of real GNP in the first quarter of 1970 would be $\pm 5.04 \, (= 2 \times 2.52)$ billion 1972 dollars. The column F^a shows the FSEs that would result if personal income and

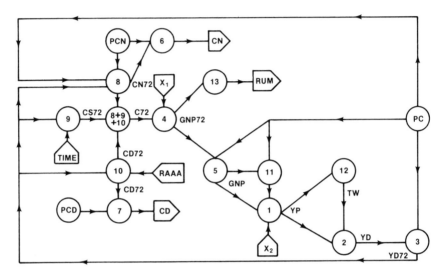

Figure 4.1
Simplified flow diagram of the experimental model (numbers refer to equations in table 4.2)

Table 4.3
Theoretical forecast standard errors for a one-quarter *ex post* forecast (billions of $)

Sample period	1960.1–1970.1			1960.1–1974.1			1960.1–1979.1		
	M	F^a	F^b	M	F^a	F^b	M	F^a	F^b
CD72	1.29	0	0	2.25	0	0	2.51	0	0
CN72	1.39	0	0	1.81	0	0	1.78	0	0
CS72	0.83	0.62	0.60	0.91	0.78	0.75	1.17	1.03	1.02
RUM	0.17	0.16	0	0.18	0.17	0	0.19	0.18	0
YCP	1.53	0.58	0.57	2.00	0.94	0.91	4.04	1.58	1.57
GNP72	2.52	0.62	0.60	3.70	0.78	0.75	4.00	1.03	1.02
YD72	2.49	0.83	0.83	2.95	0.93	0.93	4.39	3.47	3.47
YP	2.41	0	0	3.96	0	0	4.84	0	0
CD	1.26	0	0	2.56	0	0	3.51	0	0
CN	1.32	0	0	2.32	0	0	2.81	0	0

Note: M = theoretical forecast standard error of a one-quarter ahead *ex post* prediction using the experimental model. Entries are square roots of diagonal elements of the estimated Σ_v matrix.

F^a = As above, using perfect quarterly information ($\Sigma_w = 0$) on CD, CN, and YP. Entries are square roots of diagonal elements of the estimated $\Omega = (I - K\theta)\Sigma_v$ matrix.

F^b = As above, with perfect information on RUM also available.

consumption expenditures on durables and nondurables were known in advance, and equations (4.14) through (4.16) were used to pool or "filter" this information with the model forecasts.[10] For GNP72 the 95 percent confidence interval would be only ± 1.24 ($= 2 \times 0.62$). Thus a sizable gain in forecast accuracy is potentially available through the use of outside information. Similar gains in forecast precision are achieved for corporate profits (YCP) and real disposable income (YD72).

The other columns headed M and F^b show results of similar magnitude for different sample periods. Thus the rather dramatic gain in forecast accuracy achievable through the use of outside information is not peculiar to the specific parameter estimates of the 1960.1 to 1969.4 sample period. Parenthetically we observe that the forecast error variance is increasing over time. There are two reasons for this. The first is that the error variance of the structural equations of the model increases over time. The structural equations explain the data less well at the end of the sample period than at the beginning of the period. The second reason is that the model is non-linear and many of the variables are trending upward over time. These variables enter the model in such a way as to increase the forecast error variance.

As a practical matter it is useful to know what specific outside information is the most useful for improving the accuracy of econometric forecasts. This can be determined by varying the selection matrix θ in the observational model. One example is shown in the F^b columns of table 4.3, where the unemployment rate is added to the set of variables assumed to be known in advance. By comparison with F^a, the F^b columns show that the spillover effects of the unemployment rate are virtually zero. This is perhaps not too surprising because there is no simultaneous feedback from the unemployment rate to the other variables in this model. But the marginal contribution of each of the other three variables is clearly significant. This suggests that as far as this model is concerned, a high priority should be given to the development of operational observation equations for consumer expenditures on durables and nondurables and for personal income.

Table 4.4 shows estimated observation equations for these three variables, constructed as suggested by equation (4.11). (An observation model is also reported for the unemployment rate but is not used in the sequel.) These relationships will be used as in (4.12) to predict the quarterly values of these three variables in quarters for which partial monthly observations are available.

Table 4.4
Observation models: $Y(t,j) = \beta_{0j} + \sum_{i=1}^{j} \beta_{ij} y(t,i) + \varepsilon_j(t)$

j	β_0	β_1	β_2	β_3	$\bar{R}^2$	SER
Personal income (YP)						
1	-0.2602 (0.6728)	1.011 (0.0001)			0.9999	2.815
2	-0.3892 (0.3549)	0.2087 (0.0493)	0.7935 (0.0498)		0.9999	1.372
3[a]	-0.0169 (0.0092)	0.3325 (0.0013)	0.3340 (0.0018)	0.3335 (0)	1.0	0.0352
Durable consumption (CD)						
1	-0.2795 (0.4192)	1.011 (0.0038)			0.9988	1.774
2	0.1127 (0.2256)	0.3735 (0.0444)	0.6288 (0.0438)		0.9997	0.9473
3[a]	0.0082 (0.0077)	0.3342 (0.0015)	0.3318 (0.0019)	0.3392 (0.0013)	1.0	0.0321
Nondurable consumption (CN)						
1	-2.176 (0.4772)	1.015 (0.0015)			0.9998	1.818
2	-0.6017 (0.2388)	0.3450 (0.0386)	0.6595 (0.0380)		0.9999	0.8417
3[a]	0.0000 (0.0089)	0.3344 (0.0014)	0.3343 (0.0019)	0.3313 (0.0013)	1.0	0.0301
Unemployment rate (RUM)						
1	0.0418 (0.0473)	0.9903 (0.0111)			0.9897	0.1276
2	0.0325 (0.0291)	0.3883 (0.0522)	0.6027 (0.0518)		0.9961	0.0786
3	0.0000 (0)	0.3333 (0)	0.3333 (0.3333)	0.3333 (0)	1.0	0.0001

Note: Quarterly coefficients (and standard errors) estimated via OLS, 1960.1 to 1979.4.
a. Estimated standard errors are nonzero since reported monthly NIPA figures do not add exactly to reported quarterly figures.

Static Forecasts

The Realized Value of Outside Information   The parameter estimates of our experimental model were used in the previous section to determine the potential value of outside information as implied by the model. This potential may not be realized if the assumptions of the model are not satisfied. In this section we investigate the extent to which the potential improvements in forecast accuracy can be realized in practice.

A sequence of one-quarter ahead forecasts was calculated for the period 1970.1 to 1979.4, both with and without the benefit of prior knowledge of personal income and expenditures on durables and nondurables. The parameters of the model were reestimated at the end of each calendar year. Thus the forecasts are all out-of-sample predictions generated by a recently estimated model.

Table 4.5 summarizes the results of the experiment. Columns headed M show error statistics for the unadjusted model forecast. Columns F^1, F^2, and F^3 pertain to filtered forecasts obtained using the observation equations shown in table 4.4, with monthly observations on YP, CD, and CN available during the first 1, 2, and 3 months of each quarter, respectively. The final column is thus equivalent to using perfect information ($\Sigma_w = 0$) on the true quarterly values of these three variables. The error statistics of the filtered forecasts are clearly superior to those of the original model, with the superiority increasing with the amount of outside information available. Thus the forecast standard error for real GNP falls from 6.98 to 3.32 as partial data become available for the first month of the quarter, and drops further to 2.30 and 1.87 as the remaining months accrue.

Table 4.5 demonstrates that proper use of outside information yields the reductions in forecast error variances which the "potential improvement" calculations in table 4.3 led us to expect. Moreover large reductions occur even when the outside information set is comparatively small—that is, when only one or two month's worth of current quarter observations are available.[11]

The superiority of the filtered predictions is shown graphically in figures 4.2 and 4.3, which contrast the forecast errors made for two important variables, corporate profits and real GNP. The filtered (F^3) predictions enjoy a particular advantage in the late 1970s, where the model makes sizable prediction errors.

Figures 4.4 and 4.5 provide an additional insight into the ability of the models to forecast the *change* in a variable (here YCP). Figure 4.4 is a

Table 4.5
Descriptive statistics for one-quarter ahead ex post forecast errors (given YP, CD, and CN)

Variable	Minimum				Maximum				Mean				Standard deviation[a]			
	M	F^1	F^2	F^3	M	F^1	F^2	F^3	M	F^1	F^2	F^3	M	F^1	F^2	F^3
CD72	−11.18	−5.61	−3.51	−0.45	12.29	3.77	1.81	0.51	0.05	0.61	−0.08	0.07	4.64	2.02	1.20	0.20
CN72	−5.64	−3.27	−1.60	−0.83	6.29	4.38	2.96	0.52	0.15	−0.12	0.47	0.07	2.93	1.59	0.86	0.24
CS72	−4.86	−5.03	−4.98	−5.03	5.19	4.78	5.13	5.13	0	−0.29	−0.09	0.02	2.02	1.98	1.98	1.89
RUM	−0.70	−0.64	−0.65	−0.57	0.80	0.84	0.80	0.77	0.01	0.01	0.01	0	0.32	0.31	0.30	0.29
YCP	−11.81	−7.27	−9.15	−8.15	17.98	21.53	15.84	14.72	−0.14	0.52	0.49	−0.15	6.06	5.32	4.52	4.40
GNP72	−16.98	−8.70	−3.89	−5.00	17.15	9.16	4.59	5.19	0.20	0.20	0.31	0.16	6.98	3.32	2.30	1.87
YD72	−55.95	−47.64	−48.73	−47.36	32.73	33.25	31.71	26.71	0.29	−1.00	−0.12	0.12	12.56	10.23	10.19	9.67
YP	−18.12	−10.52	−4.47	−0.05	21.96	7.13	5.79	0.12	0.04	−1.44	−0.38	0.04	9.44	3.43	1.71	0
CD	−12.31	−6.00	−4.92	−0.07	16.47	5.40	2.20	0.18	−0.02	0.74	−0.15	0.04	5.79	2.35	1.43	0
CN	−9.28	−4.61	−1.42	−0.04	8.72	5.56	5.22	0.12	0.18	−0.13	0.62	0.03	3.98	2.23	1.30	0

Note: Statistics are based on forty successive one-quarter ahead forecasts from 1970.1 to 1979.4 with the model reestimated at the end of each calendar year.
M = model forecast,
F^1 = filtered forecast with data available in month 1,
F^2 = filtered forecast with data available in months 1 and 2,
F^3 = filtered forecast with data available in months 1 to 3.
a. These entries are comparable to the values reported in table 4.3.

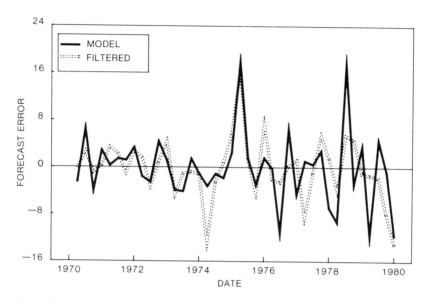

Figure 4.2
One-period ahead YCP forecast errors (model and filtered)

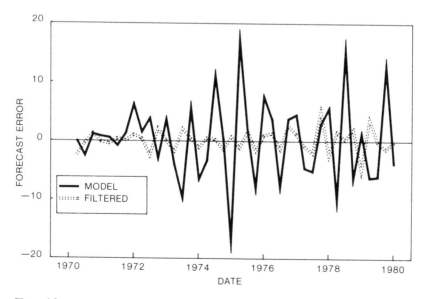

Figure 4.3
One-period ahead GNP72 forecast errors (model and filtered)

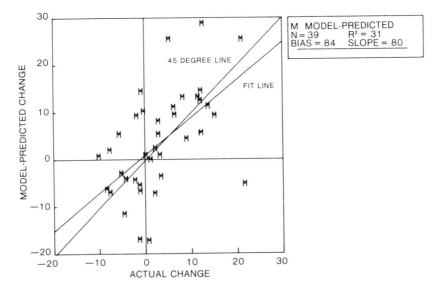

Figure 4.4
Change in YCP (actual and filter-predicted) given YP, CD, CN

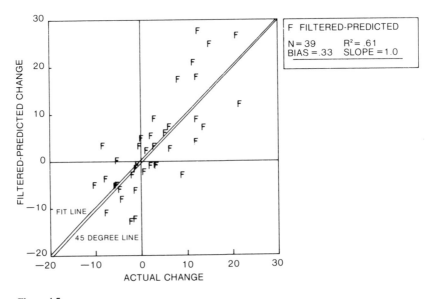

Figure 4.5
Change in YCP (actual and model-predicted) given YP, CD, CN

scatter plot where the actual change in YCP is measured horizontally, whereas the model-predicted change is measured vertically. If the forecasts were perfect, the actual and predicted changes would coincide along a 45-degree (unit slope) line through the origin. The least-squares fit through these points shows a marked deviation from this ideal. The presence of observations in quadrants 2 and 4 reflects quarters in which the predicted change was of the wrong sign. By contrast, figure 4.5 shows that the filtered (F^3) forecasts made no large errors; the fit line nearly coincides with the 45-degree line.

Dynamic Forecasts

The Potential Value of Outside Information The static forecast results indicate that outside information can make a valuable contribution to forecast accuracy. We now consider the impact of outside information on a dynamic forecast. The basic question is the extent to which the improvement due to the use of outside information in the first quarter will persist over the horizon of a four- or eight-quarter forecast.

In the absence of outside information a dynamic forecast is generated recursively using the reduced form of the model. The first-period forecast of $Y(t)$, given $Y(t-1)$ and $X(t)$, is given by

$$\hat{Y}(t) = PY(t-1) + QX(t) \tag{4.24}$$

as noted previously. Forecasts for the following periods are then obtained from

$$\hat{Y}(t+h) = P\hat{Y}(t+h-1) + QX(t+h) \tag{4.25}$$

for $h = 1, 2, \ldots$. The prediction error of $Y(t+h)$ is

$$
\begin{aligned}
\hat{V}(t+h) &= Y(t+h) - \hat{Y}(t+h) \\
&= P[Y(t+h-1) - \hat{Y}(t+h-1)] + V(t+h) \\
&= P\hat{V}(t+h-1) + V(t+h).
\end{aligned}
\tag{4.26}
$$

It follows that the prediction error covariance matrix of $Y(t+h)$ can be obtained recursively according to

$$\Sigma(h) = P\Sigma(h-1)P' + \Sigma_v \tag{4.27}$$

with the initial condition $\Sigma(0) = \Sigma_v$.

With the outside information available only in the first forecast period, the first-quarter forecast is

$$\bar{Y}(t) = \hat{Y}(t) + K[\tilde{Y}(t) - \theta \hat{Y}(t)], \tag{4.28}$$

and the forecast error covariance matrix is $\Omega = (I - K\theta)\Sigma_v$. Forecasts for the following periods are again generated recursively using (4.25) but with $\bar{Y}(t)$ as the initial value. The covariance matrix of $\bar{Y}(t + h)$ is obtained by solving (4.27) with the initial condition $\Sigma(0) = \Omega$.

It follows that the difference between these two prediction error covariance matrices is

$$\Delta(h) = P\Delta(h - 1)P' \tag{4.29}$$

with $\Delta(0) = K\theta\Sigma_v$. The solution to this matrix equation can be written explicitly as

$$\Delta(h) = P^h\Delta(0)P^{h'}. \tag{4.30}$$

Provided the econometric model is stable, it follows that

$$\lim_{h \to \infty} \Delta(h) = 0, \tag{4.31}$$

since in this case the characteristic roots of P are less than one in absolute value, which implies that $P^h \to 0$ as $h \to \infty$.[12] This shows that as the forecast horizon is extended, the outside information forecast loses its relative advantage over the pure model forecast.

The forecast standard errors for the test model are shown in table 4.6. The striking feature of this table is that the advantage of the outside information forecast diminishes very quickly with the forecast horizon. For real GNP, for example, the standard error of the two-quarter ahead model forecast is 3.35, and the outside information forecast has a standard error of 2.62. Recall that the respective one-quarter forecast standard errors are 2.52 and 0.62. Thus the rather decided advantage of the one-quarter outside information forecast is much less pronounced in the second quarter of the forecast horizon and all but disappears in the four-quarter forecast.

Summary statistics for two-, four-, and eight-quarter forecast errors are shown in table 4.7 These statistics are based on a set of eight-quarter dynamic simulations beginning with the first quarter of 1970 and running through the fourth quarter of 1979, a total of forty forecast intervals. The model was reestimated each year, and a new set of outside-sample forecasts

Table 4.6
Theoretical forecast standard errors of two-, four-, eight-quarter dynamic ex post forecasts (given YP, CD, and CN)

		1960.1–1970.1			1960.1–1974.1			1960.1–1978.1		
		2	4	8	2	4	8	2	4	8
CD72	M	1.65	2.02	2.43	3.20	4.14	4.55	3.44	4.47	5.59
	F^1	1.50	1.97	2.42	2.46	3.84	4.49	2.70	4.16	5.49
	F^3	1.35	1.94	2.41	2.27	3.78	4.48	2.56	4.11	5.47
CN72	M	1.72	2.08	2.45	2.41	3.05	3.89	2.37	3.11	4.27
	F^1	1.49	1.98	2.40	1.89	2.82	3.81	1.86	2.89	4.19
	F^3	1.40	1.94	2.38	1.82	2.79	3.81	1.81	2.88	4.19
CS72	M	1.11	1.40	1.66	1.22	1.57	1.86	1.66	2.34	3.27
	F^1	1.03	1.36	1.64	1.17	1.55	1.85	1.58	2.29	3.26
	F^3	0.99	1.34	1.63	1.15	1.54	1.85	1.56	2.28	3.25
RUM	M	0.27	0.41	0.61	0.30	0.47	0.69	0.31	0.49	0.71
	F^1	0.26	0.41	0.61	0.28	0.46	0.69	0.30	0.48	0.71
	F^3	0.26	0.41	0.61	0.28	0.46	0.69	0.30	0.48	0.71
YCP	M	1.95	2.40	2.85	2.59	3.16	5.83	5.29	6.56	7.66
	F^1	1.81	2.32	2.80	2.38	3.08	5.79	4.55	6.30	7.59
	F^3	1.63	2.26	2.77	2.16	3.01	5.78	4.33	6.23	7.58
GNP72	M	3.35	4.30	5.25	5.28	6.94	8.51	5.55	7.45	9.81
	F^1	2.84	4.07	5.15	4.00	6.39	8.36	4.36	6.93	9.63
	F^3	2.62	3.98	5.11	3.79	6.32	8.35	4.22	6.87	9.61
YD72	M	3.53	4.91	6.29	4.29	5.94	13.26	6.40	9.33	13.64
	F^1	2.93	4.57	6.12	3.30	5.43	13.15	5.87	9.03	13.50
	$1F^3$	2.67	4.43	6.05	3.14	5.35	13.13	5.82	9.00	13.49

Note: M = standard error of a two-, four- eight-quarter ahead ex post forecast implied by the model. Entries are square roots of diagonal elements of the estimated $\Sigma(h)$ matrix defined in equation (4.27), with initial condition $\Sigma(0) = \Sigma_v$.

F^1 = standard error of Kalman forecast with YP, CD, and CN known for the first month of the jump-off quarter; equations shown in table 4.4 were used to predict the remainder of the jump-off quarter. Entries are square roots of the diagonal elements of the $\Sigma(h)$ matrix defined in equation (4.27), with initial condition $\Sigma(0) = \Omega$.

F^3 = as above, with YP, CD, and CN available for all three months of jump-off quarter.

Table 4.7
Realized root mean squared errors for two-, four-, eight-quarter dynamic ex post forecasts (given YP, CD, and CN)

		Filtered, given ...			
Variable	Model	Month 1	Months 1, 2	Months 1–3	Quarter
Second-quarter dynamic forecasts					
CD72	6.19	4.36	4.16	3.70	3.71
CN72	4.92	3.23	3.10	2.65	2.64
CS72	3.16	3.13	3.06	3.05	3.05
RUM	0.45	0.44	0.44	0.43	0.42
YCP	7.78	7.24	7.06	7.01	7.00
GNP72	10.77	7.41	7.42	7.03	7.02
YD72	19.22	15.76	16.00	15.75	15.75
YP	12.67	6.72	6.65	6.77	6.77
CD	7.74	5.28	4.98	4.43	4.44
CN	6.94	4.44	4.27	3.54	3.53
Fourth-quarter dynamic forecasts					
CD72	10.63	8.71	8.18	8.29	8.29
CN72	6.91	4.97	4.90	4.62	4.61
CS72	4.19	3.98	3.96	3.94	3.93
RUM	0.70	0.68	0.67	0.67	0.66
YCP	13.49	13.39	13.30	13.27	13.25
GNP72	17.47	13.19	13.16	13.08	13.07
YD72	17.01	11.80	11.98	12.02	12.03
YP	20.83	14.91	13.60	13.48	13.50
CD	11.20	10.40	9.91	9.82	9.81
CN	9.08	5.72	5.84	5.59	5.58
Eighth-quarter dynamic forecasts					
CD72	7.50	7.48	7.47	7.47	7.46
CN72	6.48	6.18	6.01	5.43	5.42
CS72	3.59	3.59	3.40	3.33	3.32
RUM	1.22	1.21	1.21	1.20	1.20
YCP	14.69	14.61	14.58	14.20	14.19
GNP72	14.03	13.44	13.53	12.45	12.45
YD72	17.87	17.41	16.62	16.90	16.91
YP	17.47	17.40	15.85	15.29	15.26
CD	12.04	9.93	9.92	9.90	9.90
CN	8.17	7.05	6.77	6.16	6.15

Note: Entries are root mean squared errors, defined as

$$\left\{ \left(\frac{1}{n}\right) \Sigma (Y_i - \bar{Y}_i)^2 \right\}^{1/2},$$

where i ranges over all forty sample quarters, 1970.1 to 1979.4. The root mean squared errors are measured in the same units (billions of $) as the forecast standard errors in table 4.6.

was generated. These results are therefore indicative of the forecast performance that would have been observed if this model had been used continuously over this period to generate dynamic forecasts.

Two important conclusions emerge from this table. The first is that the simulation results conform to the theoretical finding that the value of current outside information diminishes as the forecast horizon lengthens. This can be seen by looking at the entries for the standard error or root mean squared error for the real GNP forecasts for two, four, and eight quarters in advance. The more dramatic finding, however, is that the standard deviations of the forecast errors are far in excess of the values given in table 4.6. As remarked previously, we expect the simulation standard errors to exceed the theoretical values if the sampling errors of the coefficients are not negligible.[13] For the one-period ahead forecasts the simulation results did exhibit this tendency, but it was not nearly so pronounced as with the four- and eight-quarter forecasts shown here. On the basis of these results, it appears to be necessary to reexamine the usual (time-series) practice of ignoring the sampling variability of coefficient estimates when evaluating the standard error of forecasts.

The 1974–75 Recession and Recovery

The performance of the dynamic forecasts of real GNP during the 1974–75 recession and recovery is summarized in table 4.8. The cyclical peak experienced in the fourth quarter of 1973 is correctly forecast seven quarters in advance by both forecasting methods. Similarly the lower turning point in 1975.1 is correctly anticipated seven quarters in advance by both forecasting procedures. Moreover there were no false turning-point forecasts generated by either forecasting procedure over this period.

The dynamic forecast paths are quite similar for both forecast procedures. The use of outside information does get the model "on track" at the beginning of each forecast period, but this has relatively little effect on where the forecast winds up four or eight quarters later. This is of course precisely what would be expected from the summary measures of dynamic forecast accuracy reviewed earlier.[14]

A striking feature of table 4.8 is that the econometric model is able to forecast the cyclical turns very well with no outside information. The major reason for this is that in the test model used here the cyclically volatile components of GNP, namely the various categories of investment expenditure, are exogenous and assumed to be known in advance. This may explain

Table 4.8
Dynamic forecasts of real GNP during the 1974–75 recession and recovery

Date	Actual	Predicted							
		M	F	M	F	M	F	M	F
1972.1	1,157	1,156	1,157						
.2	1,179	1,170	1,171						
.3	1,193	1,180	1,181						
.4	1,215	1,195	1,196						
1973.1	1,247	1,225	1,226	1,251	1,248				
.2	1,249	1,236	1,237	1,269	1,266				
.3	1,257	1,246	1,247	1,284	1,281				
.4	1,267P	1,261	1,263	1,305	1,302				
1974.1	1,255			1,291	1,288	1,258	1,254		
.2	1,256			1,290	1,287	1,253	1,249		
.3	1,249			1,279	1,275	1,236	1,232		
.4	1,232			1,262	1,258	1,229	1,225		
1975.1	1,206T					1,194	1,190	1,189	1,207
.2	1,221					1,198	1,194	1,199	1,217
.3	1,248					1,220	1,216	1,214	1,233
.4	1,260					1,229	1,225	1,220	1,238
1976.1	1,287							1,239	1,258
.2	1,296							1,250	1,267
.3	1,303							1,261	1,278
.4	1,315							1,273	1,291

Note: Entries are eight-quarter dynamic forecasts generated with the econometric model (M) and with perfect outside information (F) on YP, CD, and CN.

why the model forecasts the 1974–75 recession so well and why the value of outside information appears to deteriorate so rapidly in our simulations.

4.4 Conclusion

The results summarized in this chapter indicate that the potential gain in forecast accuracy achievable through the use of outside information is not trivial. However, this gain appears to be concentrated in near-term forecasts and is of much less importance for longer-term forecasts. Still, several important issues remain to be considered:

1. The gain in forecast accuracy using more sophisticated outside information models needs to be investigated.

2. The gain in forecast accuracy using an operating model needs to be explored, especially to see the effect of a greater degree of endogeneity.[15] 3. The approach described here could also be applied to anticipations data and possibly also leading indicators. 4. The importance of sampling variability of coefficient estimates, which is typically overlooked in studies of this kind, needs to be investigated more fully.

Despite the limitations of this study, it clearly provides the motivation for more detailed study of these issues. These further developments promise to offer new evidence on the potential for using outside information to improve the forecasting performance of econometric models.

Notes

The authors gratefully acknowledge the comments of Professors Jan Kmenta and P. A. V. B. Swamy on an earlier version of this chapter. Research on this topic has been supported by NSF Grant SOC78-09475.

1. As written, (4.6) through (4.9) assume the parameters are known. In practice, of course, the coefficients must be estimated so that (4.8), for example, should be written as

$$\hat{Y}(t) = \hat{P}Y(t - 1) + \hat{Q}X(t) \tag{4.8'}$$

and (4.9) becomes

$$Y(t) = \hat{Y}(t) + \hat{V}(t). \tag{4.9'}$$

The covariance matrix of the vector $\hat{V}(t)$ of forecast errors is Σ_v plus a positive semidefinite matrix of order $(1/T)$, where T is the size of the sample used to estimate the parameters. In the illustrative calculations that follow, the contribution of the sampling variability of the coefficients is ignored.

2. Other more sophisticated relationships such as (vector) autoregressions and econometric models are possible.

3. θ might be a partition of an identity matrix, or a more complicated matrix that selects linear combinations of the elements of $Y(t)$.

4. This theorem can be readily extended to the case where V and W are correlated. In that case the BLUP of $Y(t)$ is defined as in (4.14), but with weighting matrix

$$K = [\Sigma_v \theta' - \Sigma_{vw}][\theta \Sigma_v \theta' + \Sigma_w - \theta \Sigma_{vw} - \Sigma_{wv} \theta']^{-1}, \tag{4.15'}$$

and prediction error covariance matrix

$$\Omega = (I - K\theta)\Sigma_v + K\Sigma_{wv}, \tag{4.16'}$$

where $\Sigma_{vw} = \mathrm{cov}(v, w)$. Similarly theorem 4.1 can be generalized to accommodate biased forecasts, $E(v) \neq 0$ or $E(w) \neq 0$. The preservation-of-identities result demonstrated in theorem 4.2 also can be generalized.

5. This follows from the proposition that if A and B are positive definite and $B - A$ is positive semidefinite, then $A^{-1} - B^{-1}$ is positive semidefinite. For proof, see Dhrymes (1978), pp. 494–495.

6. For a discussion of this approach to nonlinear systems, see Schweppe (1973), chapter 13 and the references cited there. This approach relies on the "principle of continuity of approximation," which has been critiqued by Boland (1981).

7. Optimality of the combined forecast in this case is dependent on the assumption that the Taylor series remainder term, $D_t R(t)$, is indeed negligible. This seems reasonable for most applied work and can be tested empirically.

8. Given the exogenous variables in the model, the diagonal element of Σ_v are the error variances of one-quarter ahead forecasts, assuming the parameters of the structural model are known. In practice, the parameters of the model are unknown and must be estimated, and this contributes a positive semidefinite sampling variability term to Σ_v. This term is difficult to compute for a simultaneous equations model and has been omitted in this chapter.

9. Beginning in 1980, monthly estimates of nominal purchases of consumer durables, nondurables, and services are available in the Survey of Current Business.

10. The term "filtering" and the mnemonic F are suggested by the fact that (4.14) through (4.16) constitute a simplified nonrecursive Kalman filter. See Astrom (1970) and Greene (1982).

11. In practice, time lags in collecting and disseminating monthly data mean that at most the "first month" of a quarter is reported by the actual end of the calendar quarter. The significance of the findings in table 4.5 is that even this one month's worth of observations is useful in improving forecast accuracy.

12. Let R be the matrix of characteristic vectors of P, and let Λ be a diagonal matrix with the characteristic roots of P on the diagonal. Then

$$P = R\Lambda R^{-1} \quad \text{and} \quad P^h = R\Lambda^h R^{-1}.$$

Equation (4.31) follows from the fact that $\Lambda^h \to 0$ as $h \to \infty$.

13. With the usual assumptions the contribution of sampling variability of the coefficients is of the order $1/T$, where T is the sample size. With $T \geq 50$, one would ordinarily expect this source of forecast error to be small relative to the variance of the disturbances.

14. Note that dynamic accuracy is here being measured by the error in predicting GNP (or profits, or . . .) at some quarter in the future. If dynamic accuracy were somehow measured as a function of the errors in predicting quarterly changes in GNP along the time path of the forecast, relatively more benefit would be attached to the procedure which got on track more quickly for any given degree of endpoint accuracy.

15. A study that investigates points 1 and 2 is currently underway at the Federal Reserve Board, using the FRB-MIT-Penn quarterly model.

References

Aström, K. J., 1970. *Introduction to Stochastic Control Theory*. Academic Press, New York.

Boland, L. A., 1981. Satisficing in Methodology: A Reply. *Journal of Economic Literature* 29:84–86.

Dhrymes, P. J., 1978. *Introductory Econometrics*. Springer-Verlag, Berlin.

Greene, Mark N., 1982. *Macroeconomic Forecasting Using Data of Mixed Frequencies*. Ph.D. dissertation. University of Michigan, Ann Arbor.

Schweppe, Fred C., 1973. *Uncertain Dynamic Systems*. Prentice-Hall, Englewood Cliffs, N.J.

5 Centering, the Constant, First-Differencing, and Assessing Conditioning

David A. Belsley

Conditioning analysis has proved to be useful in assessing the reliability of regression estimates. Yet the form in which the data ought be in order to make such an analysis meaningful has not been widely appreciated. Here we show that to be meaningful, conditioning diagnostics must be applied to data in a form that has structural interpretability, even if the data are not kept in this form for other purposes such as estimation. This fact is illustrated in the contexts of centering and first-differencing, two important transformations often used to "improve" conditioning but which typically remove structural interpretability and produce meaningless diagnostics.

We begin with a simple example involving centering that illustrates the problems involved. The concept of structural interpretability is next introduced in section 5.2. Section 5.3, at the risk of some duplication, provides the details of the centering issue that were necessarily ignored in the opening example. The role of the constant term (and misconceptions about it) are examined in section 5.4. To this point the term centering has meant deviations about the mean (DFM), but in section 5.5 we see that similar considerations apply to most other forms of centering and many other forms of data transformations. Those problems specific to assessing the conditioning of models with first differences are examined in section 5.6, where it is seen that conditioning diagnostics applied to the first-differenced data typically will misstate the true conditioning of the least-squares estimates based on these data. This phenomenon is demonstrated using an equation for the price deflator for consumption of autos and parts from the Michigan Quarterly Econometric Model (MQEM), which is seen to be quite poorly conditioned in fact.

5.1 Round 1: An Opening Example of Centering

Confusion exists about whether data should be centered before being diagnosed for collinearity (ill conditioning). Weisberg (1980), Montgomery and Peck (1982), and Gunst (1983), for example, indicate that they should. However, Belsley, Kuh, and Welsch (1980), and Belsley (1984a) indicate that such transformations can mask the presence of the constant term in the underlying near dependencies and produce misleading diagnostics. The following example helps to establish this latter point of view, showing that collinearity diagnostics must be applied to the basic (uncentered) data

Table 5.1
Data for example

Observation	$X_i \equiv \iota$	X_2	X_3	y
1	1	0.996926	1.000060	2.69385
2	1	0.997091	0.998779	2.69402
3	1	0.997300	1.000680	2.70052
4	1	0.997813	1.002420	2.68559
5	1	0.997898	1.000650	2.70720
6	1	0.998140	1.000500	2.69550
7	1	0.998556	0.999596	2.70417
8	1	0.998737	1.002620	2.69699
9	1	0.999414	1.003210	2.69327
10	1	0.999678	1.001300	2.68999
11	1	0.999926	0.997579	2.70003
12	1	0.999995	0.998597	2.70200
13	1	1.000630	0.995316	2.70938
14	1	1.000950	0.995966	2.70094
15	1	1.001180	0.997125	2.70536
16	1	1.001770	0.998951	2.70754
17	1	1.002310	1.001020	2.69519
18	1	1.003060	1.001860	2.70170
19	1	1.003940	1.003530	2.70451
20	1	1.004690	1.000210	2.69532

including a "constant" column of ones if a constant term is specified for the model. An immediate corollary to this is that "standardized" data (zero mean, unit variance) or, equivalently, the data correlation matrix often employed for such analysis will typically produce misleading diagnostic information. Although there are legitimate reasons for centering (see section 5.5 for some), we see that assessing conditioning is not one of them, even if the centered data have been otherwise validly employed.

To see simply the issues involved, consider the model

$$y = \beta_1 X_1 + \beta_2 X_2 + \beta_3 X_3 + \varepsilon_t. \tag{5.1}$$

In table 5.1 the y series has been generated by (5.1) with the three series X_1, X_2, and X_3, an error term that is iid normal with mean zero, and parameter values $\beta_1 = 3.0$, $\beta_2 = 0.6$, and $\beta_3 = 0.9$. The X_1 series is identically 1, so that 3 is the "constant term" for this model. We shall usually denote such a vector of ones by ι, but for the moment we wish to highlight that $X_1 \equiv \iota$ is part of the basic data matrix $X = [X_1 \ X_2 \ X_3] \equiv [\iota \ X_2 \ X_3]$.

It is readily verified that the three series X_1, X_2, and X_3 are highly ill conditioned—that is, there is strong collinearity among them. If this is not obvious from examination, we note that the uncentered R^2 of X_3 regressed on X_1 and X_2 is .99999 (implying a variance inflation factor [VIF] exceeding 10^5), and the scaled condition number $\kappa(X)$ for these series is 1,342.[1] It is shown in BKW that a κ in excess of 30 is troublesome, and one as large as 1,300 is astronomical.

It is also readily verified that the two centered-data series

$$\tilde{X}_i \equiv X_i - \bar{X}_i \iota, \quad i = 2, 3, \tag{5.2}$$

are orthogonal and, in contrast to the X_i's, are perfectly conditioned. Since there is no collinearity among the centered data, they must be considered trouble free by those who would advocate centering prior to diagnosing for collinearity. This is not so, however, for, although the constant term seems to have been removed by centering ($\tilde{X}_1 \equiv 0$) along with its consequent conditioning problems, their effects have only been disguised. The ill conditioning survives in the centering transformation itself (section 5.3), and the constant is effectively redistributed among the transformed variates (section 5.4). We shall see that all of the problems arising in the estimation of (5.1) on account of the ill conditioning of the basic data also arise in the estimation of the equivalent homogeneous model

$$\tilde{y} = \beta_2 \tilde{X}_2 + \beta_3 \tilde{X}_3 + \tilde{\varepsilon}, \tag{5.3a}$$

$$\beta_1 = \bar{y} - \beta_2 \bar{X}_2 - \beta_3 \bar{X}_3 - \bar{\varepsilon}, \tag{5.3b}$$

using centered data.

The Ills of Collinearity

Before demonstrating that the ills of collinearity are not removed by centering, let us review what these ills are. We know that in the general linear model $y = X\beta + \varepsilon$ [$X n \times p, \beta p \times 1, \varepsilon n \times 1$, iid with mean zero], the OLS estimator $b \equiv (X^T X)^{-1} X^T y$ is the BLUE with variance-covariance matrix $V(b) = \sigma^2 (X^T X)^{-1}$. Collinearity among the columns of X causes crucial elements of $(X^T X)$ to be large and unstable, thus affecting both b and $V(b)$. The effect on $V(b)$ is to blow up its diagonal elements, creating inflated variances. The effect on b is to render this solution very sensitive to small changes in X—small relative changes in the elements of X can result in large relative changes in the elements of b. We now demonstrate that centering removes neither of these ills.

Some Regressions

Consider first the basic regression of y on X_1, X_2, and X_3 (standard errors are given in parentheses), giving

$$y = 3.191\ X_1 + 0.810\ X_2 - 1.302\ X_3, \tag{5.4}$$
$$\quad\ (0.784)\qquad (0.555)\qquad (0.555)$$
$$R^2 = .310, \quad \kappa(X) = 1{,}342, \quad F = 3.82,$$

and next, for comparison, the centered regression of $\tilde{y}$ on $\tilde{X}_2$ and $\tilde{X}_3$, giving

$$\tilde{y} = 0.810\ \tilde{X}_2 - 1.302\ \tilde{X}_3, \tag{5.5}$$
$$\quad\ (0.555)\qquad (0.555)$$
$$\text{with an implied constant} = \bar{y} - 0.810\bar{X}_2 + 1.302\bar{X}_3 = 3.191,$$
$$R^2 = .310, \quad \kappa(\tilde{X}) = 1.$$

The first thing we notice is that collinearity has clearly inflated variances in (5.4). Despite the facts that both X_2 and X_3 are known to be involved in the generation of y and that their joint impact, as evidenced from the F test, is significant at the 5 percent level, only one coefficient is individually significant at this level.[2]

The second thing we notice (and which should come as no surprise) is that the centered estimates (5.5) are unchanged, as are their estimated standard errors. Clearly, centering has in no way altered the estimated variances and cannot have reduced any inflated ones. Centering simply cannot aid this first ill of collinearity.

Now let us look at the second ill: the sensitivity of b to changes in the data. To do this, we perturb both the X_2 and X_3 series by a relatively small error to give new variates

$$X_i^{\circ} \equiv X_i + \eta_i, \quad i = 2, 3, \tag{5.6}$$

where the η_i's are randomly chosen and scaled so that $\|\eta_i\| = .01\|X_i\|$. Here $\|\cdot\|$ denotes Euclidean length. The regression of y on these slightly perturbed data, $X_1(\equiv \iota)$, X_2°, and X_3°, gives

$$y = 2.978\ X_1 - 0.111\ X_2^{\circ} - 0.167\ X_3^{\circ}, \tag{5.7}$$
$$\quad\ (0.173)\qquad (0.139)\qquad (0.134)$$
$$R^2 = .137, \quad \kappa(X^{\circ}) = 265.$$

Comparing (5.7) with (5.4) shows that the small relative change in the X_i's indeed results in a very large relative change in the estimates. Letting b denote the original estimates and $b°$ the perturbed, $\|b - b°\|/\|b\| =$ .4172—that is, a 1 percent relative change in the X_i's results in over a 40 percent relative change in the estimates. There is no doubt that collinearity is causing troubles.

Now we examine the corresponding perturbed, centered-data regression of y on $\tilde{X}_2°$ and $\tilde{X}_3°$, where

$$\tilde{X}_i° \equiv X_i° - \bar{X}_i°\iota, \quad i = 2, 3, \tag{5.8}$$

which gives

$$\tilde{y} = -0.111\ \tilde{X}_2° - 0.167\ \tilde{X}_3°, \quad \text{with implied constant} = 2.978, \tag{5.9}$$
$$(0.139) \qquad (0.134)$$
$$R^2 = .137, \quad \kappa(\tilde{X}°) = 1.2.$$

Again, as should be obvious but somehow goes unappreciated in this context, the estimates of the centered equation (5.9) have altered in exactly the same way as the basic equation (5.7) on account of a small relative change in the X_i's, indicating the centered-data estimates retain the same sensitivity and ill conditioning as the uncentered estimates despite the perfect conditioning of the centered-data matrix $\tilde{X}$.

An Important Conclusion

We must conclude that (1) the ill conditioning of the basic data has caused true problems to OLS estimation, giving inflated variances and extremely sensitive parameter estimates, (2) centering alters neither of these problems, and (3) diagnosing the conditioning of the centered data $[\tilde{X}_2\ \tilde{X}_3]$ (which are perfectly conditioned) would completely overlook this situation, whereas diagnostics based on the basic data $[X_1\ X_2\ X_3]$ would not.

We see later that the reason for conclusions 2 and 3 is that centering does not really alter the ill conditioning of the LS estimation problem, it merely transforms the problem into one in which the true conditioning cannot be directly observed.

The Meaning of $\kappa(\tilde{X})$

In light of the foregoing, what is the meaning of the fact that the centered-data matrix $\tilde{X} = [\tilde{X}_2\ \tilde{X}_3]$ is perfectly conditioned, having a scaled condition number $\kappa(\tilde{X})$ equal to unity? It can be shown that the scaled condition number provides an upper bound on the relative sensitivity of elements of b to relative changes in the data (a concept very akin to the economist's notion of elasticity). In the previous example the conditioning of the LS estimate with respect to the basic data X is gigantic: 1,342, indicating the great potential sensitivity of b to relative changes in X which we observe in fact. The conditioning of the LS problem with respect to the centered data $\tilde{X}$, however, is unity, and hence we should expect small relative changes in the centered data (not the basic data) to cause small relative changes in the estimates. Thus, if we were to perturb $\tilde{X}_2$ and $\tilde{X}_3$ (not X_2 and X_3) by a small relative amount, we would expect little relative change in $\tilde{b}_2$ and $\tilde{b}_3$ from (5.5).

In the next phase of our example, therefore, let us perturb $\tilde{X}_2$ and $\tilde{X}_3$ as

$$\tilde{X}_i^+ \equiv \tilde{X}_i + \phi_i, \quad i = 2, 3, \tag{5.10}$$

where the ϕ_i are randomly chosen and scaled to be small relative to $\tilde{X}_i$, so that $\|\phi_i\| = 0.01\|\tilde{X}_i\|$, $i = 2, 3$. Regressing $\tilde{y}$ on $\tilde{X}_2^+$ and $\tilde{X}_3^+$ gives

$$\tilde{y} = 0.798\ \tilde{X}_2^+ - 1.303\ \tilde{X}_3^+, \tag{5.11}$$
$$\quad (0.555) \qquad (0.554)$$
$$R^2 = .309, \quad \kappa(\tilde{X}^+) = 1.002.$$

Comparing these results to (5.5), it is clear that small relative changes in the centered data have indeed caused little relative change in the estimates of the two (not three) coefficients relevant to this LS problem. And it is the stability of this problem (not the original problem) to changes in the centered data (not the original data) that is correctly being diagnosed by the conditioning of the centered data.

Interpreting Small Relative Changes

Unfortunately knowledge of the effect of small relative changes in the centered data is not meaningful for assessing the sensitivity of the basic LS problem, for it is possible for small (and insignificant) relative changes in the basic data to produce massive relative changes in the centered data. To see this, we must ask how we interpret small relative changes. An economist, in viewing a figure of 1 trillion dollars for GNP, would readily admit that, for practical purposes, changes of 1 percent are relatively small. The economist would, however, be wholly unable to determine what constitutes

Table 5.2
Perturbation sensitivities

Year	(1) GNP (trillions of $)	(2) $\widetilde{\text{GNP}}$	(3) GNP°	(4) $\widetilde{\text{GNP}}°$	(5) $\widetilde{\text{GNP}} - \widetilde{\text{GNP}}°$
1	1.000	−0.01334	0.99137	−0.018660	0.005320
2	1.020	0.00667	1.00857	−0.001459	0.008129
3	1.020	0.00667	1.030147	0.020118	−0.134480

a small change in centered GNP, for the concept of centered GNP has no structural economic interpretation. Indeed, values for centered GNP could be large or small depending on the period of observation and therefore for reasons having nothing to do with the true meaning of the data. Suppose, for example, we had two annual GNP series, one from 1950 to 1981 and the other from 1971 to 1973. If each series had its mean removed, the centered magnitudes of the longer series would be very much larger than those of the shorter three-year series. A 1 percent change in one case is very different from a 1 percent change in the other. In order, then, to determine a "small" relative change in centered GNP, which is otherwise uninterpretable, it must be deduced from a small relative change in actual GNP, which is interpretable.

The following simple exercise displays the extremes that can arise. Consider the three element "GNP" series in column 1 of table 5.2. The corresponding centered GNP are in column 2. The basic GNP figures are perturbed in column 3 by a set of random numbers scaled so that $\| \text{GNP} - \text{GNP}° \| = .01 \| \text{GNP} \|$. The corresponding perturbed, centered data are in column 5. We calculate that $\| \widetilde{\text{GNP}} - \widetilde{\text{GNP}}° \| / \| \widetilde{\text{GNP}} \| = .6039$—that is, a 1 percent relative change in actual GNP results in a relative change of centered GNP of over 60 percent! Thus, if the 1 percent relative change in the basic data is considered small, so must be this 60 percent relative change in the centered data.

Now, returning to the data of table 5.1, we can plainly see why no information about the true conditioning of the LS problem is given by the excellent conditioning of the corresponding centered data. This latter conditioning can only guarantee that the relative changes in the estimated parameters will be small if the relative changes in the centered data are small. It is the nature of these data, however, that small relative changes in the basic data can produce immense relative changes in the centered data which can therefore cause equally immense relative changes in the centered solution.[3]

5.2   Assessing the Conditioning of Which Regression?

We noted earlier that collinearity causes two difficulties for the LS problem: a propensity for inflated variances and a potentially excessive sensitivity of the LS solution to changes in the data. These two difficulties are really related manifestations of the same problem—ill conditioning. Since it can be quite difficult to assess the presence of inflated variances (Belsley 1982), it proves easier to categorize a LS problem as ill conditioned by the presence of potential sensitivity. But sensitivity to what?

Small Relative Changes

Perturbation theory of numerical analysis has already answered this question. There, in the context of LS, it is shown that problems arise when perturbations that constitute small relative changes in the data can result in large relative changes in the LS solution.[4] Such a focus coincides with common sense, for in practice these are the conditions under which we become most concerned about the meaning and value of our LS estimates. But small relative changes in which data?

Structurally Interpretable Data

For relative changes to be meaningfully assessed as large or small, the data themselves must be structurally interpretable—that is, they must measure an autonomously conceptual aspect of the problem being modeled (Haavelmo 1944). Aggregate consumption, C, for example, in the Keynesian consumption function is structually interpretable since it is a measure that pairs up with the economically interpretable aspect of aggregate consumer behavior that is being modeled. Most economists could tell quite a bit about C. First, they could note that $C = \$0$ implies the absence of consumption—that is, there is a natural origin for its measurement. Second, measured with respect to this origin, recent consumption in current dollars is approximately 1.9 trillion dollars annually. Third, a shift of C by one-tenth of 1 percent is relatively small, both because its overall economic impact is small and because such changes are within its measurement error.

Fourth, scale changes (changes in the units of measurement) do not affect this interpretability.

But, if we were to change the origin of measurement, the resulting figure need no longer be structually interpretable. If, for example, we were to center the consumption data, little interpretation could be given to a particular value of centered consumption, $\tilde{C}$. To see this, ask the nearest economist what $\tilde{C}$ = $0 means, or $\tilde{C}$ = $1,000, or, if centered consumption were changed by 10 percent, would the change be large or small? It is clear that one would have to return to the original, interpretable data to answer these questions.

In order, then, to assess small relative changes in the data, we must first pick an appropriate origin for measurement.

Origins of Measurement

Not all variates encountered in regression analysis have natural origins as in the previous illustration. A temperature of $0°$ C, for example, does not imply the absence of temperature. And we would be hard put to know if a 10 percent change in Celsius temperature were large or small. Near the freezing point of water it could well be small but not so small near the boiling point. In general, however, one would have to know more about the structure of the problem in which the measure is being used. One can conceive of physical experiments in which the structural interpretation of temperature would be with respect to absolute zero ($0°$ K = $-273.16°$ C). In other cases the structural interpretation may in fact center around the freezing point of water, for example, a model of water viscosity. In general, it is knowledge of the structure of the underlying problem being modeled that indicates the appropriate origin of measurement against which small relative changes can be assessed.

Even variates like price, weight, profits, or acceleration that seem to have natural origins of zero might be structually interpretable with respect to different origins in certain situations. The Dow-Jones average, for example, for a long time had a psychological plateau of 800 (perhaps 1,200 these days). If one were modeling such aspects of stock-market behavior, it is quite possible that large and small relative changes should be assessed with respect to the deviation of the Dow-Jones from 800 and not from zero.

Assess the Conditioning with Respect to the Structural Data

We are now able to answer the query that heads this section. In assessing the conditioning of a given LS problem, we wish to determine the potential

sensitivity of a relative change in the LS solution (no matter how calculated) to a small relative change in the structural data. This means that
(1) the investigator must be able to pick an origin against which small
relative changes can be appropriately assessed and (2) it is the data measured relative to this origin that are relevant to diagnosing the conditioning
of the LS problem.

Point 2 does not imply the data may not be otherwise transformed
(perhaps advantageously) for estimation or other purposes. It does say,
however, that such transformed data are not, in general, relevant to diagnosing the conditioning of the LS problem.

With regard to point 1, if the investigator is unable to provide the
appropriate origin of measurement, there is an indication of an incomplete
understanding of the full problem, and the meaning of the diagnostics (if
not the estimates) must necessarily reflect this arbitrariness.[5]

5.3. Round 2: The Basic Regression and Its Conditioning

We may now explore the implications of the preceding section for assessing
the conditioning of a given regression problem. We show that it is the
condition number of the basic, or structurally interpretable, data and not
that of the centered data that provides the required diagnostic information.
To this end we define the regression problem in its basic form and examine
the conditioning of the two algorithms most often used to compute its OLS
estimates: the basic and the centered algorithms.

The Basic Regression Problem

We begin with the basic form for the regression model

$$y = \beta_1 \iota + \beta_2 X_2 + \cdots + \beta_p X_p + \varepsilon, \qquad (5.12)$$

which, in addition to the usual Gauss-Markov assumptions, is characterized by the X_i's being measured with respect to appropriate origins so that
the magnitude of relative changes in the data can be meaningfully assessed.
The $n \times p$ matrix

$$X \equiv [\iota \ X_2 \ldots X_p]$$

will be called the *matrix of basic data*. Three additional remarks apply.

First, it is assumed for the present discussion involving centering that
there is a constant term in the model and that ι is part of the basic data.

Otherwise, centering can be wholly inappropriate and cause serious problems. We shall see this in section 5.5 when we examine conditioning when structural considerations imply a homogeneous model ($\beta_1 = 0$).[6]

Second, it is assumed that the basic data are linear. Although conditioning diagnostics exist for some forms of nonlinearities (e.g., logs, see Belsley 1983b, and power series), appropriate solutions are not yet available for all forms of data and model nonlinearities.[7] These issues are beyond the scope of the present work.

Third, although origin of measurement is integral to the basic data, rescaling the X_i's clearly has no effect on relative changes in the data, and hence the units in which the X_i's are measured are irrelevant to this basic formulation.[8]

The basic regression problem is obtaining the OLS estimates of this basic model, and it is the conditioning of the various algorithms for calculating these estimates that we wish to explore. But first it is useful to provide a brief digression on the mechanics of centering, an operation integral to one such algorithm.

Centering and Its Geometry

We continue to use centering to denote DFM. Let $x = (x_1 \ldots x_n)^T$ be any n-vector and $\iota = (1 \ldots 1)^T$ be the vector of n ones. It is well known that the matrix of the linear transformation that carries x into the centered vector $\tilde{x} \equiv x - \bar{x}\iota$, where $\bar{x} = \sum x_i/n$, is

$$M \equiv I - \frac{\iota\iota^T}{n},$$ (5.13)

that is,

$$\tilde{x} \equiv Mx.$$ (5.14)

M is noted to be an idempotent $n \times n$ matrix with rank $n - 1$. The singularity of M is not always appreciated in this context, for it means that the linear transformation (5.14) is perfectly ill conditioned; small relative changes in the elements of x can cause extremely (indeed infinitely) large relative changes in $\tilde{x}$. This happens for x close to (having a small angle with) ι, the vector that spans the one-dimensional space annihilated by M, since $M\iota = 0$. We have already seen this with the data in tables 5.1 and 5.2 which, we note, were purposely made "nearly constant."

Let us see this sensitivity more generally through the geometry of center-

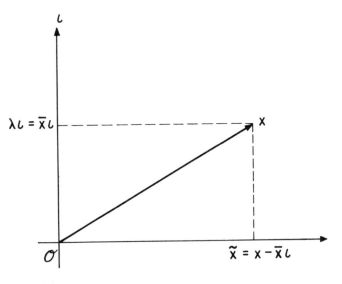

Figure 5.1
The geometry of centering

ing. In figure 5.1 are pictured the n-vector x along with the "constant" vector ι. If we project x orthogonally onto ι (which is the same as regressing x on ι), we see that the orthogonal projection $\lambda \iota$ is the vector whose elements are all $\bar{x}$, the mean of the elements of x. This is so since λ must obey $(x - \lambda\iota)^T \iota = 0$, or (recalling that $x^T \iota = \sum x_i$ and $\iota^T \iota = n$), $\lambda = \sum x_i/n = \bar{x}$. The geometric interpretation of the centered variate $\tilde{x} = x - \bar{x}\iota$, then, is simply the orthogonal projector of x onto ι shifted to emanate from the origin (see figure 5.1).

Now suppose x is collinear with ι—there is a small angle between them—as in figure 5.2. Perturb x by a vector η whose length is small relative to x, giving $x° \equiv x + \eta$. It is clear that this small relative shift in x has produced a very large relative shift in the centered $\tilde{x}$'s, which can be measured as the ratio of the lengths $\|\tilde{x}° - \tilde{x}\|/\|\tilde{x}\|$. It is also clear that such sensitivity will increase the smaller is the angle between x and ι—that is, the worse the collinearity or ill conditioning.

Estimating the Basic Regression Model

Now we may return to the OLS estimation of (5.12) and the conditioning of the two widely employed means for its calculation. The first is direct, based on

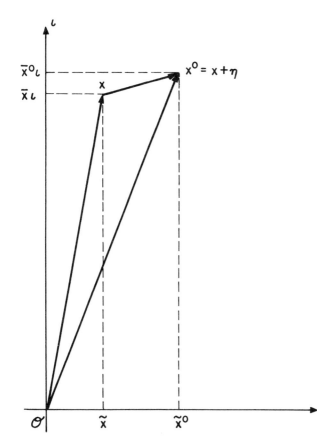

Figure 5.2
Centered and uncentered perturbations compared

$$b = (X^T X)^{-1} X^T y. \tag{5.15}$$

We shall call this the *basic algorithm*.[9] The second is a two-step sequence that first transforms the basic variates X_i into their centered counterparts[10]

Step 1: $\tilde{X}_i \equiv M X_i, \qquad i = 2, \ldots, p, \tag{5.16}$

and then calculates

Step 2: $\tilde{b} = (\tilde{X}^T \tilde{X})^{-1} \tilde{X}^T \tilde{y},$ with implicit intercept   (5.17a)

$$\tilde{b}_1 = \bar{y} - \tilde{b}_2 \bar{X}_2 - \cdots - \tilde{b}_p \bar{X}_p. \tag{5.17b}$$

We shall call the sequence of these two steps the *centered algorithm*. The $n \times (p - 1)$ matrix

$$\tilde{X} \equiv [\tilde{X}_2 \ldots \tilde{X}_p] \tag{5.18}$$

will be denoted the *matrix of centered data* which, of course, has no constant column.

It is well known (Theil 1971 and shown again in section 5.4) that these two algorithms for calculating the OLS estimates of the basic regression produce identical estimates for all parameters, that is,

$$b = \begin{bmatrix} \tilde{b}_1 \\ \tilde{b} \end{bmatrix}. \tag{5.19}$$

If, then, we perturb the basic data X, it must necessarily occur that the estimates b from the one-step basic algorithm and those from the two-step centered algorithm $\begin{bmatrix} \tilde{b}_1 \\ \tilde{b} \end{bmatrix}$ must change identically. The two algorithms must therefore be identically conditioned, yet somehow there is a feeling that centering improves the conditioning. Let us see how this misconception arises.

Determining Conditioning

The following fundamental result allows us to pair the *conditioning of a given regression* with the *condition number of its data matrix*.

A Fundamental Result on LS Conditioning   Let

$$w = Z\delta + e \tag{5.20}$$

be any regression, where w is $n \times 1$, Z $n \times p$, δ $p \times 1$, and e $n \times 1$. It is shown in BKW that the conditioning of the OLS estimate

$$d = (Z^TZ)^{-1}Z^Tw \tag{5.21}$$

with respect to the data Z is measured by the scaled condition number

$$\kappa(Z) \equiv \frac{\mu_{\max}(Z)}{\mu_{\min}(Z)} \tag{5.22}$$

of the matrix Z, where $\mu_{\max}(Z)$ and $\mu_{\min}(Z)$ are, respectively, the maximal and minimal singular values of Z after its columns have been scaled to have equal (usually unit) length.[11] In other words, the potential sensitivity of relative changes in d to relative changes in Z is measured by the scaled condition number $\kappa(Z)$ of Z.

The Conditioning of the Basic Regression   We know from section 5.2 that the only meaningful measure of conditioning for a given regression (5.12) is that which measures the potential sensitivity of small relative changes in its OLS estimates to small relative changes in the basic data X. The previous fundamental result shows that this is measured by the conditioning of (5.15), that is, the scaled condition number $\kappa(X)$ of the basic-data matrix X. Since the basic and the centered algorithms for computing these LS estimates are equivalent, $\kappa(X)$ must not only measure the conditioning of the basic algorithm (5.15) but must also measure that of the centered algorithm, the sequence of step 1 followed by step 2. Where, then, does the condition number $\kappa(\tilde{X})$ of the centered data enter?

An Enticing Alternative   When the basic-data matrix X is ill conditioned— high $\kappa(X)$—it is often noticed that the centered-data matrix $\tilde{X}$ is well conditioned. Indeed, it is shown in appendix A that the centered data cannot be worse conditioned than the basic data. It is this better conditioning $\kappa(\tilde{X})$ of $\tilde{X}$ that naturally invites attention. But $\kappa(\tilde{X})$ is telling us about the conditioning of the wrong problem!

$\kappa(\tilde{X})$: What It Means and What It Doesn't   To help us interpret $\kappa(\tilde{X})$, define the equation

$$\tilde{y} = \beta_2 \tilde{X}_2 + \cdots + \beta_p \tilde{X}_p + \eta \tag{5.23}$$

to be the centered-data model corresponding to (5.12), whose OLS estimator is clearly

$$b^* = (\tilde{X}^T \tilde{X})^{-1} \tilde{X}^T \tilde{y}. \tag{5.24}$$

The calculations (5.24) are, of course, identical to part (5.17a) of step 2 of the centered algorithm, so that $b^* \equiv \tilde{b}$. But now, in applying the previously stated fundamental result on LS conditioning to this case, we see that $\kappa(\tilde{X})$ measures the potential sensitivity of relative changes in b^* (and therefore in $\tilde{b}$) to small relative changes in the uninterpretable *centered data* $\tilde{X}$ (the wrong problem) and not to small relative changes in the interpretable *basic data* X (the correct problem). In examining $\kappa(\tilde{X})$, we are assessing the conditioning only of step 2 of the centered algorithm and are ignoring the conditioning of step 1. Step 1, of course, consists of the centering transform M, which we have already seen to be singular and therefore potentially very poorly conditioned.

Indeed, it turns out that this potentiality must always be fulfilled. In other words, if an ill-conditioned basic-data matrix X can be transformed into a well-conditioned centered-data matrix $\tilde{X}$, the centering transform itself must be ill conditioned. The basis for this result is shown in BKW (appendix B). It can also be seen as an excellent exercise in the use of the geometry employed in section 5.3. The reader is invited to show how two collinear (ill-conditioned) vectors could (but need not) produce well-conditioned (even orthogonal) centered vectors. It will then be seen that this can only occur if the two collinear vectors are themselves highly collinear with ι, which, as we have seen, is precisely the situation in which the M transform is ill conditioned. It should be no surprise that these circumstances were used to construct the data in table 5.1.

We may conclude this discussion, then, by noting that centering can indeed reduce ill conditioning of the basic data and produce a well-conditioned step 2 of the centered algorithm, but only at the cost of a poorly conditioned centering transformation in step 1. In ignoring the poor conditioning of step 1, $\kappa(\tilde{X})$ tells an incomplete and misleading diagnostic story about the conditioning of the basic regression problem which is a sequence of both steps.[12]

5.4   The Constant

Much confusion surrounding centering arises because of some commonly held misconceptions about the "constant term." This section aims at several of these issues with the goal of showing that, for the most part, the "constant" plays a role no different from any other "variate."

Structural vs. Algorithmic Roles of ι: Variates vs. Vectors

Every series X_i ($i = 1 \ldots p$) in a regression analysis, including a "constant column" ($X_1 \equiv \iota$), plays two separable roles: one structural, the other algorithmic.

The Structural Role of Variates   Structurally, a series X_i is a measured representation of some definable aspect of the underlying real situation being modeled. In this context X_i is often called a *variate* or a variable.

Sometimes this term is reserved for series that actually vary, but this is an unwarranted restriction since those structurally unchanging aspects of the underlying situation are properly measured and modeled by the "constant variate" $X_1 \equiv \iota$. In a truly linear model these constant aspects are simply the expected value of the response variate y conditional on all other X_i's being zero. If it is known a priori that there are no such constant elements, then ι should not be included. In other words, in proper modeling the decision to include a constant should be as consciously made as that to include any other variate. Often the constant is included to "sop up" excluded effects or because the model is assumed a linear approximation to a nonlinear situation.[13] This is acceptable practice if it cannot be known a priori that $\beta_1 = 0$. Often, however, the constant is included simply because the regression package automatically includes it. This convenience can lead to bad practice.

The Algorithmic Role of Vectors   Once it has been determined structurally that $X_1 \equiv \iota$ belongs in the regression, the vector ι takes on a life of its own which is in every sense the equal of any other vector X_i included. To see this, recall that a regression of y on $X \equiv [\iota \ X_2 \ \ldots \ X_p]$ is a mechanical process (having nothing to do with any underlying structural considerations) which performs an orthogonal projection of the *vector* y on the linear space S spanned by the *vectors* that comprise the columns of X. In becoming a basis vector determining one dimension of S, ι plays a role exactly the same as any other X_i. Indeed, by rotating y and all other X_i's rigidly through the same angle, the orthogonal projection problem clearly remains unchanged, but no vector is ι. In its role in the regression process, then, ι is no more or less a "constant" than any other X_i. It is a constant only in its structural interpretation.

Perturb a Constant?   The distinction between the structural and algorithmic roles of ι helps to remove the qualm that conditioning diagnostics based on perturbation analysis cannot apply to problems with ι (or any other dummy) since ι is constant and cannot be perturbed. Some use this argument as reason for diagnosing the centered data that have no constant. But we see that, among other faults, this confuses the two interpretations of ι, for ι is constant only as a structural concept but can be perturbed just like any other vector for purposes of determining the sensitivity of the output of the projection algorithm to changes in its inputs.

The Constant and Collinearity

Another misplaced use of the "constant term" occurs in some definitions of collinearity. Weisberg (1980), for example, defines two variables X_1 and X_2 as being exactly collinear if there is a linear equation such as

$$X_2 = \alpha_0 \iota + \alpha_1 X_1. \tag{5.25}$$

Although the inclusion of ι in this definition could perhaps prove adequate (albeit awkward) if all regression models had constants (including ι), it becomes unduly restrictive and even misleading in the context of homogeneous (without constant) models.

Consider a regression in the context of the two-variate homogeneous model

$$y = \beta_1 X_1 + \beta_2 X_2 + \varepsilon, \tag{5.26}$$

where $X_1 \neq \iota$ and equation (5.25) holds with $\alpha_0 \neq 0$. According to this definition there is exact collinearity between X_1 and X_2, and so, presumably, no regression should be possible. But, in fact, the data matrix $[X_1 \, X_2] = [X_1 \; \alpha_0 \iota + \alpha_1 X_1]$ will have full rank so long as $\alpha_0 \neq 0$, and a regression may indeed be properly run.[14] Of course, it would be impossible to estimate the three-vector, nonhomogeneous model

$$y = \beta_0 \iota + \beta_1 X_1 + \beta_2 X_2 + \varepsilon \tag{5.27}$$

with these data since $X = [\iota \, X_1 \, X_2]$ would have less than full rank. But this is not because there is collinearity between the two variables X_1 and X_2, rather it is because of the collinearity among the three vectors ι, X_1, and X_2.

A proper definition of exact collinearity, then, says that p vectors $X_1 \ldots X_p$ are exactly collinear if one of the X_i's may be written as a nontrivial linear combination of the others, that is, if the p vectors are linearly dependent. A "constant" enters this relation only if one of the X_i's is ι. Of course, exact collinearity is rarely of practical concern, but similar considerations arise in a proper definition of (inexact) collinearity. On this, see BKW (1980) and Belsley (1984a: Reply).

Centering Does Not Get Rid of the Constant Term

It is generally thought that centering "gets rid of the constant term." But this is not the case; centering merely redistributes the constant among all the variates so that it continues to be present but not explicitly. Begin with

$$y = \beta_1 \iota + \beta_2 X_2 + \cdots + \beta_p X_p + \varepsilon. \tag{5.28}$$

Taking means gives

$$\bar{y} = \beta_1 + \beta_2 \bar{X}_2 + \cdots + \beta_p \bar{X}_p + \bar{\varepsilon}, \tag{5.29}$$

from which we express the constant as

$$\beta_1 \equiv \bar{y} - \beta_2 \bar{X}_2 - \cdots - \beta_p \bar{X}_p - \bar{\varepsilon}. \tag{5.30}$$

Postmultiplying (5.29) by ι and substracting from (5.28), we get the centered model

$$y - \bar{y}\iota = \beta_2 (X_2 - \bar{X}_2 \iota) + \cdots + \beta_p (X_p - \bar{X}_p \iota) + (\varepsilon - \bar{\varepsilon}\iota), \tag{5.31a}$$

or

$$\tilde{y} = \beta_2 \tilde{x}_2 + \cdots + \beta_p \tilde{x}_p + \tilde{\varepsilon}. \tag{5.31b}$$

In the form (5.31b) there appears to be no constant term, but in the more transparent form (5.31a) we see through to (5.30)—the constant term is still there.[15]

In fact ι does not even play a unique role in such "reductive" transformations of the regression, for we may similarly transform (5.28) with respect to any of the explanatory variates X_i. To emphasize the parallel between ι and any other X_i in this role of "centering," we shall first (re)establish a well-known result with ι in a way that allows for immediate reapplication with X_i.

Let $b_1^*, \ldots, b_p^*$ be the LS solution to

$$y = b_1 \iota + b_2 X_2 + \cdots + b_p X_p + e, \tag{5.32}$$

and consider the corresponding transformed (centered with respect to ι) problem

$$My = b_2 M X_2 + \cdots + b_p M X_p + Me, \tag{5.33}$$

recalling that $M\iota \equiv 0$. It is easy to show the well-known result that $b_2^*, \ldots, b_p^*$ are also the LS solution to the centered problem (5.33)—for consider any other values for $b_2, \ldots, b_p$. Putting these, along with b_1^*, in (5.32) must result in a residual e° having sum of squares no less than those of the LS residual $e^* \equiv y - b_1^* \iota - b_2^* X_2 - \cdots - b_p^* X_p$. Further, since e^* results from an orthogonal projection of y into S, the linear space spanned by the X_i's (including ι), and e° results from a projection (not orthogonal) of y into the same space, there must be an $\eta \in S$, orthogonal to e^* ($\eta^T e^* = 0$), such that $e^\circ = e^* + \eta$. Thus the "centered" residual Me^* (5.33) cannot have least sum of squares since $e^{\circ T}Me^\circ = (e^* + \eta)^T M(e^* + \eta) = e^{*T}Me^* + \eta^T\eta \geq e^{*T}e^*$; recall that $Me^* = e^*$ and $\eta^T e^* = 0$. □

But we may establish an analogous result for X_i. Consider the projection matrix

$$M_{(i)} \equiv I - X_i(X_i^T X_i)^{-1}X_i^T. \tag{5.34}$$

This matrix, like M, is idempotent with rank $n - 1$ and has the readily established property that it transforms any vector $x \in R^n$ into the residuals from the regression of that vector onto X_i. It is clear that for $X_1 \equiv \iota$, (5.34) reduces to M in (5.13), so we have generalized this concept.

If we premultiply (5.32) by $M_{(i)}$, we get the model "centered" with respect to X_i,

$$M_{(i)}y = b_1 M_{(i)}\iota + b_2 M_{(i)}X_2 + \cdots + b_i M_{(i)}X_i + \cdots + b_p M_{(i)}X_p + M_{(i)}e$$

$$= b_1 M_{(i)}\iota + b_2 M_{(i)}X_2 + \cdots + 0 + \cdots + b_p M_{(i)}X_p + M_{(i)}e. \tag{5.35}$$

We have now "removed" X_i from the model (actually no more so than ι was removed before), since $M_{(i)}X_i \equiv 0$, and the new variates $M_{(i)}X_j$ are the residuals remaining after the effect of X_i has been removed. $M_{(i)}\iota$ is now, of course, no longer zero and not even "constant." One may now make use of the previous argument to show that a regression of $M_{(i)}y$ on $M_{(i)}\iota$, $M_{(i)}X_2$, ..., $M_{(i)}X_{i-1}$, $M_{(i)}X_{i+1}$, ..., $M_{(i)}X_p$ results in the LS solution b_1^*, b_2^*, ..., b_{i-1}^*, b_{i+1}^*, ..., b_p^*, and that

$$b_i^* = \alpha_y - b_1^*\alpha_1 - \cdots - b_{i-1}^*\alpha_{i-1} - b_{i+1}^*\alpha_{i+1} - \cdots - b_p^*\alpha_p, \tag{5.36}$$

where α_j is the regression coefficient of X_j regressed on X_i, and α_y of y regressed on X_i.[16] In the previous argument one need only substitute $M_{(i)}$ for M and recognize that $M_{(i)}e^* = 0$, since e^* is necessarily orthogonal to all X_i. The transformed model (5.35), then, is equivalent to the original model (5.32) in exactly the same way that the centered (with respect to ι) model (5.33) is.

Thus, any variate X_i can be used in place of ι for the purpose of "reducing" the model; there is nothing special in ι. Those who would center before diagnosing for collinearity should be quite disturbed by this result, for now it appears we could equally well (and with identical motive) transform the data by regressing on any X_i rather than ι, which is deviations from the mean (DFM). Each resulting "centered" data set would have its own condition number (better than that of the original data). Which do you pick? Fortunately we already know the answer to this question: none. These all tell the wrong story—that is, they indicate only the conditioning of the corresponding transformed regression and ignore that of the preceding regression $M_{(i)}$ which produces the transformed variates.

5.5   General Centering

Until now centering has denoted deviations from the mean. Other centers are, however, possible. Probably the most useful general definition of centering would be the removal of a constant, in some sense central to the problem, from each term in a given data series. A vector x will be said to be centered with respect to the constant α, denoted $x^{(\alpha)}$, if

$$x^{(\alpha)} \equiv x - \alpha\iota. \tag{5.37}$$

Model-Dependent vs. Data-Dependent Centering

It will prove useful to distinguish between model- and data-dependent centerings. A *data-dependent* centering occurs if $\alpha = \alpha(x)$, that is, if α is a function of the vector x being centered. Taking deviations from the mean exemplifies a data-dependent centering for which $\alpha(x) = \bar{x}$. Other descriptive values of the data, such as mode, median, maximum, or minimum, could be used as well.

Model-dependent centerings occur when α derives from model considerations independent of the data being centered. We encountered such centerings in section 5.2 when the freezing point of water (e.g., $\alpha = 32°$ F) was chosen for the origin.[17]

No Diagnostics from Data-Dependent Centered Data

All data-dependent centering processes result in data series that are equally unacceptable for diagnosing conditioning. Such centerings necessarily produce arbitrary shifts in origin, for they arise from the particular data series and can therefore have no meaning relative to the underlying model which must apply equally to all relevant series of explanatory variables X. The theory of the consumption function, for example, provides no meaning to the fact that the mean, model, or median value of disposable income is z

dollars. Thus z is structurally arbitrary, and we recall from section 5.2 that such arbitrary changes in origin transform structurally interpretable variables into uninterpretable ones. Indeed, the thrust of that discussion holds intact if we interpret centering as used there to mean any data-dependent centering.

The Conditioning of Data-Dependent Centering

Further insight into the inappropriateness of data-dependent centerings for conditioning diagnostics arises from the recognition that such centerings which employ a representative data element behave essentially like DFM when acting on variates collinear with ι and hence become ill conditioned exactly as M. To see this, center the series $x = (x_1 \ldots x_n)^T$ by any representative value α, which surely must obey $x_{min} \leq \alpha \leq x_{max}$, where x_{min} and x_{max} are, respectively, the smallest and largest elements of x. Define $z \equiv \max|x_i - \bar{x}|$. Then necessarily $\bar{x} - z \leq x_{min} \leq \alpha \leq x_{max} \leq \bar{x} + z$, and hence

$$0 \leq |\alpha - \bar{x}| < z \equiv \max|x_i - \bar{x}|. \tag{5.38}$$

Now as $x \to \iota$ (as we consider x whose elements become more nearly equal, or as the angle between x and ι decreases), $\sum(x_i - x)^2 \to 0$, and hence $(x_i - \bar{x}) \to 0$ for all i. Thus $z = \max|x_i - x| \to 0$, and from (5.38), $\alpha \to \bar{x}$.

For vectors approaching ι, then, all such data-dependent centerings are equivalent to DFM and must consequently suffer the same ill conditioning in transforming vectors collinear with ι.

The Appropriateness of Some Model-Dependent Centerings

We have already seen in section 5.2 that some model-dependent centerings are properly employed to produce data appropriate to conditioning diagnostics. Centerings that produce structurally interpretable data are not only acceptable, they are essential for meaningful conditioning diagnostics. All other centerings, data or model dependent, are improper for this diagnostic purpose (though they may possess some other computational value).

Centering When Approximating Nonlinearities

It is sometimes thought good to center when estimating a linear equation known to be a local approximation to a nonlinear model. Suppose in figure 5.3 that the true (nonlinear) model is $y = f(x) + \varepsilon$ (written in terms of the

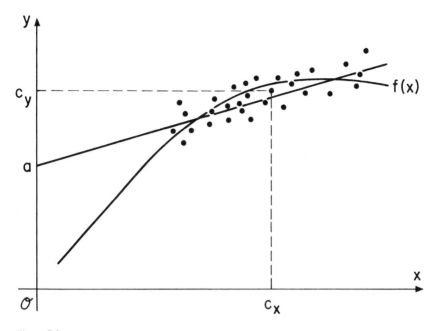

Figure 5.3
Centering in linear approximations

structurally interpretable, basic data y and x) and that the indicated data points over a local range have been generated from it.

Suppose also these points are used to estimate

$$y = a + bx + e \tag{5.39}$$

by OLS as a local approximation to f. Hence the estimate of the constant term a has no structural meaning since $x = 0$ lies outside the range of approximation. In this instance, one would obtain a more meaningful "constant" if the data were centered about locally representative values (not necessarily means) such as c_x and c_y to give $\tilde{y} \equiv y - c_y \iota$ and $\tilde{x} = x - c_x \iota$ and if $\tilde{y}$ were regressed on ι and $\tilde{x}$ as

$$\tilde{y} = a^0 \iota + b^0 \tilde{x} + e^0. \tag{5.40}$$

Since we have not necessarily taken DFM, there will in general be a constant term here, and its estimate will be interpretable as the expected centralized value of y when x takes on a representative value for the approximation.

Thus, such a transformation may indeed allow the constant, *as printed out of the regression package*, to be more readily interpreted. But it is to be emphasized that this is a computational convenience only, for clearly (5.40) and (5.39) are really the same regression with

$$a^0 = a - c_y + bc_x,$$

$$b^0 = b.$$

(5.41)

What we can learn from one regression we can equally well learn from the other through a simple linear transformation.

The question thus arises, Which data should be assessed for conditioning? $X = [\iota \ x]$, or $\tilde{X} = [\iota \ \tilde{x}]$? This is readily answered since, as always, we can only meaningfully measure the potential sensitivity in the estimates with respect to relative changes in the structurally interpretable, basic data. Therefore we seek $\kappa(X)$ and not $\kappa(\tilde{X})$.

Once again we see that, regardless of how the data may be transformed for the purposes of executing a regression, it is the basic data and not the transformed data that are relevant to diagnosing the conditioning of the regression problem, and it is this conditioning that applies to all such transformed regressions as well.[18]

Centering for Computational Advantage

The DFM centering, by reducing the number of significant digits that must be carried, is often employed in machines with short word lengths to reduce possible problems due to truncation errors. Although this concern may be justified, few problems occur as a practical matter when arithmetic is done in double precision. In any event, such centering is clearly motivated by reasons extraneous to assessing conditioning, and all conditioning diagnostics should still employ only the basic, uncentered data.

It is also thought that regression packages generally behave better when digesting the better-conditioned centered data. Doubtless this is true for certain regression packages.[19] However, well-designed regression packages (Belsley 1974) begin showing practical conditioning problems only after the scaled condition number of the basic data becomes astronomically large, of the order of 40,000.[20] Unfortunately condition numbers that are even one-fortieth of this magnitude already indicate regression results that are practically useless, even if all calculations were exact. Indeed, we saw this in the example of section 5.1, whose conditioning was 1,340. Minute changes in such data can cause massive shifts in the estimates, so "if you don't like the estimates you've got, just change the data by an insignificant amount." Thus, computational problems arise only after the data are so ill conditioned as to be effectively useless anyway. If, however, you wish still to center for computational reasons, please do, but use the basic, not the centered, data for diagnosing ill conditioning.

Centering and Assessing Conditioning When There Is No Constant

Suppose structural considerations indicate there should be no constant term in the basic regression (5.12), giving $y = \beta_1 X_1 + \cdots + \beta_p X_p + \varepsilon$ and $X_1 \neq \iota$. The fundamental result on LS conditioning of section 5.3 holds whether or not ι is in $X = [X_1 \ldots X_p]$, and hence the appropriate conditioning measure is still $\kappa(X)$.

It is illuminating, however, to see the damage that DFM centering can do if such transforms are used for computational (not diagnostic) reasons. Consider the regression

$$y = b_1 X_1 + b_2 X_2 + e \tag{5.42}$$

with the basic data matrix

$$X = \begin{bmatrix} 1 & 0 \\ 0 & 1 \\ 0 & 1 \end{bmatrix}.$$

It is clear that X_1 and X_2 are well conditioned: they are orthogonal, and their scaled condition number $\kappa(X) = 1$. If, however, we center these data about their means, we obtain

$$\tilde{X} = \begin{bmatrix} \frac{2}{3} & -\frac{2}{3} \\ -\frac{1}{3} & \frac{1}{3} \\ -\frac{1}{3} & \frac{1}{3} \end{bmatrix}, \tag{5.43}$$

a matrix that we note to be rank deficient.

We can see this situation geometrically in figure 5.4. Here X_1 and X_2 are well conditioned (an angle between them close to $90°$), whereas the centered variates MX_1 and MX_2 are exactly collinear.

Thus centering (DFM) is not generally advisable in the context of estimating homogeneous equations, certainly not for diagnosing conditioning but also not even for computational reasons.

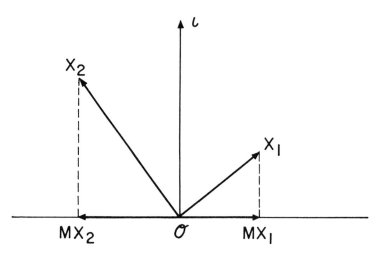

Figure 5.4
Problems from centering when there is no intercept

5.6   First-Differencing

The preceding sections have focused on issues related to centering and the difficulties this transformation creates in assessing conditioning. We are now, however, in a position to appreciate that a broader set of transformations than centering can cause similar problems. Indeed, it is clear that any transformation that renders the data structurally uninterpretable also renders them unsuitable for assessing conditioning. Centering is perhaps the most commonly encountered such transformation. First-differencing is perhaps next in line, and we turn to it now. We illustrate the main issues involved and provide an approximate solution, using the equation for the price deflator for consumption of autos and parts from the Michigan Quarterly Econometric Model (MQEM).

Differencing and Conditioning

Consider first the general first-differenced model

$$\Delta y = \beta_1 + \beta_2 \Delta X_2 + \cdots + \beta_p \Delta X_p + \varepsilon, \tag{5.44}$$

where $\Delta X_i = X_{i,t} - X_{i,t-1}$ and β_1 is an intercept that may or may not be present. Denote by ΔX the first-differenced data matrix $[\iota \ \Delta X_1 \ldots \Delta X_p]$. It is clear from sections 5.2 and 5.3 that the condition number $\kappa(\Delta X)$ assesses the relative sensitivity of the OLS estimates b to small relative changes in the differenced data ΔX_i. If the differenced data are themselves structurally interpretable, then this is the desired diagnostic information. But if, as is often the case, it is the levels data X_i that are structurally interpretable, then the differenced data will not be structurally interpretable and $\kappa(\Delta X)$ provides no meaningful diagnostic information. That the ΔX_i's lack structural interpretability in this case is readily seen by noting that one must return to the X_i's to determine whether a 1 percent shift in ΔX_i is large or small relative to the underlying situation being estimated.

Suppose, then, that it is the levels data, the X_i's, that are structurally interpretable so that $\kappa(\Delta X)$ gives an incorrect measure of the conditioning of (5.44) with respect to them. What provides a correct measure? Unfortunately no exact answer is currently available to this question. In appendix B, however, considerations are pursued that strongly suggest that an approximate lower bound for this conditioning is given by $\kappa(X)$, the condition number of the levels (or integral) data matrix $X = [\iota \; t \; X_2 \dots X_p]$. Empirical evidence so far supports this suggestion, and hence until a more exact solution is forthcoming, I adopt $\kappa(X)$ for this purpose.

The preceding naturally leads one to ask the way the incorrect measure $\kappa(\Delta X)$ relates to $\kappa(X)$ and thus the way its diagnostic information can be misleading. Unlike the case of centering where it can be shown unambiguously that $\kappa(\tilde{X}) \leqslant \kappa(X)$ (see appendix A), here we see that $\kappa(\Delta X)$ can bear any relation to $\kappa(X)$. The example

$$X = \begin{bmatrix} 1 & 0 & 0 \\ 0 & 1 & 0 \\ 0 & 0 & 1 \\ 0 & 0 & 0 \\ 0 & 0 & 0 \end{bmatrix}, \quad \Delta X = \begin{bmatrix} -1 & 1 & 0 \\ 0 & -1 & 1 \\ 0 & 0 & -1 \\ 0 & 0 & 0 \end{bmatrix},$$

provides a case where $\kappa(\Delta X) > \kappa(X) = 1$. However, for highly trended time series, the case where first-differencing is usually employed, we typically find that $\kappa(\Delta X) \ll \kappa(X)$, making the conditioning appear very much better than it is in fact. We see this to be the case in the illustration that follows.

An Illustration from MQEM

The specification of the equation for the price deflator for consumption of autos and parts in the MQEM is in first-differenced form:

$$\Delta \log \text{PCDA} = \beta_1 + \beta_2 \Delta \log \text{PPNF} + \beta_3 \Delta \log \text{PAUTO}, \tag{5.45}$$

where

PCDA = deflator for consumption of autos and parts, 1972 = 100,

PPNF = deflator for business, nonfarm GNP, 1972 = 100,

PAUTO = CPI for new autos, 1967 = 100,

and all data are quarterly 1954.1 to 1979.4.

Assessing the conditioning of models with logged (nonlinear) variates requires special treatment (see Belsley 1983b), and it will prove useful at first to treat (5.45) in its unlogged counterpart:

$$\Delta \text{PCDA} = \beta_1 + \beta_2 \Delta \text{PPNF} + \beta_3 \Delta \text{PAUTO}. \tag{5.46}$$

The results for the logged model are similar in thrust and are summarized at the end.

Consider first the estimation and conditioning of the differenced model (5.46). Ordinary least squares gives

$$\Delta \text{PCDA} = 0.208 + 0.175 \, \Delta \text{PPNF} + 0.708 \, \Delta \text{PAUTO}, \tag{5.47}$$
$$\quad\quad\quad (0.131) \quad (0.111) \quad\quad\quad (0.131)$$
$$R^2 = .652, \quad \kappa(\Delta X) = 3.$$

We immediately note that the conditioning of the differenced data matrix $\Delta X = [\iota \ \Delta \text{PPNF} \ \Delta \text{PAUTO}]$ is excellent, indicating a lack of sensitivity of the OLS estimates to changes in the first-differenced data, the ΔX's. That this same insensitivity does not, however, obtain with respect to changes in the levels data X_i is seen by perturbing the basic X's by a small relative amount. Thus, construct

$$\text{PPNF}^\circ \equiv \text{PPNF} + \eta,$$

$$\text{PAUTO}^\circ \equiv \text{PAUTO} + \phi,$$

where η and ϕ are chosen randomly but scaled so that $\|\eta\| = .01 \|\text{PPNF}\|$ and $\|\phi\| = .01 \|\text{PAUTO}\|$.

The OLS estimates of the perturbed, differenced model

$$\Delta \text{PCDA} = \beta_1 + \beta_2 \Delta \text{PPNF}^\circ + \beta_3 \Delta \text{PAUTO}^\circ + \varepsilon \tag{5.48}$$

are

$$\Delta PCDA = 0.423 + 0.151\,\Delta PPNF^{\circ} + 0.434\,\Delta PAUTO^{\circ}. \qquad (5.49)$$
$$(0.140)\quad (0.071) \qquad\qquad (0.057)$$

Letting b and b^{0} denote the unperturbed and perturbed estimates, respectively, we calculate that

$$\frac{\|b - b^{0}\|}{\|b^{0}\|} = 0.5585.$$

Thus, the 1 percent shift in the basic X's has produced over a 55 percent shift in the estimated parameters, a degree of sensitivity that is certainly not indicated by the excellent condition number of 3 belonging to the differenced matrix ΔX. This occurs of course, as it did in section 5.1 for the centered data, because small proportionate changes in the X's can produce gigantic proportionate changes in the ΔX's. For these data, for example, the 1 percent change in PPNF produced a 96 percent relative change in $\Delta PPNF$. The corresponding figure for $\Delta PAUTO$ is 82 percent. Clearly, then, we see that $\kappa(\Delta X)$ is not the desired diagnostic measure.

According to the suggestion of appendix B, however, let us consider the conditioning of the data matrix of the corresponding levels, or integral, model

$$PCDA = \beta_0 + \beta_1 t + \beta_2\,PPNF + \beta_3\,PAUTO + \varepsilon. \qquad (5.50)$$

We find that the condition number $\kappa(X)$ of this levels data matrix $X = [\iota \; t \; PPNF \; PAUTO]$ is 77, a magnitude that provides a more reasonable indication of the degree of possible sensitivity of the OLS estimates of (5.44) to small relative changes in the basic data.

The same experiment (a one percent shift in the basic data) for the logged data results in the following figures:

1. Relative change in the parameter
estimates of an equation in the
first differences of the logs   64%

2. The condition number of the first
differences of the logged data $\kappa(\Delta \ln x) = 2$

3. The condition number of the levels
(or integral) logged data $\kappa(\ln X) = 78$

Once again we note that the 64 percent actual relative change in the first-differenced estimates due to a 1 percent shift in the underlying basic data

X is completely inconsistent with the condition number of the first-differenced data $\kappa(\Delta \ln X) = 2$ but quite reasonable relative to the condition number of the levels data $\kappa(\ln X) = 78$.

Conclusions

1. When the levels data X are structurally interpretable, the first-differenced data are not, and hence $\kappa(\Delta X)$ is a meaningless diagnostic for the conditioning of the first-differenced equation with respect to the basic data X.

2. In highly trended economic time series, $\kappa(\Delta X)$ tends to understate the true conditioning of (5.44) with respect to X.

3. The condition number of the levels, or integral, data X appears to provide a more meaningful lower bound on this conditioning.

4. When properly assessed, the price-deflator equation for autos and parts in the MQEM is seen to be quite poorly conditioned.

5.7 Appendix A: Centering and Conditioning

In this appendix we examine some results on the conditioning of matrices variously related to centering. We begin with some definitions and notation. Further background, if desired, is found in Stewart (1973) and BKW (1980).

DEFINITION 5.1 The *spectral condition number* of any $n \times p$ matrix A, denoted $\chi(A)$, is the ratio of its maximal singular value, $\mu_{\max}(A)$, to its minimal, $\mu_{\min}(A)$, that is,

$$\chi(A) \equiv \frac{\mu_{\max}(A)}{\mu_{\min}(A)}, \tag{5.51}$$

or, equivalently,

$$\chi(A) \equiv \| A \| \, \| A^+ \|, \tag{5.52}$$

where $\| A \|$ denotes the spectral norm of the matrix A, and A^+ denotes the generalized inverse of A.

DEFINITION 5.2 The *scaled condition number* of any $n \times p$ matrix A, denoted $\kappa(A)$, is the ratio of the maximal to minimal singular values, after its columns have been scaled to have unit (or, equivalently, equal) length.

This, if $A = [A_1 \ldots A_1]$, $s_i = (A_i^T A_i)^{-1/2}$, and $S \equiv \text{diag}(s_1 \ldots s_p)$,

$$\kappa(A) = \chi(AS).$$ (5.53)

It is shown in BKW (1980) that the scaled condition number "tends" to be smallest among all possible column scalings AB of A, where $B \in \mathcal{D}$, the set of all $p \times p$ diagonal matrices, in the sense that

$$\kappa(A) \le \sqrt{p} \min_{B \in \mathcal{D}} \chi(AB).$$ (5.54)

In other words, $\kappa(A)$ cannot exceed the smallest such condition number (usually an unsolvable problem) by more than the typically small factor of $\sqrt{p}$. We shall denote this tendency, defined rigorously by the inequality (5.54), by the symbol $\lessapprox$, giving result 5.1.

RESULT 5.1   For any $n \times p$ matrix A, $\kappa(A) \lessapprox \chi(A)$.

It is this result, applied to $A = X$ in the LS context, that indicates the scaled number $\kappa(X)$ [not $\chi(X)$] as providing the most readily meaningful diagnostic information about the conditioning of $b = (X^T X)^{-1} X^T y$ (see BKW, ch. 3).

The following theorem now allows us to see the effect of centering on the conditioning of a matrix. I am grateful to Dr. David Gay of Bell Labs. for the basis of this proof.

THEOREM 5.1   Let the $n \times p$ matrix A be partitioned as $A = [A_1 \ A_2]$, and obtain from it $B = [A_1 \ B_2]$, where $B_2 = [I - H_1]A_2$ and $H_1 \equiv A_1(A_1^T A_1)^{-1}A_1^T$ (i.e., B_2 is the orthogonal projector of A_2 on the column space of A_1—thus, if $A_1 \equiv \iota$, B_2 is the matrix of DFM-centered variates). Then

$$\chi(A) \ge \chi(B) \ge \chi(B_2).$$ (5.55)

Proof   It suffices to consider the case where A is square and upper triangular, since we can factor $A = QR$, where $Q^T Q = I_p$ and R is square and upper triangular, and the singular values of R are the same as those of A (Stewart 1973). Thus A and A^{-1} have block forms

$$A = \begin{bmatrix} A_{11} & A_{21} \\ 0 & A_{22} \end{bmatrix} \quad \text{and} \quad A^{-1} = \begin{bmatrix} A_{11}^{-1} & A_{21}^{-1} \\ 0 & A_{22}^{-1} \end{bmatrix},$$

where $A_{21}^{-1} \equiv -A_{11}^{-1} A_{21} A_{22}^{-1}$, and B and B^{-1} have the forms

$$B = \begin{bmatrix} A_{11} & 0 \\ 0 & A_{22} \end{bmatrix} \quad \text{and} \quad B^{-1} = \begin{bmatrix} A_{11}^{-1} & 0 \\ 0 & A_{22}^{-1} \end{bmatrix}.$$

Let $\| \cdot \|$ denote the Euclidean norm when $\cdot$ is a vector and the spectral norm (the maximal singular value) when $\cdot$ is a matrix. By definition $\| B \| = \sup_{\|x\|=1} \| Bx \|$, $\| B^{-1} \| = \sup_{\|y\|=1} \| B^{-1}y \|$, and $\chi(B) \equiv \| B \| \| B^{-1} \|$. Let x^* and y^* be solutions to these two supremums, respectively. If we partition $x^* = \begin{pmatrix} x_1^* \\ x_2^* \end{pmatrix}$ and $y^* = \begin{pmatrix} y_1^* \\ y_2^* \end{pmatrix}$ commensurately with B, we show lemma 5.1.

LEMMA 5.1 It is always possible to pick x^* so that either $x_1^* = 0$ ($\| x_1^* \| = 1$) or $x_2^* = 0$ ($\| x_1^* \| = 1$), and similarly for y^*.

Proof For any $x = \begin{pmatrix} x_1 \\ x_2 \end{pmatrix}$, $\| x \| = 1$,

$$\| Bx \|^2 = \| A_{11}x_1 \|^2 + \| A_{22}x_2 \|^2 \le \max[\| A_{11} \|^2, \| A_{22} \|^2]. \qquad (5.56)$$

The first equal sign in (5.56) is due to the block diagonality of B, and the inequality is due to the fact that $\| x \|^2 = \| x_1 \|^2 + \| x_2 \|^2 = 1$.

Now suppose $\| A_{11} \| \ge \| A_{22} \|$. By definition there exists $\| x_1 \| = 1$ such that $\| A_{11}x_1 \| = \| A_{11} \|$. Letting $\hat{x} = \begin{pmatrix} \hat{x}_1 \\ 0 \end{pmatrix}$, we see that $\| B\hat{x} \| = \| A_{11}\hat{x}_1 \| = \| A_{11} \|$. Thus $\hat{x}$ allows $\| Bx \|$ to reach its upper bound $\| A_{11} \|$ among $\| x \| = 1$, and hence $x^* = \hat{x}$ and $x_2^* = 0$. A similar argument shows $x_1^* = 0$ if $\| A_{22} \| \ge \| A_{11} \|$. $\square$

Recalling that $\| Ax \| = (x^T A^T Ax)^{1/2}$, we see that for either $x_1^* = 0$ or $x_2^* = 0$,

$$\| A \| \ge \| Ax^* \| \equiv (x_1^{*T}A_{11}^T A_{11}x_1^* + 2x_2^{*T}A_{21}^T A_{11}x_1^*$$
$$+ x_2^{*T}(A_{21}^T A_{21} + A_{22}^T A_{22})x_2^*)^{1/2}$$
$$\ge (x_1^{*T}A_{11}^T A_{11}x_1^* + x_2^{*T}A_{22}^T A_{22}x_2^*)^{1/2} = \| Bx^* \| = \| B \|.$$

A similar argument in y shows that $\| A^{-1} \| \ge \| B^{-1} \|$. Thus

$$\chi(A) = \| A \| \| A^{-1} \| \ge \| B \| \| B^{-1} \| = \chi(B), \qquad (5.57)$$

and the LH inequality in (5.55) is shown.

Now for any matrix D, denote by $\mu_{\min}(D)$ the $\inf_{\|z\|=1} \| Dz \|$ and by $\mu_{\max}(D)$ the $\sup_{\|z\|=1} \| Dz \|$ (i.e., $\| D \|$). Then the second inequality in (5.55) can be seen from lemma 5.2.

LEMMA 5.2   Let the $n \times p$ matrix C be partitioned as $C = [C_1 \ C_2]$, then $\chi(C) \geq \chi(C_2)$.

Proof   Pick $\|z_2^*\| = 1$ such that $\|C_2 z_2^*\| = \mu_{min}(C_2)$ and $\|w_2^*\| = 1$ such that $\|C_2 w_2^*\| = \mu_{max}(C_2)$. From $z^* \equiv \begin{pmatrix} 0 \\ z_2^* \end{pmatrix}$ and $w^* \equiv \begin{pmatrix} 0 \\ w_2^* \end{pmatrix}$.

Now by construction and definition,

$$\mu_{min}(C_2) \equiv \|C_2 z_2^*\| = \|Cz^*\| \geq \min_{\|z\|=1} \|Cz\| \equiv \mu_{min}(C) \tag{5.58a}$$

and

$$\mu_{max}(C_2) \equiv \|C_2 w_2^*\| = \|Cw^*\| \leq \max_{\|w\|=1} \|Cw\| \equiv \mu_{max}(C) \tag{5.58b}$$

Hence

$$\chi(C) \equiv \frac{\mu_{max}(C)}{\mu_{min}(C)} \leq \frac{\mu_{max}(C_2)}{\mu_{min}(C_2)} \equiv \chi(C_2). \ \square \tag{5.59}$$

Applying this result to B in (5.55) completes the proof to theorem 5.1. $\square$

Now, since we may apply theorem 5.1 to any matrix A whose columns have already been scaled for equal length, so that $\chi(A) = \kappa(A)$, we can introduce result 5.1 to give corollary 5.1.

COROLLARY 5.1 $\kappa(A) \gtrsim \kappa(B_2)$.

In the context of LS this translates as "the centered-data matrix will strongly tend to have a lower scaled condition number than the basic-data matrix." As a practical matter, this tendency is almost invariably fulfilled.

5.8   Appendix B: $\kappa(X)$ as an Appropriate Lower Bound for the Conditioning of the First-Difference Estimates with Respect to the Basic Data X.

Consider the integral, or levels, equation corresponding to (5.44), namely

$$y = X\beta + \eta$$
$$= \beta_0 + \beta_1 t + \beta_2 X_2 + \cdots + \beta_p X_p + \eta, \tag{5.60}$$

where β_0 is the constant of integration and the term $\beta_1 t$ is the partial sum of the constant in (5.44) and will be present only if an intercept is included there. The matrix $X = [\iota \ t \ X_2 \ldots X_p]$ is the matrix of levels, or integral data.

Assume to begin with that the X and y data are such that X has full rank and a regression of y on X produces a perfect fit, that is,

$$Xb = y, \quad \text{where } b = X^+ y, \tag{5.61}$$

and we will examine the sensitivity of b to changes in X. Relaxing the assumption of perfect fit can only increase the potential sensitivity (see Hanson and Lawson 1969) so that, for this and reasons to follow, the measure we obtain can at best provide a lower bound to the true conditioning.

Consider now the set S of all rank-preserving perturbations dX of X such that $y \in C(X + dX)$, the column space of $X + dX$.[21] For this subset of perturbations we must also have, for some $b + db \neq 0$,

$$(X + dX)(b + db) = y. \tag{5.62}$$

Of course (5.61) and (5.62) must also hold when premultiplied by any reweighting matrix A of full rank, that is,

$$AXb = Ay,$$
$$A(X + dX)(b + db) = Ay. \tag{5.63}$$

Thus, any response db of b to a change $dX \in S$ that satisfies (5.61) and (5.62) must also satisfy (5.63), and hence the sensitivity of the solution to (5.63) over S must be at least that of (5.62). The relevance of this to assessing the conditioning of first differences with respect to changes in X is seen directly by noting that the first-difference equation (5.44) is derived from (5.60) with

$$A = \begin{bmatrix} -1 & 1 & 0 & \cdots \\ 0 & -1 & 1 & \cdots \\ & & & -1 & 1 \end{bmatrix}. \tag{5.64}$$

The sensitivity of the solutions, then, of both the first differences [(5.63) with A from (5.64)] and the levels (5.61) to at least some subset of permutations S is derivable from (5.62) as

$$db = -X^+ dX(b + db), \tag{5.65}$$

or from properties of matrix norms,

$$\frac{\|db\|}{\|b + db\|} \leq \kappa(X) \frac{\|dX\|}{\|X\|}. \tag{5.66}$$

Thus, among the subset of perturbations S, the sensitivity of either the first-differenced estimates or the levels estimates with respect to changes in X (not ΔX) is bounded by $\kappa(X)$. Now, if one knew the equality in (5.66) held from some $dX \in S$, then one would also know that the sensitivity of b in either (5.62) or (5.63) to the full set of perturbations on X could not be less than $\kappa(X)$, and hence that $\kappa(X)$ provides a lower bound for this measure of sensitivity. Unfortunately it has not yet been shown (showable?) that (5.66) must hold with equality. This argument can therefore only suggest that $\kappa(X)$ provides a lower bound for the desired measure of conditioning.

Notes

Without implications for any remaining errors, thanks go to David Gay, Robert Kennard, Jan Kmenta, Edwin Kuh, Donald Marquardt, Wayne Oldford, Ronald Snee, John Tukey, and Thomas Wonnacott for helpful discussions dealing with this research. Research assistance was ably provided by Ana Aizcorbe. All computation was accomplished through the TROLL system at MIT. This research was funded in part by a Mellon Grant to Boston College.

1. The concepts of centered vs. uncentered R^2 and the VIF are variously dealt with in, for example, Theil (1971), Chatterjee and Price (1977), Judge et al. (1980), and BKW (1980), the last specifically in this context.

2. On systematic means for defining inflated variances and harmful collinearity, see Belsley (1982).

3. For the data in table 5.1 we have $\|\tilde{X}_2 - \tilde{X}_2^\circ\|/\|\tilde{X}_2\| = 4.446$ and $\|\tilde{X}_3 - \tilde{X}_3^\circ\|/\|\tilde{X}_3\| = 4.459$: a 1 percent relative change in X_2 or X_3 causes over a 440 percent relative change in the corresponding centered data.

4. On these matters, see Wilkinson (1965), Stewart (1973), or BKW (1980).

5. Such arbitrariness with respect to origin will not typically affect the interpretability of the statistical analysis, at least in the linear models. It will, however, make impossible a full assessment of model validity, since various of the model's essential elements are admittedly not understood.

6. Although the homogeneous case occurs infrequently in practice, it cannot be ignored as some texts are wont to do.

7. Marquardt and Snee (1975) and Marquardt (1980) deal with some aspects of centering in polynomial models and advise centering x before generating its higher powers and estimating the model. There may be instances in which this is advisable, but the author has readily constructed cases in which it decidely is not and considers this area unresolved; see Belsley (1983a), (1984a: Reply), and (1984b).

8. In obtaining the most meaningful measure of the conditioning of the basic data, however, it is shown in BKW that the data should first be scaled to have equal length (i.e., equal $X_i^T X_i$). In BKW this is accomplished by scaling each (uncentered) column of X to have unit length.

9. Of course these calculations are not best accomplished exactly as in (5.15). A QR or SVD transformation provides the best means for carrying out these basic calculations. On this see Golub (1969), Golub and Reinsch (1970), Belsley (1974), and BKW (1980).

Belsley, D. A., 1984a. Degrading Conditioning D American Statistician 38: 73–77 and 90–93.

Belsley, D. A., 1984b. Eigenvector Weaknesses nometrics 26: 297–299.

Belsley, D. A., E. Kuh, and R. E. Welsch, 1980. Data and Sources of Collinearity. Wiley, New

Chatterjee, S., and B. Price, 1977. Regression

Christ, C. F., 1966. Econometric Models and

Golub, G. H., 1969. Matrix Decompositions tation. R. C. Milton and J. A. Nelder, eds.

Golub, G. H., and C. Reinsch, 1970. Sir Solutions. Numerische Mathematik 14: 403

Gunst, R. F., 1983. Regression Analysis w cations in Statistics A12: 2217–2260.

Haavelmo, T., 1944. The Probability A metrica 12.

Hanson, R. J., and C. L. Lawson, 196 Algorithm for Solving Linear Leas 23: 787–812.

Judge, G. E., W. E. Griffiths, R. C. onometrics. Wiley, New York.

...ely, J. W., 1967. An Appraisal the Point of View of the ...831.

...D. W., 1980. You Shou ...nal of The American S

...W., and R. D. Sne

...and E. A. P

10. The centering of y is unimportant
$(\tilde{X}^T\tilde{X})^{-1}\tilde{X}^T\tilde{y} = (\tilde{X}^T\tilde{X})^{-1}\tilde{X}^Ty$.

11. Or, equivalently, the square roots of th

12. Heuristically this can be appreciated
information: one can always go from the
centered data, one cannot retrieve the b
needed to diagnose some aspects of th
diagnostics applied to the centered data

13. In this case the situation where $X_i =$
tion in the linear approximation, even
5.5.

14. It is easily shown that $\det(X^T$
variance of the elements of $X_1 \cdot X^T X$
of which holds here.

15. In a related context (Belsley 19
collinearity (one form of data pr
form).

16. When $X_i \equiv \iota$, $\alpha_y = \bar{y}$, and $\alpha_j =$

17. The $M_{(i)}$ of (5.34) are data-
$x - \alpha X_i$, where $\alpha = X_i(X_i^T X_i)^{-1}$
such transforms, there is little
must be of the form (5.37) sinc
measuring a given variate and

18. Similar considerations app
two collinear basic variates x_1
improve conditioning. If, ho
so, and hence would not be

19. This, however, ignores
conditioned centering tran
into the fire." The less a
computational benefits fr

20. The scaled condition

21. The assumption of
perturbations but only
$(X) = \text{rank}(X + dX)$ t

References

Belsley, D. A., 1974
Specifications of G

Belsley, D. A., 19
Weak Data throu

Belsley, D. A., 1
Models. *Preprin*

Belsley, D. A., 1
Computational

6 Applications of Bounded-Influence and Diagnostic Methods in Energy Modeling

Stephen Swartz and Roy E. Welsch

6.1 Introduction

The linear model is probably the most common statistical framework used in econometric analysis. Unfortunately the majority of applied work done with this model begins and ends with the ordinary least squares (OLS) family of estimators. It is certainly true that OLS is an attractive estimator; it is very easy to compute, and, of course, it is efficient among linear unbiased estimators for problems that satisfy a certain set of assumptions. However, these assumptions seldom correspond to the situation facing us when we work with economic data. A more satisfactory approach to the linear model would still involve the OLS family of estimators, but only as a starting point around which diagnostic analysis can be used to identify assumptions that might be descriptive as well as theoretically useful. Given that understanding, the reliability of coefficient estimates and forecasts can then be enhanced by using estimators based on the assumptions we believe and robust to the breakdown of the assumptions we distrust.

The purpose of this chapter is to examine a class of estimators useful in dealing with situations in which the quality of the data/model fit is itself suspect. This is a particular problem within economics, since the forces modeled there are neither under control of the analyst nor subject t repeated sampling. Data gathered in such an environment are open to variety of sources of contamination. Errors of measurement, reporti and data entry are common within economic data; especially in large sets they are generally costly and time-consuming to correct. Experi tal design is not usually under the control of economists, which means that the sample distribution of the independent variables highly skewed. In addition the lack of controlled conditions in ec leads to contamination of the dependent variable by the spor pearance of significant yet unmodeled or unmeasurable forces these problems, notably those affecting the dependent variab thought of as being captured by the error term. It is prob appropriate to think of these things as leading to small subset that are very different from the majority of the observations; of observations are called outliers for obvious reasons.

In order to discuss the impact that outlying observations estimator, it is convenient to define the influence function

each observation has on the parameter estimates for a particular estimator. The OLS estimator performs badly in the presence of outliers because its influence function is unbounded; aberrant data can have an arbitrarily large effect on any coefficient. Imagine a model with one independent variable and no constant term. All of the independent observations lie between zero and one, and the dependent variable just equals the negative of the independent variable. Now introduce one more observation, whose independent and dependent variables are equal to one million. The OLS coefficient estimate will be close to one effectively ignoring all observations except the aberrant one. In real situations of course outliers will be less extreme—but then that also makes them much more difficult to identify. Clearly in a data set with contaminated data it would be preferable to use some estimation strategy that can limit the effect that outlying data can have on the results of estimation.

In practice, small subsets of influential observations are generally handled by the introduction of dummy variables. This method effectively corrects for a difference in mean response during a specific time period (such as during a war or a supply shock) or for a particular group of cross-sectional observations. Using dummy variables is but a hammer-and-tongs approach, for they present a number of problems. The first problem that arises in the use of dummy variables is that of identifying a priori just which groups of observations are aberrant—did the early seventies produce variation in the independent series or did it produce aberrant data? Once a group of potentially deviant data is identified, it is still not always obvious in practice just which observations belong in the group—what years did the "oil shock" effect? Even after this problem is dealt with, there is still the matter of the special structure that dummy variables impose on the data—is the effect of the "oil shock" limited to a constant increase or decrease in the dependent variable? Perhaps some of the difference in the period is "caused," and some is "contamination." Dummy variables have been used historically, despite these problems, because no easily computable alternative has been available.

Statistical research and the ever-lessening cost of computing have now made another approach to this problem practical. There are now a variety of estimators available whose influence function is either absolutely bounded or smaller for a given outlier than that of OLS. In particular, if there is an estimator that is efficient given a bound on the influence function, then the estimator developed by Krasker and Welsch (1982) can be shown to be it.

The main advantage of using these new estimators to deal with outlying observations is that the choice of the set of outliers and the degree to which they are to be trusted is made by an objective algorithm that provides consistent estimates. The weights associated with the estimators (for they can all be considered to be iterated weighted least-squares estimators) are also extremely useful as diagnostic tools; they often reveal patterns of multiple-period influence that are otherwise difficult to find. Computer programs are available to compute these estimators; the problem is no more difficult than that of calculating least absolute residual estimates.

In this chapter we illustrate the potential advantages of using these robust estimators within the context of a standard econometric model that has been used by the Department of Energy to provide energy demand forecasts to Congress. This model has been analyzed by several authors (Kuh, Lahari, and Swartz 1981 and Freedman and Peters 1984). Here we are not interested in the model itself so much as we are in the fact that it is representative of the kind of system used in practice to produce forecasts. As it happens, the use of bounded-influence (BIF) estimates improves the ability of the equations to forecast the quantity of fuels used by an average of 20 percent or more. The BIF weights also confirm our suspicions, developed earlier through the use of other diagnostic tools, that the model only imperfectly captures interregional and intertemporal behavior in energy demand. As these sorts of issues are exactly what the applied researcher must face in daily analyses, we feel that these results are both theoretically interesting and practically important.

6.2 The Model

The Regional Demand FORecasting (RDFOR) Model comes to us at the end of an evolutionary chain spanning most of the last decade. Loosely based on work done by David Knapp and David Nissen (1976), the specification underwent numerous changes both before and after it was integrated into the Midterm Energy Forecasting System (MEFS) maintained by the U.S. Department of Energy. RDFOR was used extensively by the DOE to provide forecasts of fuel demand disaggregated over DOE regions, relevant fuels, and economic sectors for several years in the mid 1970s. It has since been replaced by more complicated structural models.

RDFOR is a simple, reduced-form statistical model. It is a collection of linear equations that can be used to project trends in energy demand into the near future. As such, it is similar in kind to most econometric models used in practice. It has the advantage of simplicity; it has the disadvantage of an inherently limited scope. The relevance of the statistical parameter estimates of these models is conditional on the stability of the modeled structure over the range of the model's application. Issues of stability for linear models resolve themselves into questions concerning changes in the entire economic sector being modeled. When one uses such a model, one implicitly assumes that the market being modeled did not change "very much" during the estimation period, where very much is very loosely defined. Against these reservations, though, it's important to remember just how useful is an understanding of the central tendencies of the data. Forecasts based on projections of these kinds of tendencies have proved extremely useful in all areas of applied analysis.

The modeling strategy used in RDFOR is to separate the analysis of the demand for fuels into two distinct steps. First, the total demand for energy in each sector is specified as a function of a price index, a measure of economic activity, demographic factors, and the amount of energy demanded in the previous year. This total demand forecast is then allocated to individual fuels by equations relating the share of total demand met by each fuel to the relative price of that fuel, demographic factors, and the share of demand met by that fuel in the previous year. The model is estimated with data for the ten DOE regions over an eighteen-year period. A separate model is estimated for each major economic sector (residential, commercial, industrial, and transportation); the different models vary only in the definition of economic activity used within each submodel and in the number of fuels each submodel considers.

The Department of Energy has commissioned several studies of their operating models in the past few years. Although these cannot, by their nature, be taken as a definitive reflection of DOE practice, they offer the only available picture of the strengths and weaknesses of the specifications. Chief among the studies relevant to RDFOR are the statistical analyses of Freedman (1981) and the diagnostic analysis of Kuh, Lahari, and Swartz (1981). The Freedman study focuses on the statistical concepts behind the specification and the data base, and delimits the degree to which such a system can be a useful analytic tool. The Kuh, Lahari, and Swartz study focuses on the data-specification interface and the quality of the information available from the data base as organized by the RDFOR system.

It is useful to consider the particular problems that face the RDFOR modeling strategy, so that we can understand the problems we might encounter in estimating and forecasting the model. The system has many potential flaws. For instance, total energy demand in any sector is obtained by solving a maximizing problem that considers all prices of factors used in that sector. Changes in the relative prices of labor, capital, and raw materials, for example, would change the production plans of firms and the amount of energy demanded in the industrial sector. Since prices of complements and substitutes of energy are not included directly in the specification, their effects are relegated to the constant and the error term. It is likely that wages and interest rates are correlated with the price of fuel or total value added in the industrial sector; this correlation would bias the estimates. Any significant change in the relative prices of factors in an economic sector would make the coefficient estimates arising from data gathered before that change less meaningful, and forecasts using those coefficient estimates would not be unbiased. The RDFOR user assumes that factor input ratios in the residential and industrial sectors will remain constant, during both the estimation and and forecast periods.

Another potential problem with the RDFOR modeling strategy is that it treats all fuels symmetrically. RDFOR implicitly assumes that all fuels are perfect substitutes for each other, ignoring the fact that certain fuels cannot be easily used for certain things. Were the price of coal or liquid gas relative to electricity or natural gas to fall dramatically, for example, we would not expect consumers to begin cooking their food or lighting their homes with coal or liquid gas. RDFOR does not incorporate any such technological or habitual constraints into the problem except in the lagged dependent variables of the various equations. During an extended forecast, when the lagged dependent variable is last period's prediction, RDFOR might tend to stray significantly from the levels that casual analysis, given our knowledge of such constraints, might find reasonable.

Problems of omitted variables and limited use of technological constraints are not uncommon in linear modeling. The more forces we try to model with additional independent variables, the less power we have available within the data for any particular coefficient. There is always some practical limit to the number of series we can place on the right-hand side of an equation, although theoretically any number of series might belong there. To say that such problems are necessary is not to say that they should be ignored. Quite the contrary, it is important to be aware of the fact that any linear specification is subject to sporadic breakdown because of these issues. It is precisely because we are concerned that RDFOR is not a complete model that we are led to use robust estimators to guard against excessive contamination of the coefficients from observations in which these problems occur.

We follow closely the Kuh, Lahari, and Swartz reconstruction of the RDFOR specification, which is based in turn on a NEO draft study written in 1977. The theoretical basis for the specification is detailed there as

$$QDIV = f(PDIV, Y, HDAY, CDAY, QDIV(-1), POP), \qquad (6.1)$$

$$\frac{Q_i}{QDIV} = g_i\left(\frac{P_i}{PDIV}, GSC, \frac{Q_i(-1)}{QDIV(-1)}\right), \qquad (6.2)$$

where QDIV is a Divisia index of the quantity of energy demanded, PDIV is a Divisia index of the price of energy, Y is a measure of economic activity in a sector (value added in the industrial sector), HDAY and CDAY are heating and cooling degree days, POP is population, Q_i is the quantity demanded of the ith fuel, P_i is the price of the ith fuel, and GSC is a measure of the availability of gas service. The construction of the series used in the model will be explained later in this section.

Practical considerations have led to the imposition of a loglinear functional form onto equations (6.1) and (6.2). We have already discussed why RDFOR might be suspect in the presence of data far different from that encountered in the estimation period. The loglinear form imposes constant elasticity onto the estimation procedure, which was necessary in the MEFS framework. Constant elasticity is a good approximation as long as the data remain close to those encountered during the estimation period. The assumption therefore creates no additional problems for the model, although it does mean that the model is even less appropriate in periods with data different from that on which the model was estimated.

RDFOR is estimated on a dataset ranging over the years 1961 to 1978 and the ten DOE regions. To allow for differences in mean demand and share between regions, a dummy for each region is included. This means that we estimated fifteen coefficients for (6.1) and thirteen for (6.2). Evidence suggests that there is significant correlation among the residuals from different regions; to estimate the equations using a Zellner estimator, though, would add the burden of fifty additional coefficients to an apparently overworked data set.

In this analysis we will restrict our attention to the coal demand forecasts for the industrial sector of the model. This is done purely for rhetorical purposes; the coal demand equations behave neither better nor worse than average in the model. The specifications we use then are

$$\text{QDIV}_{it} = a_i + b * \text{PDIV}_{it} + c * \text{VADD}_{it} + d * \text{HDAY}_{it}$$
$$+ \, e * \text{CDAY}_{it} + h * \text{QDIV}(-1)_{it}, \tag{6.3}$$

$$\frac{Q_{fit}}{\text{QDIV}_{it}} = \frac{a_i + b * \text{P}}{\text{PDIV}_{fit}} + c * \text{GSC}_{it} + \frac{h * Q(-1)_{fit}}{\text{QDIV}(-1)_{it}}, \tag{6.4}$$

where all demand relationships are specified in logarithms, and

$i =$ cross-sectional index running over the DOE regions (1–10),

$t =$ time index over the years 1961–1978,

$f =$ fuel index (in the RDFOR system the fuels considered are coal, distillate fuels, electricity, liquid gas, natural gas, and residual oils; here we consider only coal),

$a_i, b, c, d, e, h =$ parameters to be estimated (note that the parameters are not constrained to be equal across the equations; we have given the same names to different coefficients for convenience, and to conform to earlier studies),

$\text{QDIV}_{it} =$ the Divisia index of quantity demanded for region i and year t, running over fuels f,

$\text{PDIV}_{it} =$ the Divisia index of energy prices for region i and year t, running over fuels f,

$\text{VADD}_{it} =$ value added by the industrial sector in region i in year t,

$\text{HDAY}_{it} =$ heating degree days in region i for year t,

$\text{CDAY}_{it} =$ cooling degree days in region i for year t,

$Q_{fit} =$ quantity of fuel f demanded in region i in year t,

$P_{fit} =$ price of fuel f demanded in region i in year t,

$\text{GSC}_{it} =$ the number of customers that have gas service in region i in year t.

The data available are of poor quality; this severely impacts OLS estimates and is yet another reason that robust estimators are called for. The data used with RDFOR is from the SEDS data base, which has been discussed in Wood (1981). Since that data base only has state data in it and all our work has been done with regional data, a brief note on data construction is in order. Fuel quantities, value-added, and gas service customer data are all direct sums over the states in each region. Fuel prices are weighted sums of state prices, with the weights being the quantity of that fuel for that state divided by the sum of the quantities over that region (it's worth noting that the state price data was constructed by a method called "geographical interpolation" from data on prices in a small number of cities). Heating and cooling degree days for a state are then number of degree/days that the temperature was above or below a benchmark level. Regional data for these series is built up as a population-weighted sum of the state data. The Divisia indexes are calculated from the constructed regional quantity and price data in the standard way.

As it happens, the exogenous data are relatively stable over the forecast period. Given any sort of reasonable estimated elasticities for the equations, they simply cannot account for much of the variability in the endogenous series. As a result the specification effectively reduces to a simple difference equation, with the effective constant term equal to the estimated constant plus the sum of the current period exogenous series times their respective coefficients. The dynamic properties of the model depend totally on the estimated magnitude of the coefficient on the lagged term—given some shock in the exogenous series, forecasts will merely converge to some steady state depending on the mean exogenous values and the coefficient estimates. The data are not adequate to measure these forces, since the estimation period does not contain a completed shock-response cycle. Further the coefficient on the lag term is burdened with the responsibility of simultaneously determining the adjustment speed of all ten DOE regions. In prior analysis Kuh, Lahari, and Swartz found that relaxing the cross-sectional constraints on the coefficients significantly improved the forecasting performance of the model, although it did produce "absurd" coefficient estimates.

In summary, the RDFOR specification and the SEDS data base are both likely to have episodic breakdowns of some magnitude. The SEDS data base is extremely problematic; the RDFOR model is structured in such a way as to be very sensitive to those problems. This is not to say that it cannot provide useful benchmark forecasts; rather, it suggests that we must be careful in estimation to minimize the potential impact of the contamination we are likely to find.

6.3   OLS Estimates

The RDFOR system as we have described it here evolved in a production
situation in which the most important output of the model was its baseline
forecasts. As is true in most production work, the people making these
forecasts estimated the model first with OLS and then explored the standard extensions of that estimator (i.e., serial correlation corrections or
more complicated lag structures) until coefficients were found that were
presentable and produced adequate forecasts. This practice led to reported
coefficients for the model which changed several times a year and has made
it very difficult to "replicate" earlier work on the model.

   As we mentioned earlier, we do not believe that this is an appropriate
estimation methodology, neither for research purposes nor in a production
environment. Ordinary least squares is a useful starting point for a model
like RDFOR, not because slight extensions of OLS can produce a wide
range of coefficient estimates from which to choose but because it is the
estimator for which we have the greatest number of diagnostic tools
available. In this section we'd like to illustrate what we consider appropriate use of OLS. We present OLS coefficients and diagnostics then to point
out the actual (as opposed to potential) problems with the estimator; we
later use these coefficients to produce forecasts that we can use for comparison after further analysis.

   A brief word on our diagnostic frameworks is in order. We find it useful
to discuss the numerical and statistical problems with OLS separately.
Numerical problems (multicollinearity) arise when the exogenous data are
involved in exact or nearly exact linear relationships of their own. Of course
such problems will be reflected in enlarged standard errors for the OLS
estimates; beyond that, round-off error in the computer algorithms used to
calculate the coefficients and standard errors adds a further degree of
inaccuracy which is far less easy to accommodate in analysis. A flag for the
existence of numerical instability is the condition number of the matrix X,
which is equal to the square root of the ratio of the highest to the lowest
eigenvalue of $(X'X)^{-1}$. In practice, a condition number higher than 30
seems to indicate instability. At that point differences in the fifth and sixth
decimal position of the data can alter the coefficient estimates.

   Once collinearity is indicated by a high condition number, we turn to the
variance decomposition of the matrix $(X'X)^{-1}$ to discover which series are
involved in the contaminating relationships. That diagnostic tool can be

used to portion out each coefficient's variance to the independent series in the model. Near relationships among the exogenous series cause an inflation of these variances; if a group of series contributes a large amount of variance to any coefficient, that group turns out to be involved in a collinear relationship. Details of the variance decomposition, and of its use as a diagnostic tool, can be found in chapter 3 of Belsley, Kuh, and Welsch (1980).

The diagnostic framework we use to uncover statistical problems in an OLS framework is described in detail in chapter 2 of Belsley, Kuh, and Welsch (1980). We again provide a summary here. The OLS coefficient estimates are of course $b = (X'X)^{-1}X'y$. It is useful to consider the projection matrix $H = X(X'X)^{-1}X'$; we call it the hat matrix, since we know that $\hat{y} = Xb = Hy$. The predicted value of the ith dependent observation is $\hat{y}_i = \sum_{k=1}^{n} h_{ik}y_k$. The Cauchy-Schwarz inequality tells us that the diagonal elements of the matrix H dominate the off-diagonal elements, so we conclude that the element $h_{ii}(\equiv h_i)$ dominates this sum. A straightforward algebraic manipulation shows that strong leverage points (those with large h_i) come to dominate predicted or fitted values. We therefore use these h_i as a diagnostic to locate potentially influential observations. H is a projection matrix, so we know that all of these h_i are between 0 and 1 and that their sum is equal to p, the number of coefficients in the model. A perfectly balanced X matrix—with equal leverage for all observations—is one for which $h_i = p/n$. We find that $2p/n$ or $3p/n$ are useful cutoff values for identifying influential observations using the hat matrix diagonal elements.

Large residuals have often been used as an indication of regression problems. If the errors of a least-squares model are assumed to be spherically distributed, then the variance for the ith observation is $\sigma^2(1 - h_i)$. Instead of using the raw residuals as a diagnostic tool, we prefer to scale them by $\hat{\sigma}^2(1 - h_i)$, where we typically use $s(i)$ which is an estimate of the variance σ made with all the observations except the ith so that the scaling factor is stochastically independent of the residual to be scaled. Doing this, we obtain the (externally) studentized residual $e_i^* = e_i/s(i)(1 - h_i)^{1/2}$, which has the t distribution when the residuals have a normal distribution.

One other set of measures of the influence of an individual data row on OLS results arises when one compares OLS regression quantities based on the full data set with the corresponding quantities based on a data set with the row deleted. We focus on two such quantities arising from the deletion

Table 6.1
Coefficient estimates for the total demand equation of the industrial sector

Coefficient	Estimate	Standard error	t statistic	$PROB > |t|$
A01	−3.895	0.644	−6.053	0
A02	−4.144	0.658	−6.3	0
A03	−4.047	0.651	−6.218	0
A04	−4.004	0.634	−6.316	0
A05	−4.339	0.675	−6.427	0
A06	−3.782	0.621	−6.095	0
A07	−3.762	0.643	−5.851	0
A08	−3.362	0.624	−5.39	0
A09	−3.904	0.616	−6.335	0
A10	−3.573	0.621	−5.759	0
B	−0.009	0.019	−0.488	0.626
C	0.295	0.035	8.482	0
D	0.105	0.058	1.805	0.073
E	0.02	0.027	0.749	0.455
H	0.659	0.038	17.16	0

Note: NOB = 180   MAX HAT = 0.188
CRSQ = 0.965   SSR = 0.242
COND(x) = 572.082   MAX RSTUDENT = 3.066
NOVAR = 15   DW(0) = 1.851
SER = 0.038   MAX DFFITS = −0.946

of any row i: $DFFIT_i$, the scaled difference in the predicted value, and $DFBETAS_i$, the scaled difference in the coefficient estimates. Computational formulas exist that make these values straightforward to calculate without actually doing the deletions; they are available (as are the hat values and the studentized residuals) within most of the more popular econometric and statistical packages.

OLS coefficient estimates for equation (6.3) appear as table 6.1. The most noteworthy estimates are the insignificant price coefficient b (corresponding to a long-run price elasticity of only 0.02) along with a strong positive income coefficient of 0.295 (corresponding to a reasonable long-run income elasticity of 0.86). The lack of a significant price response has been considered a problem by people estimating this model. It can be explained away if one characterizes the industrial sector as a fixed-coefficient production process in the short run or in periods of uncertainty; in that case one might expect a lack of a price response during the sample period. Another reason why we might have a hard time measuring the price effect here is the inclusion of a value-added term. Presumably changes in

Table 6.2
Variance decomposition proportions for the total demand equation of the industrial sector

Singular value	Condition index	Constants	B	C	D	E	H
0.004	572.082	0.986	0.002	0.126	0.765	0.197	0.104
0.007	296.425	0.01	0.046	0.842	0.218	0.002	0.703
0.015	138.554	0.004		0.032	0.017	0.801	0.013
0.617	3.412		0.77				0.085
0.903	2.332		0.103				0.042
1	2.106						
1	2.106						
1	2.106						
1	2.106						
1	2.106						
1.001	2.103						
1.003	2.099						
1.034	2.037		0.054				
1.137	1.852		0.012				0.053
2.106	1.		0.012				

the real price of factors will systematically affect the total value of productive activity. Thus the value-added series might capture the combined effect of changes in the prices of all factors, a force otherwise omitted from the specification. If the price effect occurs in concert with the effects of other factors' prices, then it might be captured by the value-added term instead of the price index itself.

The variance decomposition for equation (6.3) is presented as table 6.2. Although it indicates the existence of three strong collinear relationships within the data, it is significant to note that none of them involve the price term. Two independent relationships exist between the weather variables and the constant term; one exists between the value-added and lagged dependent variable. The conditioning analysis would therefore argue against the idea that the price term is lost to the value-added term in a direct manner; it has nothing to say of the proposition that the latter series, by combining information on other prices, better captures that effect.

Significant diagnostics from the estimation of (6.3) appear as table 6.3. We distinguish between "large" and "small" diagnostics with intuitively plausible cutoffs, which appear at the top of the chart. Several things are worth noting. First, there are many more large studentized residuals than

Table 6.3
Significant diagnostics for the total demand equation of the industrial sector

	RSTUDENT	HAT	DFFITS	Constant	B	C	D	E	H
Region 1, 1964								−0.152	
Region 1, 1973								0.215	−0.214
Region 1, 1975					−0.151				
Region 1, 1976	2.895		0.806	−0.157	0.375	0.25			
Region 1, 1977					0.205				
Region 2, 1962	3.066		0.886					−0.395	
Region 2, 1971	−2.489		−0.654						
Region 2, 1973									
Region 2, 1975	−2.356		−0.774	−0.341	−0.23	0.299	−0.161		−0.224
Region 2, 1976	2.336		0.696		0.343		0.251		−0.206
Region 2, 1978					−0.21				
Region 3, 1967								0.214	
Region 3, 1973							−0.156		
Region 3, 1974				−0.15					
Region 3, 1975				−0.204	0.165	0.204			−0.189
Region 3, 1976						−0.216			
Region 4, 1962									
Region 4, 1968				0.227			−0.225		
Region 4, 1969				0.166			−0.155		
Region 4, 1974				−0.173			0.2		
Region 4, 1976					0.184				
Region 4, 1978				0.151					
Region 5, 1967								0.206	
Region 6, 1962						−0.24			
Region 6, 1973					−0.186	−0.24			
Region 6, 1975	−2.947		−0.946	−0.264	−0.356		0.232	0.244	0.172
Region 6, 1978		0.188	−0.74	0.488	−0.316		−0.398	−0.191	0.168

Region 7, 1961		−0.637					0.163	
Region 7, 1967	−2.341	−0.812	−0.342			0.262	0.542	
Region 7, 1976	2.768	0.779			−0.208			0.287
Region 7, 1978						−0.183		
Region 8, 1965							0.209	
Region 8, 1967	−2.009						0.164	
Region 8, 1970	−2.037			0.155			−0.215	
Region 9, 1976			0.196			−0.195		
Region 9, 1978	−2.166	−0.811		−0.464	−0.246	0.22	−0.159	0.211
Region 10, 1972	2.219	0.582		−0.174				

Note: Cutoffs: DFBETAS = 0.143071, DFFITS = 0.57735, HAT = 0.166667, RSTUDENT = 2.

Table 6.4
Coefficient estimates for the coal share equation in the industrial sector

Coefficient	Estimate	Standard error	t statistic	PROB > $|t|$
A01	0.156	0.185	0.845	0.4
A02	0.507	0.267	1.899	0.059
A03	0.577	0.283	2.043	0.043
A04	0.53	0.257	2.058	0.041
A05	0.695	0.343	2.024	0.045
A06	0.53	0.262	2.022	0.045
A07	0.438	0.235	1.868	0.063
A08	0.321	0.167	1.922	0.056
A09	0.473	0.223	2.119	0.036
A10	0.26	0.148	1.759	0.08
B	0.008	0.042	0.19	0.85
C	−0.097	0.063	−1.541	0.125
H	0.952	0.026	36.796	0

Note: NOB = 180   MAX HAT = 0.224
   CRSQ = 0.999 SSR = 4.501
   COND(x) = 46.383 MAX RSTUDENT = 8.613
   NOVAR = 13   DW(0) = 2.025
   SER = 0.164   MAX DFFITS = 2.304

diagonal elements in the hat matrix; this indicates that the majority of the problems we will face arise from the dependent series, as opposed to the independent data. (The one significant hat element in fact is from an observation in region 6, which has been independently verified by Wood 1980 to have a large number of errors in the data.) Second, there are strong regional patterns in the diagnostics. The DFBETAS for the lagged dependent variable (the coefficient H), for instance, indicate that the eastern and southeastern states had a strong downward (i.e., toward zero) influence on that coefficient, whereas the western states had the opposite effect. Region 2, in particular, has a number of aberrant endogenous observations. Third, there are strong intertemporal patterns in the diagnostics. Roughly two-thirds of the influential observations come from about one-third of the data, those being the post-1973 values. The large number of significant diagnostics indicates problems with the model/data fit, a problem we must confront in further estimation.

Coefficient estimates for the coal share equation (6.4) are given in table 6.4. Note again that we do not have a significant price effect; the fit of the equation arises almost totally from the lagged share and the constant terms. The degree of collinearity here is acceptable; this is not surprising, given that the large collinear effects involved the weather variables in (6.3) and that the Divisia index appears in the denominator of a fraction here.

Significant diagnostics for the coal share equation appear as table 6.5. The regional patterns in the diagnostics are even more striking here; region 1 (New England) and the western states perform very badly. New England has a strong positive influence on the lagged share coefficient; another data error in region 6 produces a residual with a scaled magnitude more than eight times as large as the standard error of the regression.

The lesson learned from the diagnostics, in general, is that there is a great variation across regions in the ability of the model to explain the data. The total demand equation might be reacting poorly to data from the early 1970s; the coal share equation seems to fit some regions much less well than others. The effort of OLS to fit the few outlying or incorrect observations at the expense of the rest of the data might lead to a situation where the ability to forecast in general is lessened in order to fit a few hard-to-measure observations slightly better. Some manner of weighting or dummying to avoid contamination from the bad observations is obviously called for.

6.4   Alternative Estimation Procedures

The OLS estimator of the coefficients of the classical linear regression model has a number of desirable qualities. Under the appropriate assumptions (e.g., see Theil 1971) it is the maximum likelihood estimator, unbiased, consistent and asymptotically normal. The salient argument favoring the use of OLS, though, seems to be the Gauss-Markov theorem: among all unbiased linear estimators of the regression model, the OLS estimator is BLUE (best linear unbiased estimator) in that its covariance matrix differs from the covariance matrix of any other linear estimator by a positive definite matrix.

The Gauss-Markov theorem establishes that for at least one choice criterion (linear, unbiased), OLS is the optimal estimator of the coefficient of the linear model. What is often overlooked in the econometrics literature is that other criteria exist by which to judge estimators. Many of these are at least as important as efficiency. For example, OLS and many other commonly used maximum likelihood techniques have an unbounded influence function; any small subset of the data can have an arbitrarily large influence on their coefficient estimates. In a world of fat-tailed or asymmetric

Table 6.5
Significant diagnostics for the coal share equation in the industrial sector

	RSTUDENT	HAT	DFFITS	Constant	B	C	H
Region 1, 1961							0.385
Region 1, 1962				−0.227			0.258
Region 1, 1963				−0.152			0.181
Region 1, 1965							0.163
Region 1, 1967	2.091		0.575				0.257
Region 1, 1970	−3.36		−0.857	−0.183	−0.199	−0.152	
Region 1, 1973							0.165
Region 1, 1974	3.219		1.144	0.485			−0.79
Region 1, 1976	−2.237		−0.769	−0.255	0.159		0.473
Region 1, 1977		0.158	0.578	0.324		−0.175	−0.426
Region 1, 1978		0.152	−0.591	−0.345		0.2	0.43
Region 6, 1961	−2.212		−0.592		−0.215		
Region 6, 1971					−0.158		
Region 6, 1973	8.613	0.165	2.304	0.455	0.369	0.28	−0.807
Region 6, 1977		0.154		0.201	0.4	0.162	
Region 6, 1978						0.158	−0.163
Region 7, 1972							
Region 8, 1962							
Region 9, 1961	2.492		0.722				
Region 9, 1962	−2.514		−0.639	0.293	0.215	−0.321	
Region 9, 1973		0.151			0.181		−0.15
Region 9, 1976		0.224	0.589	−0.157	−0.466		
Region 9, 1977					−0.378		
Region 9, 1978						−0.18	
Region 10, 1961				0.186			
Region 10, 1972				0.202			
Region 10, 1974				−0.172			
Region 10, 1975				0.169			
Region 10, 1976			0.583	0.197	−0.4		
Region 10, 1977					0.193		

Note: Cutoffs: DFBETAS = 0.149071, DFFITS = 0.537484, HAT = 0.1444444, RSTUDENT = 2.

error distributions, data errors, and imperfectly specified models, it is just those data in which we have the least faith that often exert the most influence on the OLS estimates.

Estimators whose influence functions are not unbounded are known collectively as bounded-influence (BIF) estimators. They are members of a larger family of statistical techniques (robust techniques) that are designed to safeguard against model failure by sacrificing efficiency (and linearity) in the absence of deviations from the statistical model in favor of decreased sensitivity to the presence of such problems. In the linear regression model BIF estimators have a number of advantages. They safeguard against increases in estimated parameter variance caused by fat-tailed error distributions unrelated to the explanatory variable data. When there is reason to believe that the error contamination is related to the data (keypunch errors that are associated with large data values, or breakdown in the specification at extreme values of the data), then bias as well as variability are a concern. Bounded-influence estimators control the bias inherent in such situations by limiting the influence that aberrant data can have on the final estimates. Subject to a constraint on the influence any data point can have, the BIF estimator recently developed by Krasker and Welsch (1982) can be shown to meet the necessary conditions for an efficient estimator.

We will illustrate the gains that can be had through the use of BIF estimators by considering the forecasts developed with the RDFOR specification. Using coefficient estimates based on the first three quarters of the time-series data associated with the models, we have found that ex post forecasts based on BIF estimates are significantly better than those based on OLS estimates. BIF estimates seem to lead to a decrease in the largest errors of the OLS based forecasts while providing virtually the same accuracy in other instances. Since we are chiefly concerned with avoiding very large errors in applied work, this result argues that BIF estimators deserve consideration when developing forecasts with the standard linear regression model.

Because RDFOR is a reduced-form model, and because of the structural problems mentioned earlier, it cannot be expected to fit the demand patterns manifested by the real economy in any exact way. The Kuh, Lahiri, and Swartz analysis found RDFOR particularly bad at fitting the response to the energy price shocks of the early 1970s. Moreover the specification does not perform well for the very early data values in the time range. Large and systematic trends in various diagnostic measures indicate that potential biases mar the accuracy of the OLS coefficient estimates. The collinearity of the data both magnify the effect of these biasing forces and increase the sensitivity of forecasts to whatever biases occur. For these reasons we are skeptical of the ability of the OLS estimator to produce good forecasts. Bounded-influence estimators should perform better in an environment such as this.

We have organized our exposition in this section as follows. First we attempt to present a coherent intuitive explanation of the various robust and bounded-influence estimators available in the BIF package on TROLL; a more technical exposition is contained in Peters, Samarov, and Welsch (1983). Then, we give OLS and BIF estimates of the equations necessary to produce estimates of coal demand in the industrial section, a comparison of forecasts based on these results, and a discussion of additional or complementary insights such ex post BIF forecasts provide within the context of our analysis. Our emphasis is on the ability of BIF to provide diagnostic insights, rather than on the potential of BIF estimates to "rescue" the model.

Bounded-Influence Estimators

The OLS estimator can be intuitively justified from a number of perspectives.[1] Geometrically it can be viewed as a projection operator into the space spanned by the exogenous data series considered as n vectors (where there are n observations). Statistically OLS is of course the maximum likelihood estimator of the linear regression model for iid normally distributed errors. Due to the special nature of these operations, they are both computationally equivalent to minimizing the sum of the squared residuals with respect to the coefficients of the regression model—hence the estimator's name.

That the influence function of the OLS estimator is unbounded can also be understood from a variety of perspectives. The following thought experiment is typical. Suppose that we knew the "real" coefficients. We could identify some subset of observations that was fitted least well by those coefficients. Allow that subset of the data to become more and more aberrant. As it does so, the associated "real" residuals grow without bound. The least-squares estimator will shift its estimates of the true values of the coefficients in such a way that these large residuals are reduced at the expense of the smaller residuals. Ordinary least squares will adjust its coefficient estimates based on information from a small, aberrant set of data points; OLS therefore has an unbounded influence function.

Accurate identification of influential observations relies on prior knowledge of the true coefficient values of the model. Our thought experiment was simplified by the fact that we assumed perfect information regarding the "real" coefficient values, which enabled us to pick out influential observations. Finding such observations in a real sample is problematic because the very aberrations we are looking for cloud our conception of the true coefficient values and make aberrations less obvious; influential data often hide when least squares is used. A feasible strategy in the absence of perfect foreknowledge of the coefficient values (a common situation) is to develop some concept of the central tendency of the model that is robust to potentially influential observations and use that concept to identify candidate influential observations. Downweighting these "bad" data, we would develop a new idea of the model's central tendency, identify "bad" data within this new view, revise our outlook once again, and so on. Huber (1973, 1975, 1981) worked out the procedures necessary to implement this iterative process and proved its convergence in some specific cases.

We have been discussing influential observations as though they were a phenomena having to do only with the residuals of the model. Actually influential observations enter into the computation of the OLS coefficient estimates as both a function of the residual and the magnitude of the X data. The solution to the problem of minimizing the sum of the squares of the residuals is equivalent to the problem of solving a set of equations, called normal equations, which are the derivatives of the sum of the squared residuals with respect to the coefficient estimates (because at the minimum of a function that function's derivatives must be zero). The normal equations of the OLS estimator contain terms in both the residuals and the X data; most bounded influence estimators downweight both outlying X data and observations corresponding to large residuals in order to achieve boundedness.

Corresponding to these two sources of unboundedness are two distinct mathematical techniques that simultaneously downweight influential observations in the calculation of most BIF coefficient estimates. The first involves changing the function through which residuals enter the sum which is minimized to find the estimates. By convention this function is called the robustifying criterion function; we refer to it as the ρ function. OLS corresponds to an estimator for which the ρ function is always quadratic. Minimum absolute error estimators are occasionally used, for which the ρ function is always the absolute value. For robust estimation of the linear model a cutoff value related to the number of data values and the desired efficiency of the estimator in well-behaved circumstances is calculated and used to identify residuals as large. As implemented first by Huber (1974, 1977) and later in all of the BIF estimators we shall consider, the ρ function of choice is to allow a residual to enter the sum as a function of its square if it is less than the cutoff and as a function of its absolute value if it is greater than the cutoff. Here greater than and less than previously refer to the absolute value of the residual. In the robust estimator due to Huber, this is the only kind of downweighting that occurs. Since the X data could also be aberrant, the Huber estimator still has an unbounded influence function.

When we say that the cutoffs are determined as a function of the desired efficiency of the BIF estimator, we are referring to the relative efficiency with respect to the OLS estimator. Since the comparison of efficiencies involves placing an ordering on square matrices, and since no clear and widely accepted ordering is known, a number of proxies is implemented by various researchers. One suggestion is to compare the determinants of the OLS and BIF covariance matrices. Another is to use the ratio of the greatest eigenvalues of the two matrices. These two measures cover a range of plausible relative efficiencies relating to sums and averages of the eigenvalues of the different matrices. Since economists seem to think more in terms of the determinants of the covariance matrices, we have used that measure in our analysis.

The second mathematical technique used to downweight influential observations in the calculation of BIF coefficient estimates involves the identification of outlying values in the space of the exogenous series. Bounded-influence estimators are differentiated by the sophistication of the tools they use to determine whether or not a particular observation is "different" from the other "typical" observations. We will discuss the methods used by the various estimators in turn.

The BIF estimation procedure due to Mallows (1973, 1975) uses two separate iterative processes, governed by two separate cutoffs, to downweight influential observations. The first iterative process calculates X weights based on a robust distance measure in a manner similar to the iterative process we described earlier. Initial X weights are calculated to downweight outliers; the revised X matrix is analyzed, and new X weights are calculated; and so on. This weighted X matrix is used in the second iterative procedure, where further downweighting occurs corresponding to the size of the residuals arising from coefficient estimates developed from the most recent version of the X matrix. As a data-analytic tool the Mallows estimator is intuitively clear. The choice of separate cutoffs for the separate sources of contamination (X outliers and large residuals) allows the user a greater degree of flexibility than can be had from the other BIF estimators. Remember, though, that outlying data that fits well increases the efficiency of the estimates. Any downweighting of X data that does not take account of the quality of the fit of that X data cannot produce efficient estimates because the outlying points, if they contain good information, would contribute much to the precision of the estimates. Since the Mallows estimator develops its X weights before it even considers the fit of the data, the other BIF estimators are to be preferred on purely statistical grounds.

The Schweppe BIF estimator (see Handschin et al. 1975) uses a relatively simple algorithm to develop initial X weights but provides bounded influence and does not downweight "good" outliers. It accomplishes this feat through the use of the diagonal elements of the OLS projection matrix $X(X'X)^{-1}X'$, called the HAT values. The HAT values are used to compute initial X weights through a simple, noniterative process. Although the quality of the outliers influences the initial X weights, this simple algorithm does not optimally combine information about outliers in X space and poorly fit observations. For example, the Schweppe algorithm is not sophisticated enough to identify nearly replicated outliers well. Imagine one outlier in X space duplicated over and over in the sample. As the outlier appears more often, it seems less different in some naive way (there are lots of other points like it in the sample!), and the Schweppe algorithm downweights the outliers less severely. This and other problems indicate that the Schweppe algorithm is too simple to be consistently useful as a BIF estimator.

Given the bound on efficiency arising from the cutoff value of the ρ function, but otherwise completely buying the statistical model, the BIF estimator developed by Krasker and Welsch (1982) can be shown to meet the necessary conditions for an efficient BIF estimator. If one wants to use a bounded influence estimator but otherwise stick closely to the world view underlying the OLS estimator, then the Krasker-Welsch estimator with its efficiency properties and its minimal violation of the data is clearly the estimator of choice. If, on the other hand, one is more interested in data analysis and skeptical about efficiency results of all kinds, then the Mallow's estimator is more appealing. Since the different estimators use different methods to guard against model failure, they can provide different kinds of information about the data and the fit; one cannot easily choose arbitrarily among the estimators.

The boundedness criterion is intuitively attractive and should enter into the decision regarding an estimator for the linear model. Even the most noninterventionist analyst among us should have some limit, albeit large, on the amount of influence any one data point can have on the coefficient estimates; one cannot trust the data or oneself too much after all. As a practical matter then some very lenient cutoff associated with a very moderate loss in efficiency vis-à-vis the OLS estimator is probably always called for. Should there be no problem at all within the data set, BIF estimates will turn out to be quite close to OLS estimates. The small reduction in the power of inference is not often likely to be important; the reduction of uncertainty concerning some of the model assumptions which impacts on the usefulness of the inference is often likely to be important. This gain, plus the diagnostic information available as a result of BIF estimation, argues strongly for using BIF estimators for the linear model.

The Empirical Results

When choosing a reduced-form, econometric model over a structural, "engineering" model for forecasting purposes, one sacrifices detail and scope for simplicity and inexpensiveness. Unfortunately in complicated situations the basic assumptions prerequisite to empirical analysis using relatively unsophisticated estimators are often flagrantly violated. Using more advanced estimators can be infeasible because of a lack of good data, further breakdown of statistical assumptions, and so on. Either the simplicity and moderate cost originally desired will not be achieved through the means of the econometric model, or the results obtained will be questionable on methodological and practical grounds.

Guarding against potential statistical problems by including them in the specification or in the estimator can cause difficulties because, without a reasonable framework, one's imagination can find hideous problems in even the most innocent of error processes. Robust estimators provide a desirable alternative in that they usually require little more from the data than do the simpler estimators they replace, and they generally guard against a wider range of potential problems than do parametric specification tests—not by "correcting" for them but by minimizing the damage they can create. The type of robust procedure chosen should correspond to the class of problems one anticipates in the data and model being used. In subsequent analysis of results based on both simple and robust estimators, differences in estimates or forecasts can flag instances where one's fears were well founded. The robust procedure is then justified both practically and diagnostically, and one can pinpoint the areas of the analysis that should be taken skeptically.

For the RDFOR model Kuh, Lahiri, and Swartz (1981) found little right among the assumptions behind the coefficient estimates used to develop forecasts of energy demand with the model. A logical extension of their work is the use of alternative estimators. Bounded-influence estimators were chosen because the quality of the data and specification seemed to be the greatest single problem with the OLS RDFOR results. It was hoped that BIF estimates would eliminate or mitigate strange patterns of time and regional sensitivity manifested in the OLS results. In a limited sense that hope proved well founded. Ex post forecasts of industrial fuel demand (using data from 1960 to 1974 to create coefficients and then forecast demand for 1975 to 1978) have been significantly improved in terms of percent error using BIF estimates. Generally, BIF performed better in the eastern and midwestern DOE regions but worse in the western regions. Odd behavior in the western regions seemed to reduce our ability to forecast accurately behavior in the eastern regions; improvement in the eastern forecasts led to a significant increase in the accuracy of total U.S. forecasts since these regions consume the largest share of fuel. We present a detailed comparison of the ex post forecasts following a look at the coefficient estimates and the diagnostic information that best explains the difference among them.

Adjusted coefficient estimates for the RDFOR total demand equation using OLS and the various BIF estimators tuned to the 95% efficiency level are presented in table 6.6.[2] Remember, when using the RDFOR specification for forecasting, the region-specific constant terms (A1–A10 in the chart) must be adjusted for the fact that the series proxying heating and cooling demand are dropped. Thus reported values for A1–A10 are actually estimated values for those coefficients plus the in-region mean of the heating and cooling degree days series times their coefficients (D and E, respectively).[3]

Except for the constant terms, and their associates the weather coefficients, these coefficients show little variation over the estimators we used. The constant terms are always at least a little bit less negative in the

Table 6.6
Adjusted coefficient estimates for the RDFOR total demand equation

	Estimates from OLS	BIF estimates			
		Huber	Schweppe	Krasker-Welsch	Mallows
A1	−2.689	−2.594	−2.594	−2.605	−2.629
A2	−2.915	−2.813	−2.814	−2.827	−2.852
A3	−2.832	−2.731	−2.732	−2.744	−2.769
A4	−2.845	−2.745	−2.745	−2.757	−2.781
A5	−3.097	−2.988	−2.989	−3.001	−3.028
A6	−2.632	−2.541	−2.541	−2.552	−2.574
A7	−2.564	−2.470	−2.471	−2.481	−2.504
A8	−2.174	−2.094	−2.095	−2.104	−2.123
A9	−2.767	−2.669	−2.669	−2.681	−2.705
A10	−2.965	−2.690	−2.690	−2.724	−2.809
B	−0.050	−0.063	−0.063	−0.062	−0.057
C	0.278	0.268	0.268	0.269	0.272
D	0.040	0.017	0.017	0.019	0.025
E	0.033	0.033	0.033	0.034	0.037
H	0.662	0.669	0.669	0.669	0.668

columns corresponding to the BIF estimators. The price coefficients B are slightly more negative, the value-added coefficients C slightly less positive, and the lagged endogenous coefficients H slightly closer to 1 in the BIF columns. Comparing these coefficients, we conclude that aberrant data accounts for a small overprediction of aggregate industrial demand.

The adjusted coefficient estimates for the RDFOR coal share equation, presented as table 6.7, embody quite a bit more variation among the different estimators. Whereas OLS finds the share of energy demand allocated to coal to be a difference process with a positive constant and an autoregressive coefficient of .9, BIF ignores virtually all information and sets the constant terms AC1–AC10 to zero, the relative price effect SC to zero, and the autoregressive parameter TC to 1. BIF seems to say, almost across the board, that the best available guess as to the share of total energy demand that will be met by coal is last period's share.

New England (region 1) provides an interesting example of the kind of insight one can develop from an analysis of these coefficients. In the BIF estimates AC1 is the only significantly nonzero constant term. Apparently New England alone among its regional peers has experienced a significant reduction in the share of its energy needs met by coal. We would be

Table 6.7
Adjusted coefficient estimates for the RDFOR coal share equation

	Estimates from OLS	BIF Estimates			
		Huber	Schweppe	Krasker-Welsch	Mallows
AC1	0.007	−0.195	−0.204	−0.222	−0.162
AC2	0.350	−0.000	−0.012	−0.036	0.050
AC3	0.468	0.035	0.020	−0.005	0.103
AC4	0.395	0.028	0.015	−0.007	0.087
AC5	0.498	0.028	0.012	−0.012	0.093
AC6	0.273	−0.018	−0.026	−0.034	0.009
AC7	0.255	−0.029	−0.039	−0.055	0.020
AC8	0.263	0.019	0.010	−0.013	0.072
AC9	0.279	0.027	0.018	0.001	0.061
AC10	0.339	0.096	0.088	0.073	0.154
GC	−0.148	−0.088	−0.086	−0.082	−0.087
SC	−0.081	0.007	0.009	−0.002	0.039
TC	0.921	0.992	0.994	0.996	0.986

surprised if New England consumed much coal at all; the data bears us out. Nonetheless, since the magnitudes of the various shares are similar regardless of the magnitude of aggregate demand in the regional data, a region like New England can have an impact on the share equation disproportionate to its share of total coal consumption. Compared to the BIF estimates, it seems as though the OLS coefficients interpret at least some of the drop in New England consumption as evidence that the coefficient of autoregression of shares (TC) should be further from 1—that is, that shares are influenced by included series other than the lagged endogenous share—and/or that the relative price effect should matter. Since the evidence from region 1 seems relatively different than that from other regions, BIF ignores it and finds that neither price nor (except in a few regions) the constant term seems to matter.

Differences in the coefficient estimates among the OLS and BIF estimators extend diagnostic insight available from other sources. Since BIF estimators downweight observations that have a large influence on the final coefficient estimates, the information they contain is most similar to that contained in the diagnostic DEFITS.[4] DFFITS is a measure of the impact an observation has on its own fitted value. It can be broken into two components: one (HAT) that measures the degree to which the observation is an outlier in X space, and one that is the scaled residual (RSTUDENT) associated with the observation. Should data associated with a high DFFITS have a large impact on any specific coefficient estimate, it can be detected through a measure (DFBETAS) of the impact an observation has on a parameter estimate. Diagnostic analysis using these measures is complementary to that using the various BIF estimators; one can either develop BIF estimates and then use the diagnostics to pinpoint sources and effects of whatever differences in coefficients occur, or one can first check for trouble in the diagnostics and then study the results when the damages are limited in a controlled way.

Within the context of the BIF coefficient estimates the diagnostics corresponding to the coal share equation presented as table 6.8 serve as a useful means of confirming the channels through which BIF and OLS interpret the data differently. The fact that the diagnostics are distributed unevenly across the ten DOE regions confirms our suspicions about cross-regional problems. The preponderance of large positive DFBETAS associated with region 1 on the lag share coefficient show that region 1 data generally have the effect of making that coefficient lower than it otherwise would be (the deletion diagnostics are a scaled difference between coefficients estimated without and with the specific observation). The observation corresponding to region 1 for 1974 is noteworthy as an observation that OLS interprets in the constant term instead of as caused change; this is an interpretation that BIF reverses. Also noteworthy is the observation from region 6 for 1973. The residual from that observation is almost eight times as large as the standard error of the error distribution. We have since determined that the data error is in the endogenous "share" series for that observation.

An alternative way of presenting diagnostic information like the BIF weights or DFFITS which can be broken into two separate components, as mentioned before, is in the form of contour plots. Figure 6.1 contains a contour plot of DFFITS for the coal share equation. The contours are equi-DFFITS lines broken into the effects due to RSTUDENT (the scaled residual) and to M distance (outliers in X space). Notice that except for the on observation on the far right of the plot (which is the observation associated with region 1, 1974, and which is the point in X space most deviant from the other data), most of the problems with the results are due to poorly fitting endogenous observations as opposed to aberrant exogenous data. This might suggest that various important series have been omitted from the regression, that coefficient constraints restrict the speci-

Table 6.8
Significant diagnostics from OLS estimation of the RDFOR coal share forecast equation

	RSTUDENT	HAT	DFFITS	DFBETAS			
				Constant	Relative price	Gas available	Lag share
Region 1, 1961	1.3957	0.1466	0.5785	-0.1439	0.0472	-0.0150	0.3926
Region 1, 1962	0.9867	0.1383	0.3952	-0.0917	0.0323	-0.0013	0.2602
Region 1, 1970	-3.5097	0.0891	-1.0979	-0.2884	-0.0761	-0.4102	0.2391
Region 1, 1972	-1.1784	0.1569	-0.5083	-0.2330	0.0225	-0.0769	0.3464
Region 1, 1973	-1.3777	0.2027	-0.6947	-0.3875	0.1340	0.0139	0.5462
Region 1, 1974	2.7484	0.3082	1.8346	1.0232	-0.5923	-0.6423	-1.4371
Region 6, 1961	-2.1552	0.0924	-0.6875	-0.0586	0.0669	-0.2600	-0.1105
Region 6, 1973	8.6989	0.0856	2.6609	0.0924	0.0352	-0.7166	-0.6510
Region 8, 1972	0.7050	0.1449	0.2902	-0.1387	0.1922	0.0860	0.0508
Region 8, 1973	0.8995	0.1443	0.3694	-0.2204	0.2590	-0.0068	0.0822
Region 9, 1961	2.6315	0.0977	0.8661	0.3834	-0.3610	0.2384	-0.1725
Region 9, 1962	-2.2730	0.0832	-0.6846	0.1904	-0.0906	0.1047	-0.2399
Region 9, 1966	-1.7975	0.0820	-0.5374	0.0540	0.0283	0.1700	-0.0840
Region 9, 1973	1.6866	0.1268	0.6426	0.0602	0.0974	0.4055	-0.0892
Region 10, 1961	1.6533	0.1328	0.6469	0.1850	-0.1275	0.4005	-0.0107
Region 10, 1968	-1.0820	0.1606	-0.4733	0.0881	0.0127	0.3518	-0.0422
Region 10, 1969	-1.4764	0.1479	-0.6150	0.0641	0.0427	0.4409	0.0110
Region 10, 1974	1.3256	0.1073	0.4594	0.0952	0.0194	0.2262	-0.1361

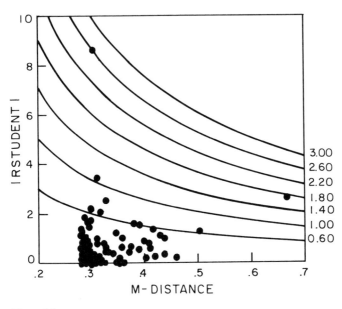

Figure 6.1
DFFITS contour plot

fication from representing important interregional variation, or that the aggregate demand/share modeling strategy is inadequate to the task of predicting energy demand.

Another important repository of the diagnostic information arising out of the BIF estimation procedure are the final weights with which BIF scales the exogenous data. Table 6.9 lists the thirty worst points as measured by the OLS DFFITS and the weights each of the BIF estimators assigned to those points. Immediately obvious in this chart is the preponderance of downweighted data from regions 1, 6, 9, and 10. Note that not all of the "bad" points from the point of view of OLS and DFFITS remain "bad" points from the point of view of BIF. For example, it seems that down-weighting data from region 1 for 1970 and 1974 was sufficient to alleviate whatever was wrong with data from region 1 for 1972 and 1973; the latter two points were not downweighted at all by any of the algorithms except the Mallows procedure. This suggests perhaps that the data from 1972 and 1973 were still fairly outlying in X space but fit reasonably well after the other data were properly downweighted.

Just as the OLS DFFITS can be broken down into components due to aberrant X data and large residuals, so can these BIF weights be broken

Table 6.9
Final weights from BIF estimates of the RDFOR coal share equation, ordered by the OLS DFFITS

	OLS DFFITS	BIF final weights			
		Huber	Schweppe	Krasker-Welsch	Mallows
Region 6, 1973	2.6609	0.1079	0.1083	0.1290	0.1415
Region 1, 1974	1.8346	0.2388	0.2059	0.1190	0.2167
Region 1, 1970	−1.0979	0.2539	0.2561	0.2712	0.3294
Region 9, 1961	0.8661	0.3180	0.3170	0.3507	0.4212
Region 1, 1973	−0.6947	1.0000	1.0000	1.0000	0.8580
Region 6, 1961	−0.6875	0.4447	0.4441	0.5100	0.5738
Region 9, 1962	−0.6846	0.3403	0.3420	0.4172	0.4501
Region 10, 1961	0.6469	0.5528	0.5433	0.5228	0.7819
Region 9, 1973	0.6426	0.5266	0.5170	0.4908	0.7220
Region 10, 1969	−0.6150	0.7408	0.7218	0.5825	0.9801
Region 1, 1961	0.5785	0.8961	0.8722	0.7582	1.0000
Region 1, 1967	0.5631	0.4347	0.4366	0.5047	0.5668
Region 9, 1966	−0.5374	0.4525	0.4559	0.5692	0.6020
Region 6, 1971	−0.5170	0.6234	0.6290	0.7930	0.7974
Region 1, 1972	−0.5083	1.0000	1.0000	1.0000	0.9923
Region 10, 1968	−0.4733	1.0000	1.0000	0.7629	1.0000
Region 10, 1972	−0.4609	0.5719	0.5763	0.6564	0.7079
Region 10, 1974	0.4594	0.5662	0.5616	0.5944	0.8041
Region 6, 1967	−0.4182	0.8041	0.8136	1.0000	1.0000
Region 7, 1972	0.3926	0.7458	0.7367	0.7537	1.0000
Region 6, 1964	0.3822	0.4320	0.4359	0.5672	0.5720
Region 8. 1973	0.3694	1.0000	1.0000	0.9896	1.0000
Region 10, 1966	0.3384	0.7162	0.7202	0.8308	0.9661
Region 2, 1971	−0.3377	0.6707	0.6792	0.9228	0.8839
Region 8, 1962	−0.3273	0.7639	0.7669	0.9291	1.0000
Region 10, 1971	0.2893	0.6610	0.6636	0.7877	0.9176
Region 2, 1963	0.2609	0.9903	1.0000	1.0000	1.0000
Region 1, 1968	−0.2574	0.8477	0.8615	1.0000	1.0000
Region 10, 1965	−0.2561	0.9027	0.8844	0.8499	1.0000
Region 6, 1970	0.2258	0.5955	0.6003	0.7812	0.7929

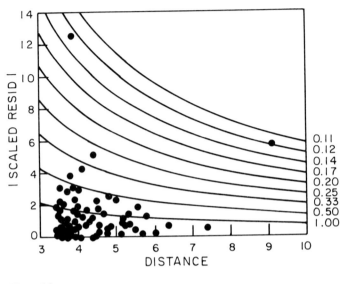

Figure 6.2
BIF weight contour plot

into components due to X outliers and large residuals. A contour plot of the
BIF weights for the Krasker-Welsch estimator is presented as figure 6.2.
The Krasker-Welsch algorithm gives the smallest weight to the region 1,
1974, observation, which again (compare with figure 6.1) is on the right-
hand side of the diagram. By and large the BIF algorithm expands the
scaled residuals of the more aberrant data points, which is what we would
expect of BIF—we sacrifice some fit of the worst points in order to fit better
the majority of points. Again we find that the majority of downweighting is
due to poorly fit left-hand side data.

   In considering the various diagnostic possibilities attendant to the BIF
estimators, it should be clear that we have done more than would the
average analyst. Practically one would seldom use all of these different
diagnostic techniques simultaneously. Depending on intent and the arena
in which results are to be presented, one might choose the coefficients
generated by the BIF algorithm, the weights used to create those coefficients, or the diagnostics arising directly from the OLS algorithm to
analyze potential weaknesses in the statistical model. Charts of the diagnostics have the advantage of thoroughness, yet they are often overwhelm-

ing to the casual user; the contour plots are both easy to use and informative of the nature of the breakdown encountered in the original model.

Our present purpose in amassing diagnostic information is to assess the reliability of energy demand forecasts for coal based on the RDFOR equation system. We might conclude that although RDFOR's OLS forecast of aggregate energy demand seems fairly robust to data problems of the kind that BIF estimators can correct for (remember the total demand equation's coefficients changed only slightly in a direction that would produce lower forecasts of total energy demand when using the BIF algorithms), the share equations seem more sensitive to data errors. Regions with lower absolute energy demand will have just as much impact on the OLS forecasts of share equation coefficients as will regions using a great deal of energy. We should remember that a large data error in region 6 might hurt the OLS forecasts in that region. Regions 1, 6, 9, and 10 fit very poorly in the OLS estimation process. Since none of these regions is an especially heavy coal consumer, relaxing their influence on the rest of the data might have a significant impact on the overall accuracy of energy demand forecasts. Finally, we remarked earlier that it was possible that important forces were omitted from the RDFOR specification. If those forces are dependent on time, as is the case with the increasing impact of conservation or supply-side forces or a change over time in the reaction to relative price, then our forecasts are irrecoverably damaged. The best we can hope for from BIF coefficients in this situation is that the time-dependent forces were prevalent over the majority of our data points and that our estimation procedure can therefore discard information from those points that do not seem to fit as well.

In order to test the forecasting ability of the RDFOR specification, we have constructed ex post forecasts using actual exogenous series and coefficient estimates corrected for the omission of the weather and gas availability series. Percent errors of forecasts of energy demand for the years 1975 to 1978 are presented in table 6.10.

Given our expectations as to the quality of these forecasts (based on the diagnostic evidence that we have presented) the patterns of improvement in our forecasts that can be gained through use of BIF coefficient estimates are hardly surprising. Using BIF coefficients improves the ability of the specification to forecast demand in regions 1 to 5, the regions where most U.S. coal is used. It also improves forecasts in region 6, where we identified one large data error. These gains were achieved at the expense of forecasts

Table 6.10
Percent errors of forecast using OLS and BIF coefficient estimates of the
RDFOR industrial coal demand forecasting model (percent)

| | OLS | BIF | | | |
		Huber	Schweppe	Krasker-Welsch	Mallows
Region 1					
1975	17.681	−0.172	−0.869	−1.444	−0.282
1976	62.502	15.088	13.403	12.239	14.405
1977	37.106	−19.281	−21.116	−22.273	−20.122
1978	87.407	−7.730	−10.596	−12.400	−8.898
Region 2					
1975	27.409	20.459	20.231	19.851	19.418
1976	−5.776	−15.776	−16.100	−16.583	−17.169
1977	21.316	−0.439	−1.086	−1.517	−3.777
1978	51.841	17.854	16.835	16.119	13.012
Region 3					
1975	1.566	−2.381	−2.484	−2.356	−2.741
1976	−1.199	−7.200	−7.365	−7.313	−7.243
1977	19.750	4.928	4.546	5.131	3.497
1978	24.214	6.151	5.661	6.223	4.933
Region 4					
1975	8.674	4.329	4.217	4.355	4.250
1976	16.532	7.232	6.991	7.293	7.054
1977	24.434	4.963	4.491	5.533	3.017
1978	7.397	−13.197	−13.712	−12.677	−15.042
Region 5					
1975	−0.694	−4.244	−4.348	−4.315	−4.260
1976	9.561	−2.152	−2.458	−1.911	−3.469
1977	16.154	−4.690	−5.210	−4.062	−7.463
1978	34.130	2.074	1.284	3.086	−2.231
Region 6					
1975	0.613	−4.896	−4.775	−4.053	−5.492
1976	3.451	−13.065	−12.975	−10.995	−15.978
1977	13.432	−17.962	−17.980	−14.475	−23.893
1978	51.073	−4.573	−4.720	1.180	−14.935
Region 7					
1975	0.501	−3.239	−3.354	−3.428	−2.508
1976	−12.409	−24.898	−25.215	−24.651	−25.642
1977	−14.683	−34.182	−34.659	−33.701	−35.691
1978	0.549	−30.913	−31.654	−30.066	−33.696
Region 8					
1975	−10.418	−11.757	−11.812	−11.997	−12.071
1976	−13.805	−17.815	−17.949	−18.117	−18.793
1977	−18.096	−26.980	−27.231	−27.055	−29.270
1978	−9.910	−22.165	−22.520	−22.306	−25.185

Table 6.10 (Continued)

	OLS	BIF			
		Huber	Schweppe	Krasker-Welsch	Mallows
Region 9					
1975	−7.213	−6.221	−6.236	−6.967	−5.132
1976	−18.871	−28.790	−29.050	−28.827	−30.857
1977	−28.176	−43.754	−44.131	−43.468	−47.150
1978	−0.721	−29.635	−30.314	−28.936	−35.885
Region 10					
1975	−45.936	−40.304	−40.406	−41.816	−44.345
1976	−62.968	−61.592	−61.820	−62.812	−66.883
1977	−56.047	−56.965	−57.375	−58.509	−64.631
1978	−42.499	−45.588	−46.258	−47.767	−56.286
U.S. totals					
1975	1.408	−2.316	−2.417	−2.382	−2.517
1976	2.910	−6.314	−6.552	−6.265	−7.190
1977	13.664	−4.703	−5.153	−4.282	−7.121
1978	23.916	−1.845	−2.479	−1.274	−5.070

for regions 7 to 9, whose BIF forecasts are somewhat worse. Apparently region 10's data are difficult to make sense of with either algorithm's interpretation of the data. Note that the overall effect of the changes in predictive accuracy is to produce remarkable improvement in aggregate coal demand forecasts; BIF forecasts were off by from 1.25 to 5 percent, as opposed to a 24 percent forecast error in the OLS forecast after four years.

Just as large charts of diagnostic information are somewhat imposing, so are large charts of diagnostic percent error deviations imposing. In a situation where distributions of numbers need to be compared, a useful didactic tool is the box plot, an example of which is presented as figure 6.3. The box plot is best considered as an aerial view of a distribution—in this case the distribution of the absolute values of the percent errors of forecast arising out of each of the estimators we have examined. The line in the center of the plot for each series is the median of that series. The lower and upper line of the box containing the median line are the first and third quartiles, respectively; their difference is called the midspread. The lines attached to the top and bottom of the box represent the extent of the third quartile plus the midspread and the first quartile minus the midspread. The dots and squares, finally, are the points that are respectively between 1 and

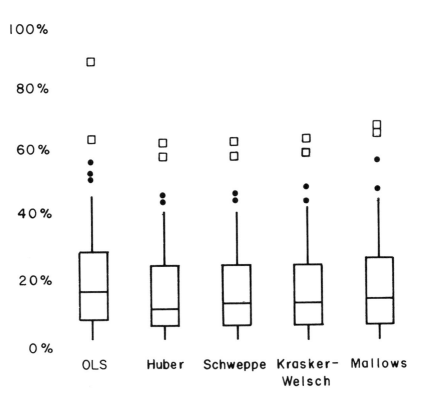

Figure 6.3
OLS and BIF percent errors of forecast of industrial coal demand in the RDFOR model,
presented as a group of box plots

1.5 midspreads from the region spanned by the box and more than 1.5
midspreads from that region.

The box plot of figure 6.3 graphically represents the superiority of the
BIF-based forecasts over the OLS-based forecasts. The median OLS absolute percent error is approximately 17 percent; the median Huber absolute percent error of forecast is 11 percent. The range of percent errors
was improved by the BIF coefficients. We can conclude that the problems
encountered in producing forecasts of energy demand using the RDFOR
specification can be lessened through use of more resistant estimators such
as the BIF estimators considered in this chapter.

In the RDFOR model it is hard to distinguish between the various BIF
algorithms. In general, since there are few aberrant X observations, we

might expect the Huber algorithm (which ignores the exogenous data completely) to do slightly better than the other three estimators. Under these circumstances it is not possible to distinguish among the three BIF estimators. Another confusing factor is the experimental nature of the efficiency calibration algorithms for the various estimators; the same efficiency level can lead to markedly different average weights and aggregate downweighting. In any case it is not likely that any one of these estimators will dominate the others; each should be a useful tool for the analyst.

Although it is hard to defend a model such as RDFOR as an accurate device for creating forecasts to be used for policy analysis such models have their place among the portfolio of tools that should be available to the analyst. Such specifications are easier to develop and validate than more complicated structural tools and certainly much cheaper to run and alter during the construction of specific policy prescriptions. Exactly because of their simplicity, though, they are likely to be subject to a variety of ills related to their interaction with the real world through the data with which we provide them. We have demonstrated a range of tools that are useful to catalog the various failures occurring in the specific model being used. If the list of problems includes potential data errors; inconsistency of small parts of the data with other, larger segments; occasional, unpredictable, yet significant departures of the behavior being modeled from the specification, and so on, then the potential for improved performance at a small additional cost through the use of diagnostics and bounded-influence estimators should be seriously considered.

Notes

This chapter reflects the view of the authors and is not approved by the Federal Reserve Board where Swartz is an economist. The research was supported, in part, by the National Science Foundation, U.S. Department of Energy, U.S. Army Research Office, and IBM, The help and advice of Edwin Kuh and Supria Lahiri is gratefully acknowledged.

1. This section is intended to be intuitive rather than rigorous. For a more complete technical development of this material, and for a description of software that implements these estimators, see Peters, Samarov, and Welsch (1983).

2. Results here in section 6.4 are not comparable with the results in section 6.3, since here the time bounds omit data for 1975 to 1978.

3. Full statistical information on these coefficients is provided elsewhere; see Kuh, Lahiri, and Swartz (1981).

4. The reader is again referred to Belsley, Kuh, and Welsch (1980) for details.

References

Belsley, D. A., 1981. Collinearity and Forecasting. CCREMS Technical report no. 27. MIT, Cambridge, Mass.

Belsley, D. A., E. Kuh, and R. E. Welsch, 1980. *Regression Diagnostics: Identifying Influential Data and Sources of Collinearity.* Wiley, New York.

Freedman, D., 1981. Analysis Quality Report on Midterm Energy Demand: The RDFOR Model Industrial Sector. Prepared for the NBS under Contract NB80 SBCA 0492.

Hampel, F. R., 1971. A General Qualitative Definition of Robustness. *Annals of Mathematical Statistics* 42 : 1887–1896.

Hampel, F. R., 1974. The Influence Curve and Its Role in Robust Estimation," *Journal of the American Statistical Association* 69 : 383–394.

Handschin, E., J. Kohlas, A. Fiechter, and F. Schweppe, 1975. Bad Data Analysis for Power System State Estimation. *IEEE Transactions on Power Apparatus and Systems* PAS-94 (2) : 329–337.

Hartman, R. S., 1979. Frontiers in Energy Demand Modeling. *Annual Review of Energy.* 4.

Huber, P. J., 1964. Robust Estimation of a Location Parameter. *Annals of Mathematical Statistics* 35 : 73–101.

Huber, P. J., 1977. *Robust Statistical Procedures.* SIAM, Philadelphia.

Huber, P. J., 1981. *Robust Statistics.* Wiley, New York.

Krasker, W. S., 1980. Estimation in Linear Regression Models with Disparate Data Points. *Econometrica* 48 : 1333–1346.

Krasker, W. S., E. Kuh, and R. E. Welsch, 1982. Estimation for Dirty Data and Flawed Models. *Handbook of Econometrics.* Z. Griliches and M. D. Intrilligator, eds. North-Holland Amsterdam, pp. 651–698.

Krasker, W. S., and R. E. Welsch, 1982. Efficient Bounded-Influence Regression Estimation. *Journal of the American Statistical Association* 77 : 596–604.

Kuh, E., Lahari, S., and Swartz, S., 1981. Diagnostics for the RDFOR Residential and Industrial Demand—An Interim Report, CCREMS. MIT Cambridge, Mass.

Mallows, C. L., 1973. Influence Functions. Talk at NBER Conference on Robust Regression, Cambridge, Mass.

Mallows, C. L., 1975. On Some Topics in Robustness. Memorandum. Bell Telephone Laboratories, Murray Hill, N.J.

NE077, 1977. Draft Report on the RDFOR Model, typescript.

Peters, S., A. Samarov, and R. E. Welsch, 1983. Computational Procedures for Bounded-Influence and Robust Regression. Technical Report No. 30. MIT Center for Computational Research in Economics and Management Sciences, Cambridge, Mass.

Synergy, Inc., 1979. The Demand Analysis System. Prepared for the DOE, Contract EC-78-C-01-8560 MOD(20). Washington, D.C.

Theil, H., 1971. *Principles of Econometrics.* Wiley, New York.

7 A Comparison of the Michigan and Fair Models: Further Results

Ray C. Fair and Lewis S. Alexander

7.1 Introduction

This chapter examines the equation-by-equation accuracy of the Michigan Quarterly Econometric Model (MQEM) and the Fair model using the method in Fair (1980). Emphasis is placed on examining the possible misspecification of the equations. In an earlier study, Fair and Alexander (1984), we used the method to examine the accuracy of the complete models. In the present study we are interested in the accuracy of the individual equations when considered in isolation from the rest of the model.

7.2 The Method

Although the main use of the method in Fair (1980) is to compare complete models, it can be used to examine individual equations. When the method is applied to complete models, it accounts for the four main sources of uncertainty of a forecast: uncertainty due to (1) the error terms, (2) the coefficient estimates, (3) the exogenous variables, and (4) the possible misspecification of the model. Because it accounts for these four sources, it can be used to make comparisons across models. For present purposes we are not interested in the uncertainty from the exogenous variables. All variables in the individual equations being examined, both exogenous and endogenous, except for the dependent variable and lagged values of the dependent variable, are assumed to be known with certainty.[1] The following is a brief outline of the method as it pertains to individual equations. See Fair (1980) or chapter 8 in Fair (1984) for a complete discussion of the method.

Assume that the equation being examined has p coefficients to estimate. Let s^2 denote the variance of the error term, and let V denote the covariance matrix of the coefficient estimates. V is $p \times p$. An estimate of s^2, say $\hat{s}^2$, is $(1/T)uu'$, where u is a $1 \times T$ vector of estimated error terms. T is the number of observations. The estimate of V, say $\hat{V}$, depends on the estimation technique used. Let $\hat{\alpha}$ denote a p-component vector of the coefficient estimates, and let u_t denote the error term for period t.

Uncertainty from the error terms and coefficient estimates can be estimated in a straightforward way by means of stochastic simulation. Given assumptions about the distributions of the error terms and coefficient estimates, one can draw values of both error terms and coefficients. For each set of values the equation can be solved for the period of interest. Given, say, J trials, the estimated forecast mean and estimated variance of the forecast error for each period can be computed. Let $\tilde{y}_{itk}$ denote the estimated mean of the k-period ahead forecast of variable i, where t is the first period of the forecast, and let $\tilde{\sigma}_{itk}^2$ denote the estimated variance of the forecast error. $\tilde{y}_{itk}$ is simply the average of the J predicted values from the J trials, and $\tilde{\sigma}_{itk}^2$ is the sum of squared deviations of the predicted values from the estimated mean divided by J.

It is usually assumed that the distributions of the error terms and coefficient estimates are normal, although the stochastic-simulation procedure does not require the normality assumption. The normality assumption has been used for the results in this paper. Let u_t^* be a particular draw of the error term for period t, and let α^* be a particular draw of the coefficients. The distribution of u_t^* is assumed to be $N(0, \hat{s}^2)$, and the distribution of α^* is assumed to be $N(\hat{\alpha}, \hat{V})$.

Estimating the uncertainty from the possible misspecification of the equation is the most difficult and costly part of the method. It requires successive reestimation and stochastic simulation of the equation. It is based on a comparison of estimated variances computed by means of stochastic simulation with estimated variances computed from outside-sample (i.e., outside the estimation period) forecast errors. Assuming no stochastic-simulation error, the expected value of the difference between the two estimated variances for a given period is zero for a correctly specified equation. The expected value is not in general zero for a misspecified equation, and this fact is used to try to account for misspecification effects.

Without going into details, the basic procedure is to estimate the equation over a number of different estimation periods and for each set of estimates to compute the difference between the two estimated variances for each length ahead of the forecast. The average of these differences for each length ahead provides an estimate of the expected value. Let $\bar{d}_{ik}$ denote this average for variable i and length ahead k. Given $\bar{d}_{ik}$, the final step is to add it to $\tilde{\sigma}_{itk}^2$. This sum, which will be denoted $\hat{\sigma}_{itk}^2$, is the final estimated variance. Another way of looking at $\bar{d}_{ik}$ is that it is the part of the forecast-error variance not accounted for by the stochastic-simulation estimate. Some of the specifics of the above procedure will become apparent in the discussion of the computations in section 7.4.

7.3   Some Features of the Models

Before considering the individual equations, it will be useful to give a brief discussion of some of the differences between the two models. The MQEM has 61 stochastic equations and 50 identities, and the Fair model has 30 stochastic equations and 98 identities. Even though the MQEM has more stochastic equations than does the Fair model, it is to some extent less structural. The Fair model accounts for all balance-sheet constraints and flows of funds among the sectors, which the MQEM does not. This is an important difference. It means that a variable like corporate profits is determined by an identity in the Fair model (revenue minus costs) and by a stochastic equation in the MQEM. There are a number of variables in the MQEM that are determined by stochastic equations that would be determined by identities if all the flow-of-funds constraints were meet.

The MQEM is also less structural in its determination of the unemployment rate. In the Fair model there are three stochastic equations explaining the labor force (equations for prime age men, prime age women, and all others), a stochastic equation explaining the number of people holding two jobs, and a stochastic equation explaining the demand for jobs by the firm sector. The unemployment rate is determined by an identity. It is equal to one minus the ratio of total employment to the total labor force. Total employment is equal to the total number of jobs minus the number of people holding two jobs. In the MQEM the unemployment rate is determined by a stochastic equation. It is a function of a dummy variable, a time trend, and one minus the employment rate of adult men. The employment rate of adult men is determined by a stochastic equation. It is a function, among other things, of real GNP.

The MQEM has more disaggregation with respect to the expenditure variables. The differences pertain to consumer durable expenditures and nonresidential fixed investment. In the MQEM durable expenditures are disaggregated into four components: new autos, motor vehicles and parts less new autos, furniture and household equipment, and all other. There is one stochastic equation for each of these components. In the Fair model there is one stochastic equation explaining total durable expenditures. Nonresidential fixed investment is disaggregated into four components in the MQEM: structures, producers' durable equipment in production, producers' durable equipment in agriculture, and producers' durable equipment except in agriculture and production. There is one stochastic equation for each of these components. In the Fair model there is one stochastic equation explaining total nonresidential fixed investment. There is also a separate equation in the MQEM explaining the number of new car sales, which is used as an explanatory variable in the automobile expenditure equation. Considerable work has gone into the MQEM in explaining automobile expenditures.

There is a heavy use of dummy variables in the MQEM, and many of the dummy variables are subjective in nature. Two of the more subjective variables are a dummy variable to reflect increased awareness of gas mileage in the cost of running a new car and a dummy variable to reflect auto rebates and reaction to higher auto prices. Of the 345 estimated coefficients in the MQEM, 70 are coefficients of dummy variables or variables that are a function of dummy variables, which is 20.3 percent of the total. These coefficients appears in 29 different stochastic equations.

Dummy variables play a much less important role in the Fair model. There are 11 dummy variables, 6 of which account for the effects of the dock strikes in the import equation. The other 5 dummy variables appear in four different stochastic equations. Of the 169 estimated coefficients in the Fair model, 13 are coefficients of dummy variables or variables that are a function of dummy variables, which is 7.7 percent of the total.

The heavy use of dummy variables in the MQEM poses a problem for the comparison method. One problem, which is not of concern here, is that it is difficult to account for exogenous-variable uncertainty with respect to dummy variables, since it is difficult to know how to estimate the uncertainty of these variables. Another problem is simply that it is difficult to know what to make of an equation that is heavily tied to dummy variables. Even though an equation like this may do well in tests, the use of dummy variables may have biased the results in favor of the equation. In some sense the more an equation is based on dummy variables, the less it has explained.

An example of this problem is the following. As noted previously, a dummy variable links the employment rate of adult men to the overall unemployment rate. The former is much easier to explain than the latter because the labor force of adult men fluctuates much less than does the labor force of other groups. The MQEM thus links a relatively easy-to-explain variable to a relatively hard-to-explain variable by the use of a time trend and a dummy variable. It is not clear how much of the unemployment rate is actually explained by this procedure, even though the equation fits well and (as will be seen) does well in tests.

Another example of the dummy variable problem concerns the key price equation in the MQEM, equation A2, which determines PPNF, the private nonfarm deflator. There are two dummy variables in the equation that pertain to the price freeze, and there is a productivity trend variable that is a function of three other dummy variables. One of the latter three variables takes on a value of 1 between 1954.1 and 1967.4 and 0 otherwise; one takes on a value of 1 between 1968.1 and 1973.4 and 0 otherwise; and one takes on a value of 1 between 1979.1 and 1979.4 and 0 otherwise. The specification of this equation may mean that a fairly large part of the fluctuations in the price deflator is explained by the dummy variables, and if this is true, the method will underestimate the uncertainty from the price equation.

The MQEM has also used what seem to be some questionable explanatory variables. For example, the discount rate is used as an explanatory variable in the bill rate equation. It is by far the most significant variable in the equation. On a quarterly basis the two variables are highly correlated, but this is because the discount rate generally follows the bill rate with a lag of a few weeks. The discount rate is not generally the policy instrument used by the Fed to influence short-term rates. It is simply a passive instrument. Another example of this type is the use of the minimum wage in the wage rate equation. It seems more likely that the aggregate wage rate affects the minimum wage rate rather than vice versa. Both the discount rate and the minimum wage are exogenous in the model.

7.4 The Equations Analyzed

The equations that have been analyzed are listed in table 7.1. In some cases a group of equations has been analyzed rather than a single equation, and the groups are also presented in the table. The groups for the MQEM are the following. Five equations are used to explain consumer expenditures on durables: an equation explaining new car sales and four equations for four categories of durable goods. The new car sales variable is an explanatory variable in the first two expenditure equations. Four equations are used to explain nonresidential fixed investment, one equation for each of four categories of investment. Inventory investment is determined by a stochastic equation and an identity. The identity determines the stock of inventories. The stock of inventories appears as an explanatory variable in the inventory investment equation with a lag of one quarter. The unemployment rate for the MQEM is determined by three stochastic equations and

Table 7.1
The MQEM and Fair model Equations analyzed

	Equation
MQEM	
Individual equations, variable	
Consumer expenditures, services (CS72)	C7
Consumer expenditures, nondurables (CN72)	C6
Housing investment (IRC72)	C13
Imports (M72)	C16
Private nonfarm deflator (PPNF)	A2
Wage rate (JCMH)	A1
Bill rate (RTB)	E2
Sets of equations, variable	
Consumer expenditures, durables (CD72)	CD72 = CDAN72 + CDAO72 + CDFE72 + CDO72
Units of retail new car sales (AUTOS)	C1
Consumer expenditures, new autos (CDAN72)	C2
Consumer expenditures, motor vehicles and parts less new autos (CDAO72)	C3
Consumer expenditures, furniture and household equipment (CDFE72)	C4
Consumer expenditures, durable goods less CDAN72 + CDAO72 + CDFE72(CDO72)	C5
Nonresidential fixed investment (IBF72)	IBF72 = IBFNC72 + IPDQ72 + IPDO72 + IPDAG72
Structures (IBFNC72)	C8
Producers' durable equipment in production (IPDQ72)	C10
Producers' durable equipment except in agriculture and production (IPDO72)	C11
Producers' durable equipment in agriculture (IPDAG72)	C12
Inventory investment (IINV72)	C15
Stock of business inventories (SINV72)	$SINV72 = SINV72_{-1} + IINV72$
Global unemployment rate (RUG)	B3
Output per manhour (QMH77)	B1
Employment rate, males 20 and over (REM)	B2
Unemployment rate, males 20 and over (RUM)	RUM = 100 − REM
Money supply (M1BPLUS)	E11
M2 plus short term treasury securities (M2PLUS)	E1

Table 7.1 (continued)

	Equation
Fair model	
Individual equations, variable	
Consumer expenditures, services (CS)	1
Consumer expenditures, nondurables (CN)	2
Consumer expenditures, durables (CD)	3
Imports (IM)	27
Private nonfarm deflator (P_f)	10
Wage rate (W_f)	16
Bill rate (RS)	30
Sets of equations, variable	
Housing investment (IH_h)	4
Stock of housing (KH)	$KH = (1 - \delta_H)KH_{-1} + IH_h$
Nonresidential fixed investment (IK_f)	12
Stock of capital (KK)	$KK = (1 - \delta_K)KK_{-1} + IK_f$
Inventory investment (IV_f)	$IV_f = V - V_{-1}$
Production (Y)	11
Stock of inventories (V)	$V = V_{-1} + Y - X$
(Note: X = total sales, X is determined elsewhere in the model.)	
Civilian unemployment rate (UR)	$UR = U/(L1 + L2 + L3 - J_m)$
Labor force, males 25–54 ($L1$)	5
Labor force, females 25–54 ($L2$)	6
Labor force, all others ($L3$)	7
Number of moonlighters (LM)	8
Number of jobs in the firm sector (J_f)	13
Total employment, civilian and military (E)	$E = J_f + J_g + J_m + J_s - LM$
Number of people unemployed (U)	$U = L1 + L2 + L3 - E$
(Note: J_g = federal government civilian jobs, J_m = federal government military jobs, J_s = state and local government jobs. These variables are exogenous.)	
Money supply ($M1$)	$M1 = M_h + M_f + M_r + M_s$
Demand deposits and currency, household sector (M_h)	9
Demand deposits and currency, firm sector (M_f)	17
(Note: M_r = demand deposits and currency, foreign sector; M_s = demand deposits and currency, state and local government sector. These variables are exogenous.)	

Note: All equation numbers are for stochastic equations. See Belton, Hymans, and Lown (1981) for a description of the MQEM variables and equations. See Fair (1984) for a description of the Fair variables and equations.

an identity. This specification was discussed before. The output per man-hour variable is an explanatory variable in the equation determining the employment rate of males 20 and over. Finally, the money supply is determined by two stochastic equations.

The groups of equations for the Fair model are the following. Housing investment is determined by a stochastic equation and an identity. The identity determines the stock of housing, which appears in the housing investment equation with a lag of one quarter. Nonresidential fixed investment is also determined by a stochastic equation and an identity. The identity determines the stock of capital, which appears in the investment equation with a lag of one quarter. Inventory investment is determined by a stochastic equation, which explains the level of production, and two identities. Given the level of sales and the level of production, the identities determine the stock of inventories and inventory investment. The stock of inventories appears in the production equation with a lag of one quarter.

The unemployment rate is determined by five stochastic equations and three identities. The stochastic equations determine three labor force categories, the number of moonlighters (people holding two jobs), and the number of jobs in the firm sector. Total employment is equal to the total number of jobs less the number of moonlighters. Total unemployment is equal to the total labor force less total employment. The unemployment rate is the ratio of unemployment to the civilian labor force.

The money supply is determined by two stochastic equations and an identity. The two stochastic equations determine the demand deposits and currency of the household and firm sectors. The money supply variable is the sum of these two plus the demand deposits and currency of the foreign and state and local government sectors.

7.5   Calculations of the Results

Many steps were involved in obtaining the final results, and it is easiest to discuss the computation of the results in the order in which they are done. The results for the MQEM will be discussed first.

Duplication of the Basic Estimates

Data for the MQEM were taken from the TROLL version of the model that was current at the beginning of 1983.[2] The specification of this version of the model is in Belton, Hymans, and Lown (1981), which we term BHL estimates. The first step was to duplicate the basic set of estimates. For none of the 61 equations were the differences between our estimates and the BHL estimates large enough to call into question our duplication of the results.

Uncertainty with Respect to the Error Terms and Coefficient Estimates

Given the basic coefficient estimates, V and s^2 were estimated for each equation. When a group of equations was considered, the covariance matrix of the coefficient estimates was taken to be block diagonal, where the blocks are the V matrices for the individual equations. Similarly the covariance matrix of the error terms for a group of equations was taken to be diagonal, where the diagonal elements are the s^2 estimates for the individual equations.

Table 7.2 contains the main results of this paper. The values in the a rows are stochastic-simulation estimates of the forecast standard errors based on draws of the error terms only. The values in the b rows are based on draws of both error terms and coefficients. The results are based on 250 trials for each of the two stochastic simulations. The simulation period is 1978.1 to 1979.4. In terms of the notation in section 7.2, the b-row values are values of $\tilde{\sigma}_{itk}$.[3] The values in the left half of the table are for the individual equations or groups of equations. The values in the right half of the table are for the whole model.

Uncertainty from the Possible Misspecification of the Model

For the misspecification results the MQEM was estimated and stochastically simulated 27 times. For the first set, the estimation periods ended in 1974.4 and the simulation period began two quarters later in 1975.2. For the second set, the estimation periods ended in 1975.1 and the simulation period began in 1975.3. For the final set, the estimation periods ended in 1981.2, and the simulation period began in 1981.4. The beginning quarters for the estimation periods remained unchanged from those for the basic period. The length of the first 20 simulation periods was eight quarters. Since the data ended in 1981.4, the length of the twenty-first simulation period, which began in 1980.2, was only seven quarters. Similarly, the length of the twenty-second period was six, and so on through the length of the twenty-seventh period, which was only one quarter. For each of the 27 sets of estimates, new estimates of the V matrices and the s^2 values were obtained. Each of the 27 stochastic simulations was based on 50 trials.

These results produced for the one-quarter ahead forecast for each

Table 7.2
Estimated standard errors of forecasts for 1978.1 to 1979.4 for three models

		Individual equations or groups								Complete models							
		1978				1979				1978				1979			
		1	2	3	4	1	2	3	4	1	2	3	4	1	2	3	4
Consumer expenditures, services																	
MQEM	a	0.27	0.38	0.44	0.50	0.55	0.60	0.63	0.67	0.28	0.39	0.47	0.54	0.59	0.65	0.70	0.74
	b	0.29	0.39	0.48	0.56	0.61	0.67	0.71	0.75	0.30	0.41	0.52	0.62	0.67	0.74	0.80	0.85
	d	0.46	0.70	0.88	1.06	1.23	1.41	1.64	1.82	0.48	0.74	0.93	1.15	1.37	1.63	1.94	2.21
	d/b	1.59	1.79	1.83	1.89	2.02	2.10	2.31	2.43	1.60	1.80	1.79	1.85	2.04	2.20	2.43	2.60
Fair	a	0.32	0.42	0.51	0.59	0.67	0.71	0.74	0.81	0.30	0.40	0.53	0.61	0.72	0.81	0.89	1.00
	b	0.31	0.43	0.54	0.62	0.72	0.79	0.84	0.92	0.30	0.41	0.55	0.67	0.81	0.93	0.99	1.10
	d	0.40	0.46	0.56	0.67	0.76	1.05	1.39	1.50	0.35	0.55	0.87	1.19	1.41	1.68	1.94	2.21
	d/b	1.29	1.07	1.04	1.08	1.06	1.33	1.65	1.63	1.25	1.34	1.58	1.78	1.74	1.81	1.96	2.01
AR8	a	0.28	0.40	0.49	0.60	0.69	0.72	0.78	0.81								
	b	0.30	0.44	0.54	0.64	0.76	0.84	0.95	1.05								
	d	0.51	0.81	1.05	1.31	1.61	1.90	2.27	2.56								
	d/b	1.70	1.84	1.94	2.05	2.12	2.26	2.39	2.44								
Consumer expenditures, nondurables																	
MQEM	a	0.48	0.59	0.65	0.65	0.70	0.70	0.75	0.71	0.54	0.70	0.85	0.98	1.14	1.18	1.27	1.38
	b	0.46	0.58	0.69	0.73	0.78	0.82	0.84	0.84	0.52	0.70	0.88	1.02	1.14	1.25	1.39	1.45
	d	0.77	1.03	1.13	1.21	1.36	1.50	1.58	1.65	0.86	1.28	1.55	1.78	2.10	2.43	2.86	3.28
	d/b	1.67	1.78	1.64	1.66	1.74	1.83	1.88	1.96	1.65	1.83	1.76	1.75	1.84	1.94	2.06	2.26
Fair	a	0.57	0.66	0.69	0.81	0.75	0.77	0.70	0.76	0.58	0.73	0.82	0.99	0.99	1.07	1.07	1.16
	b	0.68	0.73	0.82	0.87	0.89	0.88	0.84	0.91	0.70	0.78	0.96	1.07	1.11	1.17	1.23	1.33
	d	0.85	0.95	1.03	1.23	1.41	1.49	1.53	1.66	0.84	0.94	1.02	1.21	1.25	1.16	1.03	0.98
	d/b	1.25	1.30	1.26	1.41	1.58	1.69	1.82	1.82	1.20	1.21	1.06	1.13	1.13	0.99	0.84	0.74
AR8	a	0.57	0.89	1.07	1.26	1.37	1.43	1.45	1.48								
	b	0.61	0.97	1.16	1.33	1.51	1.62	1.71	1.81								
	d	0.88	1.35	1.37	1.12	1.28	1.50	1.73	1.88								
	d/b	1.44	1.39	1.18	0.84	0.85	0.93	1.01	1.04								

Consumer expenditures, durables

MQEM	a	1.12	1.34	1.42	1.47	1.57	1.76	1.79	1.73	1.15	1.53	1.82	2.20	2.36	2.73	2.98	3.18
	b	1.30	1.72	1.88	2.13	2.40	2.63	2.79	3.11	1.31	1.93	2.32	2.77	3.33	3.85	4.30	4.85
	d	3.28	2.89	2.82	0.99	i	i	i	i	3.52	3.97	4.91	4.55	5.23	6.40	7.84	8.99
	d/b	2.52	1.68	1.50	0.46	—	—	—	—	2.69	2.06	2.12	1.64	1.57	1.66	1.82	1.85
Fair	a	2.15	2.29	2.16	2.13	2.30	2.22	2.25	2.34	2.17	2.44	2.79	3.26	3.72	3.69	4.09	4.25
	b	2.08	2.39	2.56	2.53	2.54	2.47	2.70	2.56	2.11	2.55	3.16	3.52	3.94	4.15	4.40	4.61
	d	3.44	4.44	5.16	5.38	4.74	3.84	4.30	3.64	3.09	3.58	5.09	6.40	7.95	8.97	10.20	11.66
	d/b	1.65	1.86	2.02	2.13	1.87	1.55	1.59	1.42	1.46	1.40	1.61	1.82	2.02	2.16	2.32	2.53
AR8	a	1.91	2.60	3.15	3.36	3.60	3.92	4.18	4.19								
	b	2.13	2.82	3.39	3.83	3.80	4.45	4.69	5.12								
	d	4.32	5.54	6.39	6.64	6.93	7.97	9.09	9.92								
	d/b	2.03	1.96	1.88	1.73	1.82	1.79	1.94	1.94								

Housing investment

MQEM	a	2.09	3.02	3.51	4.26	4.65	4.91	5.01	5.09	2.09	3.07	3.68	4.69	5.54	6.41	7.16	7.40
	b	2.23	3.19	3.86	4.62	5.20	5.76	6.22	6.89	2.24	3.22	3.98	4.86	5.93	7.20	8.61	10.37
	d	5.35	8.49	9.82	10.74	11.99	13.57	14.94	15.29	5.36	8.54	9.42	9.93	12.13	15.26	18.79	21.49
	d/b	2.40	2.66	2.54	2.32	2.31	2.36	2.40	2.22	2.39	2.65	2.36	2.04	2.05	2.12	2.18	2.07
Fair	a	2.70	4.40	5.77	6.49	7.15	7.50	7.44	7.64	2.71	4.71	6.36	7.25	8.19	8.99	9.39	10.38
	b	2.82	4.82	6.41	7.57	8.39	8.80	9.15	9.68	2.80	4.83	6.83	8.46	9.58	10.77	11.88	13.35
	d	4.91	7.74	7.37	6.20	5.38	7.37	8.01	7.29	4.78	7.28	7.56	7.64	9.45	11.57	13.13	15.34
	d/b	1.74	1.61	1.15	0.82	0.84	0.84	0.88	0.75	1.71	1.51	1.11	0.90	0.99	1.07	1.11	1.15
AR8	a	2.61	4.22	5.92	7.06	7.66	8.02	8.21	8.23								
	b	2.78	4.68	6.20	7.42	8.53	8.96	9.34	9.42								
	d	6.43	11.25	12.24	10.89	9.58	10.35	12.46	12.77								
	d/b	2.31	2.40	1.97	1.47	1.12	1.16	1.33	1.36								

Table 7.2 (continued)

		Individual equations or groups								Complete models							
		1978				1979				1978				1979			
		1	2	3	4	1	2	3	4	1	2	3	4	1	2	3	4
Nonresidential fixed investment																	
MQEM	a	1.13	1.38	1.47	1.49	1.62	1.75	1.79	1.83	1.13	1.47	1.71	1.94	2.20	2.51	2.79	3.09
	b	1.08	1.51	1.65	1.79	2.00	2.11	2.16	2.09	1.08	1.57	1.85	2.16	2.56	2.88	3.22	3.40
	d	2.52	4.15	5.18	5.21	4.53	5.36	9.20	15.05	2.53	4.28	5.60	5.76	4.86	6.27	13.47	29.18
	d/b	2.33	2.75	3.14	2.91	2.27	2.54	4.26	7.20	2.34	2.73	3.03	2.67	1.90	2.18	4.18	8.58
Fair	a	1.50	1.88	2.14	2.30	2.35	2.26	2.39	2.53	1.72	2.25	2.60	2.92	3.24	3.32	3.49	3.66
	b	1.50	1.99	2.21	2.33	2.56	2.74	2.85	2.98	1.81	2.56	2.97	3.05	3.48	3.77	4.00	4.09
	d	2.24	2.57	2.74	2.91	3.40	3.49	3.75	3.85	2.69	3.24	4.00	4.19	5.24	6.08	6.75	7.54
	d/b	1.49	1.29	1.24	1.25	1.33	1.27	1.32	1.29	1.49	1.27	1.35	1.37	1.51	1.61	1.69	1.84
AR8	a	1.24	2.13	2.75	3.29	3.80	4.21	4.30	4.46								
	b	1.42	2.05	2.78	3.68	4.27	4.92	5.15	5.45								
	d	2.26	2.35	3.41	3.35	2.69	2.03	i	i								
	d/b	1.59	1.15	1.23	0.91	0.63	0.41	—	—								
Inventory investment																	
MQEM	a	3.71	3.87	3.95	4.47	4.25	3.81	4.32	4.44	3.86	4.20	4.38	5.18	5.06	4.81	5.17	5.33
	b	4.38	4.21	4.00	4.35	4.10	4.17	4.43	4.26	4.59	4.75	4.53	5.10	4.76	5.11	5.45	5.57
	d	6.36	6.83	7.05	7.06	6.82	6.74	7.04	7.09	6.28	6.93	7.37	7.87	7.12	6.10	6.47	7.33
	d/b	1.45	1.62	1.76	1.62	1.66	1.62	1.59	1.66	1.37	1.46	1.63	1.54	1.50	1.19	1.19	1.32
Fair	a	4.70	5.35	4.88	6.55	5.92	5.47	5.21	5.32	4.66	5.22	5.10	5.52	6.12	5.54	5.38	5.77
	b	4.62	5.17	5.46	5.30	5.21	6.04	5.85	5.90	4.50	5.05	5.52	5.60	4.99	5.93	5.90	6.23
	d	4.76	5.40	5.69	5.51	5.42	6.18	6.00	6.10	4.64	5.28	5.80	5.88	5.35	6.23	6.22	6.58
	d/b	1.03	1.04	1.04	1.04	1.04	1.02	1.03	1.03	1.03	1.05	1.05	1.05	1.07	1.05	1.05	1.06
AR8	a	5.22	5.45	5.81	5.72	5.69	6.41	6.02	6.38								
	b	5.33	6.18	6.45	6.75	6.64	6.67	6.75	7.32								
	d	6.67	7.66	7.92	7.51	7.78	8.12	8.18	8.61								
	d/b	1.25	1.24	1.23	1.11	1.17	1.22	1.21	1.18								

Imports

MQEM	a	2.44	3.45	3.82	3.95	3.98	3.85	3.70	3.55	2.47	3.42	3.68	3.80	3.80	3.65	3.64	3.67
	b	2.70	3.45	3.75	3.90	4.23	4.17	4.33	4.48	2.65	3.49	3.64	3.90	4.42	4.47	4.63	4.78
	d	3.73	4.96	5.70	6.41	7.07	7.28	7.88	8.45	3.66	5.01	5.64	6.29	6.98	7.67	9.12	10.69
	d/b	1.38	1.44	1.52	1.64	1.67	1.75	1.82	1.89	1.38	1.44	1.55	1.61	1.58	1.72	1.97	2.24
Fair	a	2.06	2.60	2.67	2.61	2.67	2.78	2.57	2.73	1.90	2.46	2.60	2.67	2.72	2.71	2.61	2.97
	b	2.15	2.61	2.90	3.03	3.10	3.26	3.39	3.32	2.22	2.44	2.66	2.76	2.81	3.28	3.56	3.70
	d	3.85	6.05	8.22	10.09	11.87	13.44	15.69	17.42	4.00	5.74	7.54	8.94	10.24	11.11	12.56	13.10
	d/b	1.79	2.32	2.83	3.33	3.83	4.12	4.63	5.25	1.80	2.35	2.83	3.24	3.64	3.39	3.53	3.54
AR8	a	2.63	3.53	3.98	4.64	4.71	4.87	5.14	5.22								
	b	2.79	3.61	4.33	4.91	5.43	5.58	5.77	5.96								
	d	5.04	7.54	9.69	11.70	13.11	13.71	14.25	15.26								
	d/b	1.81	2.09	2.24	2.38	2.41	2.46	2.47	2.56								

Private nonfarm deflator

MQEM	a	0.27	0.40	0.50	0.56	0.64	0.70	0.77	0.79	0.27	0.40	0.51	0.59	0.70	0.79	0.90	0.99
	b	0.28	0.41	0.51	0.62	0.67	0.77	0.84	0.92	0.28	0.40	0.53	0.66	0.74	0.88	1.01	1.17
	d	0.34	0.41	0.43	0.59	0.63	0.72	0.90	1.01	0.34	0.40	0.45	0.62	0.68	0.79	0.93	1.11
	d/b	1.21	1.00	0.84	0.95	0.94	0.94	1.07	1.10	1.21	1.00	0.85	0.94	0.92	0.90	0.92	0.95
Fair	a	0.39	0.54	0.67	0.76	0.83	0.97	0.89	0.92	0.38	0.55	0.68	0.77	0.84	0.91	0.92	0.98
	b	0.41	0.56	0.69	0.81	0.88	0.93	0.98	1.04	0.41	0.57	0.70	0.84	0.91	0.99	1.09	1.21
	d	0.68	1.13	1.58	2.07	2.50	2.85	3.27	3.69	0.66	1.12	1.55	2.05	2.44	2.80	3.17	3.49
	d/b	1.66	2.02	2.29	2.56	2.84	3.06	3.34	3.55	1.61	1.96	2.21	2.44	2.68	2.83	2.91	2.88
AR8	a	0.30	0.48	0.70	0.91	1.11	1.27	1.39	1.50								
	b	0.34	0.53	0.77	1.05	1.30	1.55	1.78	1.99								
	d	0.70	1.18	1.72	2.57	3.24	3.75	3.98	3.74								
	d/b	2.06	2.23	2.23	2.45	2.49	2.42	2.24	1.88								

Table 7.2 (continued)

		Individual equations or groups								Complete models							
		1978				1979				1978				1979			
		1	2	3	4	1	2	3	4	1	2	3	4	1	2	3	4
Unemployment rate																	
MQEM	a	0.21	0.28	0.34	0.40	0.43	0.47	0.50	0.53	0.23	0.35	0.44	0.54	0.58	0.65	0.72	0.76
	b	0.22	0.30	0.35	0.41	0.46	0.50	0.54	0.59	0.25	0.36	0.45	0.54	0.61	0.66	0.74	0.84
	d	0.26	0.37	0.43	0.46	0.45	0.43	0.41	0.41	0.34	0.52	0.67	0.74	0.71	0.51	0.62	1.07
	d/b	1.18	1.23	1.23	1.12	0.98	0.86	0.76	0.69	1.36	1.44	1.49	1.37	1.16	0.77	0.84	1.27
Fair	a	0.40	0.54	0.63	0.65	0.67	0.71	0.76	0.77	0.24	0.38	0.48	0.54	0.61	0.65	0.65	0.68
	b	0.40	0.59	0.67	0.73	0.77	0.85	0.86	0.87	0.26	0.42	0.52	0.61	0.70	0.77	0.78	0.80
	d	0.32	0.56	0.75	0.90	1.05	1.22	1.35	1.45	0.39	0.61	0.86	1.05	1.16	1.25	1.30	1.39
	d/b	0.80	0.95	1.12	1.23	1.36	1.44	1.57	1.67	1.50	1.45	1.65	1.72	1.66	1.62	1.67	1.74
AR8	a	0.29	0.58	0.81	0.97	1.06	1.11	1.17	1.23								
	b	0.29	0.56	0.83	1.04	1.19	1.30	1.37	1.41								
	d	0.31	0.37	0.39	0.29	i	i	i	i								
	d/b	1.11	0.66	0.47	0.28	—	—	—	—								
Wage rate																	
MQEM	a	0.31	0.42	0.58	0.64	0.71	0.78	0.82	0.88	0.31	0.42	0.59	0.66	0.78	0.87	0.97	1.10
	b	0.35	0.46	0.56	0.68	0.79	0.88	0.98	1.07	0.35	0.47	0.59	0.72	0.86	1.00	1.15	1.32
	d	0.28	0.42	0.54	0.67	0.71	0.80	0.89	1.07	0.28	0.43	0.59	0.75	0.83	0.99	1.14	1.37
	d/b	0.80	0.91	0.96	0.99	0.90	0.91	0.91	1.00	0.80	0.91	1.00	1.04	0.97	0.99	0.99	1.04
Fair	a	0.56	0.79	0.92	0.98	0.99	1.05	1.10	1.19	0.56	0.86	1.00	1.13	1.20	1.30	1.32	1.38
	b	0.59	0.79	1.02	1.18	1.35	1.47	1.59	1.67	0.59	0.84	1.01	1.15	1.35	1.48	1.70	1.85
	d	0.50	0.60	0.84	1.00	1.31	1.60	1.89	2.16	0.37	0.49	0.60	0.72	0.98	1.07	1.44	1.76
	d/b	0.85	0.76	0.82	0.85	0.97	1.09	1.19	1.29	0.63	0.58	0.59	0.63	0.73	0.72	0.85	0.95
AR8	a	0.21	0.33	0.43	0.53	0.60	0.63	0.68	0.73								
	b	0.26	0.44	0.58	0.73	0.86	0.95	1.04	1.14								
	d	0.43	0.75	1.04	1.35	1.75	2.11	2.51	2.96								
	d/b	1.65	1.70	1.79	1.85	2.03	2.22	2.41	2.60								

Bill rate

MQEM	a	0.43	0.50	0.62	0.77	0.73	0.72	0.82	0.92	0.41	0.48	0.58	0.70	0.69	0.71	0.80	0.91
	b	0.43	0.61	0.81	1.11	1.28	1.37	2.29	3.57	0.41	0.57	0.73	0.96	1.03	1.06	1.26	1.49
	d	0.67	0.81	1.01	1.32	1.50	1.58	2.26	3.53	0.64	0.89	1.02	1.26	1.38	1.35	1.17	0.97
	d/b	1.56	1.33	1.25	1.19	1.17	1.15	0.99	0.99	1.56	1.56	1.40	1.31	1.34	1.27	0.93	0.65
Fair	a	0.67	0.96	1.10	1.15	1.27	1.34	1.31	1.35	0.71	1.00	1.07	1.13	1.17	1.21	1.17	1.19
	b	0.65	0.94	1.12	1.19	1.30	1.42	1.44	1.52	0.73	0.94	1.04	1.03	1.15	1.26	1.31	1.45
	d	1.31	1.75	1.88	1.77	2.38	2.70	3.08	3.37	1.37	2.13	2.38	2.49	2.66	2.83	3.00	3.22
	d/b	2.02	1.86	1.68	1.49	1.83	1.90	2.14	2.22	1.88	2.27	2.29	2.42	2.31	2.26	2.29	2.22
AR8	a	0.52	0.82	0.92	0.97	1.00	1.08	1.17	1.23								
	b	0.54	0.86	1.00	1.13	1.22	1.35	1.39	1.40								
	d	1.52	2.51	2.72	3.08	3.39	3.65	3.89	4.09								
	d/b	2.81	2.92	2.72	2.73	2.78	2.70	2.80	2.92								

Money supply

MQEM	a	0.74	1.23	1.69	1.96	2.32	2.73	3.01	3.29	0.76	1.28	1.74	1.99	2.29	2.57	2.77	2.89
	b	0.77	1.42	1.97	2.40	2.76	3.07	3.42	3.94	0.83	1.51	2.10	2.67	3.11	3.42	3.87	4.58
	d	1.34	2.07	3.54	4.00	4.84	5.62	6.34	7.46	1.57	4.26	5.68	5.97	5.17	6.54	13.64	29.34
	d/b	1.74	1.46	1.80	1.67	1.75	1.83	1.85	1.89	1.89	2.82	2.70	2.24	1.66	1.91	3.52	6.41
Fair	a	1.04	1.41	1.51	1.62	1.75	1.84	1.95	1.88	0.98	1.35	1.49	1.66	1.82	2.00	2.03	1.98
	b	1.04	1.46	1.65	1.86	2.08	2.18	2.20	2.24	0.95	1.37	1.51	1.77	2.11	2.32	2.38	2.54
	d	1.43	2.23	3.03	3.88	4.78	5.82	7.14	8.30	1.40	1.84	1.88	2.13	2.31	2.39	2.37	1.92
	d/b	1.36	1.53	1.84	2.09	2.30	2.67	3.25	3.71	1.47	1.34	1.25	1.20	1.09	1.03	1.00	0.76
AR8	a	0.57	1.11	1.55	1.95	2.43	2.91	3.42	3.92								
	b	0.57	1.17	1.68	2.33	3.08	3.89	4.83	5.77								
	d	2.10	3.50	4.26	5.27	5.91	7.05	8.85	10.39								
	d/b	3.68	2.99	2.54	2.26	1.92	1.81	1.83	1.80								

Table 7.2 (continued)

Note: a = uncertainty due to error terms,

b = uncertainty due to error terms and coefficient estimates,

d = uncertainty due to error terms, coefficient estimates, and the possible misspecification of the model,

i = the total estimated variance was negative.

There were 250 trials for each stochastic simulation. Errors are in percentage points except for inventory investment, where the errors are in billions of 1972 dollars at an annual rate. Errors for all variables except the unemployment rate, the bill rate, and inventory investment are percents of the forecast means. The exact variables tabled for each model are the following. See Belton, Hymans, and Lown (1981) for the MQEM notation, and see Fair (1984) for the Fair notation. The variables for the autoregressive model are the same as those for the MQEM.

	MQEM	Fair
Consumer expenditures, services	CS72	CS
Consumer expenditures, nondurables	CN72	CN
Consumer expenditures, durables	C72-CS72-CN72	CD
Housing investment	IRC72	IHH
Nonresidential fixed investment	IBF72	IKF
Inventory investment	IINV72	IVF
Imports	M72	IM
Private nonfarm deflator	PPNF	PF
Unemployment rate	RUG	UR
Wage rate	JCMH	WF
Bill rate	RTB	RS
Money supply	M1BPLUS	M1

endogenous variable 27 values of the difference between the estimated forecast-error variance based on outside-sample errors and the estimated forecast-error variance based on stochastic simulation. The average of these 27 values was taken for each variable. In terms of the notation in section 7.2, this average is $\bar{d}_{i1}$, where the i refers to variable i, and the 1 refers to the one-quarter ahead forecast. The total variance of the one-quarter ahead forecast of variable i is $\tilde{\sigma}_{it1}^2 + \bar{d}_{i1}$, which in terms of the notation in section 7.2 is $\hat{\sigma}_{it1}^2$. For the results in Table 7.2, t is 1978.1, and the d-row value for 1978.1 for each variable is the square root of $\hat{\sigma}_{it1}^2$. The calculations for the two-quarter ahead forecasts are the same except that there are only 26 values of the difference between the two estimated variances for each variable. Similarly there are only 25 values for the three-quarter ahead forecast, and so on.

Results for the Fair Model

A procedure similar to that for the MQEM was followed for the Fair model. The version of the model used is the one in Fair (1984). The d-row values for the Fair model are also based on 27 sets of estimates of the equations. The same ending quarters were used here as for the MQEM results.

Results for the Autoregressive Model (AR8)

The MQEM data base was used for the autoregressive model. The estimation periods are the same as those for the MQEM. The model consists of a set of eighth-order autoregressive equations with a constant term and time trend, with one equation per each variable of interest. The equations are completely separate. The same steps were followed for the autoregressive model as were used for the MQEM except that there were 100 rather than 50 trials for each of the 27 sets of stochastic simulations.

Results for the Complete Models

The results for the complete models are presented in the right half of table 7.2. These results are taken from Fair and Alexander (1984). In this earlier study uncertainty from the exogenous variables was also estimated and "c-row" values were presented. These values were estimated standard errors based on draws of the error terms, coefficient estimates, *and* exogenous-variable values. The d-row values were then computed using the c-row values as the base. In the present case there are no c-row values, and the d-row values are computed using the b-row values as the base. Otherwise, the present results are identical to those in the earlier study.

The d/b Ratios

Table 7.2 also contains ratios of the d and b rows. The larger this ratio is for a given variable and length ahead of the forecast, the larger is the mean of the differences between the two estimated variances, $\bar{d}_{ik}$. In the following discussion these ratios will be referred to as measures of the misspecification of the equations or groups of equations. It should be noted, however, that this terminology is not quite right. Misspecification also affects the b-row values, and the ratios of the d and b rows measure the misspecification that is not already reflected in the b-row values. It should be noted that no tests of the hypothesis that the equations are correctly specified are made. It is merely assumed that the hypothesis is false. Given this, the objective is to estimate by how much the equations are misspecified. The estimates of misspecification are the $\bar{d}_{ik}$ values. Standard errors of these estimates are not available because the distribution of $\bar{d}_{ik}$ is not known.

A Note about Computer Work

The Fair-Parke program (1984) was used for all the computations in this chapter. Once a model is set up in the program, all the estimation and stochastic simulation that are needed for the results in table 7.2 can be done with a few commands. The program provides an easy way to debug the setting up of the model, and once this debugging has been done, few other errors are likely to arise.

7.6   Discussion of the Results

It should first be noted that the present results cannot be used to compare the predictive accuracy of the three models because exogenous-variable uncertainty has not been taken into account for the MQEM and Fair models. In other words, the d-row values in table 7.2 cannot be compared across models. The appropriate comparisons were made in Fair and Alexander (1984), which show, among other things, that the MQEM is heavily tied to the use of exogenous variables. What we are interested in here is the size of the d/b values for a given equation and how sensitive these values are to the inclusion of the equation in the complete model.

MQEM

MQEM does extremely well with respect to the private nonfarm deflator, the unemployment rate, the wage rate, and the bill rate. The d/b values for these variables are close to one. One would conclude from these results that the equations are well specified. As noted earlier, however, the equations for the private nonfarm deflator and the unemployment rate are heavily tied to dummy variables, and the equations for the wage rate and the bill rate have questionable explanatory variables. It is not clear how much the present results should be trusted with respect to these equations.

The worst variable for MQEM is nonresidential fixed investment. The d/b values average 3.43 separately and 3.45 when the entire model is used. This suggests that the estimated variances of the error terms and coefficient estimates substantially overestimate the predictive accuracy of the equations. Thus the determination of this variable appears to be highly misspecified.

The results for consumer durable expenditures are not sensible. It sometimes turns out in the successive reestimation and stochastic simulation of the model that some of the stochastic simulation estimates of the variances are much larger than the estimates based on outside-sample errors. This may result in large negative values of $\bar{d}_{ik}$, and these values, when added to the square of the b-row values, can yield negative values of the total variance. What this means is that the sample is not large enough to produce sensible results. This was the case for consumer durable expenditures for MQEM.

The remaining variables for MQEM have d/b values around 2. From this group the best results are for inventory investment. This variable has an average d/b value of 1.62 individually and 1.40 when it is included in the entire model. The worst results from this group are for housing investment. The average d/b values for this variable are 2.40 and 2.23.

In general, the results are not sensitive to the inclusion of the equations in the complete model. There is, however, one important exception. The average d/b value for the money supply increases by 65 percent when the equations are included in the complete model. In Fair and Alexander (1984) the ability of the MQEM to predict the money supply was shown to be much worse than that of either the Fair model or the AR8 model. The current results suggest that not all of the MQEM'S poor performance can be blamed on the specification of the two equations jointly determining the money supply. It appears that specification errors made in determining other endogenous variables substantially worsen the results for the money supply.

Results for the other variables, however, are not sensitive to their inclusion in the complete model. Excluding the money supply results, the average deviation of the individual equation d/b values from the d/b values for the complete model is only 9 percent.

Fair Results

Fair does well or reasonably well for consumer service expenditures, consumer nondurable expenditures, housing investment, nonresidential fixed investment, inventory investment, the unemployment rate, and the wage rate, where the ratios are generally closer to 1 than to 2. The three worst equations are the equations for imports, the private nonfarm deflator, and the money supply. The remaining equations, for consumer durable expenditures and the bill rate, generally have ratios that are closer to 2 than to 1.

The results for the Fair model are generally more sensitive to being included in the entire model than are those for the MQEM. The extreme case is once again the money supply, although in this case the results are better when the equations are included in the complete model. The average d/b value is cut in half when the equations are included in the model. This suggests that errors in predicting other endogenous variables partly offset the errors in the equations determining the money supply.

Even excluding the money supply results, the Fair model results are more sensitive to being included in the model. For example, the average d/b value for consumer expenditures for services increases by 33 percent when that equation is included in the model. Also, the average d/b value for the wage rate decreases by 28 percent when it is included in the model. Excluding the money supply results, the average deviation of the d/b values for the individual equations from the d/b values for the complete model is 21 percent.

The difference in the sensitivity of the results for the two models to whether the equations are included in the complete model is consistent with results reported in Fair and Alexander (1984). These earlier results show that the MQEM is closely tied to exogenous variables—that is, the predictive accuracy of the model is sensitive to alternative corrections for exogenous variable uncertainty. These results and the present results suggest that the Fair model is more "endogenous" than the MQEM.

Autoregressive Results

The autoregressive results are not sensible for nonresidential fixed investment and the unemployment rate (again, a small sample problem). For the remaining variables the autoregressive model does best for consumer nondurable expenditures and inventory investment, where the ratios are closer to 1 than to 2. Otherwise, the ratios are closer to 2. Excluding the results for nonresidential fixed investment and the unemployment rate, the average of the d/b values is 2.14. This suggests that any equation in a structural model that has d/b values above about 2 should be a cause for concern.

Conclusion

The method presented in Fair (1980) is capable of measuring the misspecification of equations. One can glean from the misspecification results in table 7.2 the parts of the models that need the most improvement. One such part for MQEM is clearly the equations for nonresidential fixed investment. Two such parts for the Fair model are the equation for the private nonfarm deflator and the equation for imports. In general, it would seem that any d/b value that is greater than 2 is cause for some concern and more work. There is also some concern for MQEM that the use of dummy variables has given a misleading impression of the quality of some of the equations.

Notes

1. An exception to this is when groups of equations are examined. In these cases all the variables determined within the group are endogenous.

2. We are indebted to Edwin Kuh and Steve Swartz for providing us with a tape of the data. We are also indebted to Joan Crary for answering a number of questions about the model. None of these individuals is accountable for the results in this chapter. We assume responsibility for all errors.

3. As indicated in the note to table 7.2, most of the errors are in units of percent of the forecast mean. See the discussion in chapter 8 of Fair (1984) for the exact way in which the percentage errors are computed.

References

Belton, T., S. H. Hymans, and C. Lown, 1981. The Dynamics of the Michigan Quarterly Econometric Model of the U.S. Economy. Discussion paper R-108.81. Department of Economics, University of Michigan, Ann Arbor, December.

Fair, R. C., 1980. Estimating the Expected Predictive Accuracy of Econometric Models. *International Economic Review* 21 (June): 355–378.

Fair, R. C., 1984. *Specification, Estimation, and Analysis of Macroeconometric Models.* Harvard University Press, Cambridge, Mass.

Fair, R. C., and L. S. Alexander, 1984. A Comparison of the Michigan and Fair Models. Cowles Foundation discussion paper no. 703. New Haven, Conn.

Fair, R. C., and W. R. Parke, 1984. The Fair-Parke Program for the Estimation and Analysis of Nonlinear Econometric Models. Mimeograph. Cowles Foundation, New Haven, Conn.

8 Linear Analysis of Large Nonlinear Models and Model Simplification

Edwin Kuh, John Neese, and Peter Hollinger

8.1 Model and Theory Background

A systems theory that permits a deep understanding of linear dynamic equation models has been well understood for many years and has been a working tool in engineering applications. Yet these ideas have seldom been applied to economic models that are especially hard to understand because of their size and complexity. Thanks to Wilkinson (1965) and the EISPACK code (B. T. Smith et al. 1976), studying the linearized dynamic behavior of large systems has become feasible. Extensions of the basic EISPACK code and theory have been merged with the broad set of modeling utilities in the TROLL econometric modeling system. These are now part of a new TROLL task called LIMO (1984), which overcomes several major barriers to studying sizable (in contrast to toy-sized) nonlinear economic models.

Figure 8.1 schematically describes the familiar econometric setting and some notation as a starting point. We are especially interested in parameter perturbations, even though more commonly used multiplier analysis is valuable for understanding model structure.

Prices Wages and Productivity in MQEM

This chapter reports on some aspects of a more comprehensive study of inflation (Kuh, Neese, and Hollinger 1985). We apply several methods, linear and nonlinear, to the price-wage-productivity sector of the Michigan Quarterly Econometric Model (MQEM).[1] These methods are spelled out more fully in Kuh et al. (1985) where we likewise use linear analysis to understand what does and does not matter in sizable econometric models by exploring in detail one aspect of a serious medium-size econometric model.

The MQEM has 117 equations that are rather evenly divided between definitional and stochastic behavioral equations. As seen in figure 8.2, there is one major private-sector price equation which is driven by unit labor costs (a combination of a lagged annual rate of change in the wage rate with averaged man-hour productivity) and by a measure of economic slack capacity that includes manufacturing and labor-force utilization rates. Exogenously determined crude materials (mainly petroleum) and

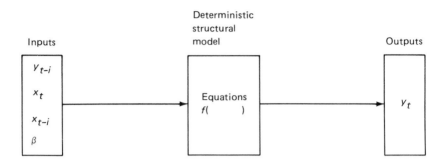

Deterministic structural nonlinear equation model notation: $f(y_t, y_{t-i}, x_t, x_{t-i}, \beta) = 0$,
y = endogenous variable vector, x = exogenous variable vector, β = parameter vector

Analytical approaches

Multiplier Endogenous variable changes in response to exogenous variable changes
(black box)

Parameter perturbation Endogenous variable changes in response to parameter
changes (structural)

Figure 8.1
Economic model terminology

food prices are also arguments in this main price equation. Final demand-
sector prices in turn are driven by this price equation, along with a one-
period (quarter) own-lag and miscellaneous sector-specific variables.

Wages depend on the two-period rate of change of the consumer price
deflator[2] and an average of its preceding six periods' quarterly percent rate
of change, the unemployment rate, and the minimum wage. It is evident
that unit labor costs drive prices. In turn, wages are coupled to prices
through the consumption price deflator. Although the precise configura-
tion of wage-price interaction differs among models, the process described
typifies most macroeconomic models; prices also appear as arguments in
final-demand equations for consumption and as elements of the cost of
capital in investment-demand equations.

Linear Analysis

A linear approximation to the model's nonlinear structural form around
the baseline model solution path is[3]

$$D_t \Delta y_t = E_t \Delta y_{t-1} + F_t \Delta x_t + G_t \Delta \beta, \tag{8.1}$$

where

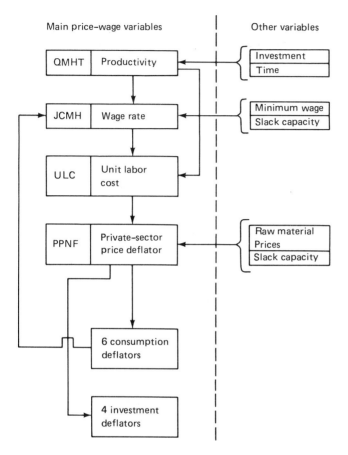

Figure 8.2
Sketch of price-wage structure

$\Delta y_t, \Delta y_{t-1}, \Delta x_t, \Delta\beta$ = vectors of deviations around the baseline solution,

$$D_t(y_t, y_{t-1}, x_t, \beta) \equiv (\partial f/\partial y_t), \tag{8.2}$$

$$E_t(y_t, y_{t-1}, x_t, \beta) \equiv -(\partial f/\partial y_{t-1}), \tag{8.3}$$

$$F_t(y_t, y_{t-1}, x_t, \beta) \equiv -(\partial f/\partial x_t), \tag{8.4}$$

$$G_t(y_t, y_{t-1}, x_t, \beta) \equiv -(\partial f/\partial\beta). \tag{8.5}$$

Although the D, E, F, and G matrices are generally time varying as noted, we will drop the time subscript for now.

Assuming that the square coefficient matrix D is invertible (the usual case in econometric models), we have the reduced-form deviations model:

$$\Delta y_t = D^{-1}E\Delta y_{t-1} + D^{-1}F\Delta x_t + D^{-1}C\Delta\beta, \tag{8.6}$$

$$\Delta y_t = A\Delta y_{t-1} \quad\quad + B\Delta x_t \quad\quad + C\Delta\beta. \tag{8.7}$$

Dynamics

Multipliers

Parameter perturbations

A linearized model's time response is conveniently expressed in terms of its reduced form in equation (8.7). Given initial conditions Δy_{t_0}, and time paths for exogenous variables and coefficient perturbations Δx_s, $\Delta\beta_s$ for $t_0 < s \le t_0 + n$, $(n \ge 1)$, Δy_{t_0+n}, the endogenous variable response at $t_0 + n$, is given by the familiar equation:

$$\Delta y_{t_0+n} = A^n\Delta y_{t_0} + \sum_{s=0}^{n-1} A^s\{B\Delta x_{t_0+n-s} + C\Delta\beta_{t_0+n-s}\}. \tag{8.8}$$

When $\Delta y_{t_0} = 0$ and $\Delta\beta_s = 0$ $(s = t_0, \ldots, t_0 + n)$, we have the familiar formula for standard multiplier analysis.

A more effective way to study a linearized model's dynamic behavior is to reexpress equation (8.8) using characteristic roots and vectors of the dynamics matrix A. These are defined by[4]

$$Ar_g = r_g\lambda_g \ (g = 1, \ldots, G), \tag{8.9}$$

$$l'_gA = \lambda_g l'_g \ (g = 1, \ldots, G), \tag{8.10}$$

where λ_g = a characteristic root of A (a complex-valued scalar),

r_g = the right characteristic vector associated with λ_g,

l_g = the left characteristic vector associated with λ_g.

Equations (8.9) and (8.10) are equivalent to

$$AR = R\Lambda, \tag{8.11}$$

$$L'A = \Lambda L', \tag{8.12}$$

where $\Lambda = $ a $G \times G$ diagonal matrix with the characteristic roots on its diagonal,

$R = $ the $G \times G$ matrix of right characteristic vectors,

$L = $ the $G \times G$ matrix of left characteristic vectors.

We are free to normalize the characteristic vectors so that

$$L'R = RL' = I, \tag{8.13}$$

where I is the $G \times G$ identity matrix.

From equations (8.11) through (8.13) we can express A in terms of its characteristic roots and vectors:

$$A = R\Lambda L' = \sum_{g=1}^{G} r_g \lambda_g l'_g. \tag{8.14}$$

A corresponding expression for powers of the A matrix relates its roots and vectors to the dynamic behavior of the linearized model:

$$A^s = R\Lambda^s L' = \sum_{g=1}^{G} r_g \lambda_g^s l'_g. \tag{8.15}$$

Substituting equation (8.15) into the convolution formula in equation (8.8) yields

$$\Delta y_{t_0+n} = \sum_{g=1}^{G} r_g \left\{ \lambda_g^n l'_g \Delta y_{t_0} + \sum_{s=0}^{n-1} \lambda_g^s l'_g (B\Delta x_{t_0+n-s} + C\Delta \beta_{t_0+n-s}) \right\}. \tag{8.16}$$

Thus for any single root, λ_g, the portion of endogenous variable response associated with λ_g is

$$(\Delta y_{t_0+n} | \lambda_g) = r_g \left\{ \lambda_g^n l'_g \Delta y_{t_0} + \sum_{s=0}^{n-1} \lambda_g^s l'_g (B\Delta x_{t_0+n-s} + C\Delta \beta_{t_0+n-s}) \right\}. \tag{8.17}$$

When the response of a particular endogenous variable associated with a given root is large, we have isolated an association that warrants further scrutiny, and we will want to know its origin in the model structure:

$$\Delta \lambda_g \cong \sum_{i=1}^{G} \sum_{j=1}^{G} \frac{\partial \lambda_g}{\partial a_{ij}} \Delta a_{ij}, \tag{8.18}$$

$$\lambda_g = \sum_{i=1}^{G} \sum_{j=1}^{G} \frac{\partial \lambda_g}{\partial a_{ij}} a_{ij}. \tag{8.19}$$

If the partial derivative notation of (8.19) is replaced by Δ for purely didactic purposes, each individual relative contribution can be thought of as $\Delta\lambda_g/(\Delta a_{ij}/a_{ij})$, that is, the change in λ_g associated with a (small) percent change in the coefficient a_{ij}. It follows immediately that the elasticities $(\partial\lambda_g/\partial a_{ij})\cdot(a_{ij}/\lambda_g)$ sum to unity over i and j, which offers another interesting normalization.

Although in principle all variables might affect each other (sometimes with delays), in practice econometric model coefficient matrices tend to be sparse and sometimes are approximately block triangular. Either or both properties can readily lead to simplified structures. Furthermore, dynamics are usually straightforward—that is, most "own" dynamics are first-order or Koyck lags. Because of the foregoing and the relatively mild nonlinearity of the current model, we propose to use linear analysis to discover the main elements of the inflationary structure in MQEM. We shall see how much of this information is obtainable by using parameter perturbations to locate the major coefficients that strongly influence the central PPNF equation.

The procedure adopted here is schematized in figure 8.3. It suggests how to utilize linear-systems analysis to understand the essential elements of macromodels that are not strongly nonlinear, a condition that is certainly true for MQEM and many others. In a more extended treatment one should validate inferences made from the linear analysis by comparing full model nonlinear simulations with partial nonlinear simulations in which the least influential parameter/variable combinations are neutralized.

First, the MQEM model is linearized. The parameters are then numerically evaluated in 1973.2, a quarter which occurs shortly after the beginning of food price escalation and immediately prior to the first oil price shock. To avoid unusual short-term variable fluctuations influencing the linearized coefficients, exogenous variables were given trend values which in turn caused endogenous variables to have smooth time paths. Second, the model is put into state-variable form (see equations 8.1 and 8.6). Third, the characteristic root/vector decomposition is calculated with LIMO using methods that diminish numerical difficulties with vector computations when there are multiple roots. As a practical matter these most often occur when there are zero or near-zero roots, so that vectors associated with small (less than 0.30) roots are not calculated. Fourth, linear parameter perturbations in all equations and their partial-root decompositions (see equations 8:16 and 8.17) for PPNF are calculated. Fifth, these results reveal

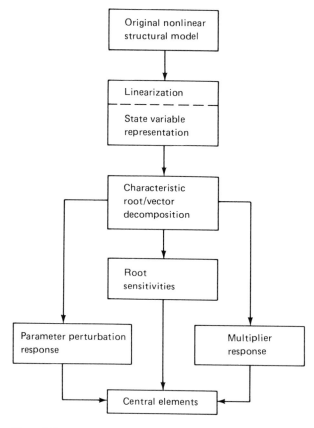

Figure 8.3
Steps in analysis

quantitatively those equations and coefficients that dominate inflation dynamics in the MQEM, thus achieving a principal objective of this chapter.

When the time differences in (8.7) are infinitesimal, we can write it as

$$dy_t = Ady_{t-1} + Bdx_{t-1} + Cd\beta. \tag{8.20}$$

Given an infinitesimal perturbation in a single parameter β_j at time $t_0 + 1$, an initial condition for y_{t_0} together with (8.20) indicates that

$$\frac{dy_t}{d\beta_j} = \begin{cases} 0, & \text{for } t = t_0, \\ A_t(dy_{t-1}/d\beta_j) + (C)_{.j}, & \text{for } t \geq t_0 + 1, \end{cases} \tag{8.21}$$

where $(C)_{\cdot j}$ denotes the jth column of C and where it is assumed that the initial condition y_{t_0} and the exogenous variable time paths x_t are independent of the parameters.

The elasticity of y_g with respect to β_j is derived from equation (8.21) as

$$\eta(y_g, \beta_j)_t \equiv \frac{dy_{gt}}{d\beta_j} \frac{\beta_j}{y_{gt}} = \begin{cases} 0, & \text{for } t = t_0, & (8.22a) \\ (A)_{g\cdot}(dy_{t-1}/d\beta_j)(\beta_j/y_{gt}) + c_{gj}(\beta_j/y_{gt}), & (8.22b) \end{cases}$$

for $t > t_0 + 1$ where $(A)_{g\cdot}$ denotes the gth row of A and where c_{gj} denotes the (g,j)th entry of C. Moreover, since

$$\frac{dy_{i,t-1}}{d\beta_j}\left(\frac{\beta_j}{y_{gt}}\right) \equiv \frac{y_{i,t-1}}{y_{gt}}\eta(y_i, \beta_j)_{t-1}, \tag{8.23}$$

the first term on the right-hand side of equation (8.22b) can be expressed in terms of previous-period elasticities. Consequently equation (8.22) can be rewritten as

$$\eta(y_g, \beta_j)_t = \begin{cases} 0, & \text{for } t = t_0, & (8.24a) \\ \sum_{i=1}^{G}(a_{gi}y_{i,t-1}/y_{gt})\eta(y_i, \beta_j)_{t-1} + c_{gj}\beta_j/y_{gt}, & \text{for } t > t_0 + 1 \\ & (8.24b) \end{cases}$$

where a_{gi} is the (g, i)th entry of A and there are G state variables $g = 1, \ldots, G$.

In the general parameter perturbation case, an elasticity has a useful "shares" interpretation. The general $\eta(y_g, \beta_j)$'s homogeneous dynamics depend on the previous-period elasticity of each endogenous variable in a proportion which is a *first-order approximation* to that variable's share in determining y_{gt}—that is, $(a_{gi}y_{i,t-1}/y_{gt})$. Likewise its forcing function is a first-order approximation to β_j's share in determining y_{gt}—that is, $(c_{gj}\beta_j/y_{gt})$.

8.2   Empirical Results of Parameter Perturbations

As a convenient way to summarize parameter perturbation, we shall initially describe major results in two categories. The first includes elasticity responses to an impulse perturbation in an equation's autoregressive terms. These are often quite powerful. Second, we describe large endogenous responses for the remaining coefficient perturbations. In each row of table 8.2, equations are designated in the first column by the endogenous variable

Table 8.1
Symbols and definitions of a subset of MQEM endogenous variables

MQEM equation[a]	symbol	Behavior equation
A. Wages and prices		
A1	JCMH	Compensation per man-hour, business nonfarm sector, 1977 = 100
A6	PCN	Deflator for nondurable consumption, 1972 = 100
A7	PCS	Deflator for consumption of services, 1972 = 100
A11	PG	Deflator for total government purchases of goods and services, 1972 = 100
A9	PINC	Deflator for business fixed investment, nonresidential structures, 1972 = 100
A2	PPNF	Deflator for business nonfarm GNP, 1972 = 100
		Identities
	DLJCMH[b]	Logarithmic growth rate of JCMH
	DLPPNF[b]	Logarithmic growth rate of PPNF
B. Productivity and employment		
B1	QMH77	Index of output per hour of all persons, business nonfarm sector, 1977 = 100
		Identities
	DLQMH77[b]	Logarithmic growth rate of QMH77
C. Consumption and investment		
C1	AUTOS[c]	Units of new auto retail sales
C3	CDAO72[c]	Other auto consumption expenditures, 1972 $
C4	CDFE72	Consumption of furniture and household equipment, 1972 $
C5	CDO72	Consumption of other durables, 1972 $
C6	CN72	Consumption of nondurables, 1972 $
C7	CS72	Consumption of services, 1972 $
C9	IBFNC72	Nonresidential investment, structures, 1972 $
C10	IINV72	Inventory investment, 1972 $
C14	IPDO72	Real nonresidential investment, producers' durables, other, 1972 $
C19	IPDQ72	Real nonresidential investment, producers' durables, production, 1972 $
C11	IRC72	Residential fixed investment, 1972 $

Table 8.1 (continued)

MQEM equation[a]	symbol	Behavior equation
C13	M72	Imports, 1972 $
		Identities
	C72	Personal consumption expenditures, 1972 $
	FS72	Final sales, 1972 $
	FSMF72	Final sales of manufactured goods, 1972 $
	FSNMF72	Final sales of nonmanufactured goods, 1972 $
	GNP72	Gross national product, 1972 $
	GNPAVEQ	Six-quarter moving average of GNP72
	SINV72	Real business inventories = (4 × current stock)
D. Income flows		
D7	YPDIV	Corporate dividend payments
D1	YPWS	Private wages and salaries
		Identities
	YD72	Disposable personal income = YD/(PC/100), 1972 $
E. Monetary sector		
E16	M1BPLUS	M1B plus savings accounts (measured as ratio of M2PLUS)
E1	M2PLUS	M2 plus short-term Treasury securities (not held by money market mutual funds)
E11	RAAA	Corporate AAA bond interest rate, long-term private sector rate
E15	RCD	Ninety-day certificate of deposit rate, market yield
E2	RTB	Ninety-day Treasury bill rate
F. Output composition		
F3	JCAP	Index of available capacity in manufacturing
F2	JIPM	Federal Reserve index of industrial production in manufacturing, 1967 = 100
F1	SERVE72	Services component of GNP, 1972 $
Exogenous variables		
	MBASE	Inclusive monetary base
	RDIS	Discount rate, Federal Reserve Bank of New York

Table 8.1 (continued)

Note: Unless otherwise noted, national income account flow variables are at annual rates, measured in billions of current dollars and seasonally adjusted. All interest rates are measured as percent per annum. Symbols are listed alphabetically, so that MQEM Equation numbers (column one) are not in numerical order.

a. Coefficient symbols within a given equation that first appear here follow the equation number, e.g., A1.1, A1.2, ... , etc.

b. These definitions were computed as $\log z_t = \ln z_t - \ln z_{t-1}$, where $\ln z_t - \ln z_{t-1} = \ln(z_t/z_t - 1) \cong (z_t - z_{t-1})/z_{t-1}$. Inclusion of these variables allows us to examine model response in terms of growth rates by key endogenous variables.

c. Estimated with first-order autoregressive correction.

in whose equation the perturbed coefficient appears, in the second column by the coefficient symbol, and in the third column by the coefficient's variable for which a coefficient is being perturbed. The variable names and definitions appear in table 8.1.

The parameters are perturbed by 1 percent shifts. To help focus our attention on the most important reactions, only those responses with elasticities in excess of 0.10 are reported, a cutoff that is considered conservative. Results for periods 1 to 8, 12, 16, and 24 are given. We have normalized variables to have a unit impact elasticity by using the construct $z_t = \Delta \ln p_t$ so that, for example, the price variable appears as $\Delta \ln$ PPNF. Since inflation, not price levels, are of principal interest, this change of variables seems the correct way to describe results.

Among the own-dynamics parameter-perturbation responses for $\Delta \ln$ PPNF, the preponderance of large ones is associated with perturbations in final demand: five consumption sectors, four investment sectors, and the import sector. Parameters in manufacturing production and capacity also matter, as do four monetary variables: RTB, RAAA, RCD, and M1BPLUS/M2PLUS. These comments are based on table 8.2

Impact elasticities are plausibly small and reach a peak eight quarters later. Consumption effects have largely attenuated after period 12. Investment in plant and manufacturing capacity (capital stock) reaches a maximum around period 8, and RAAA effects attain a maximum in period 12. The M1BPLUS/M2PLUS term in the M1BPLUS equation peaks in period 16. Some effects persist into period 24. The $\Delta \ln$ PPNF begins to respond first to final demand and subsequently to investment and monetary variables. Enough impulse responses remain strong for long periods to lend credence to the concept of borderline inflationary instability.

Table 8.2
Parameter perturbation elasticity responses of $\Delta \ln \mathrm{PPNF}$

Equation elements			Period										
Left-hand side	Coefficient	Right-hand side variable	1	2	3	4	5	6	7	8	12	16	24
QMH77	B1.0	INTERCEPT							0.11	0.16	0.24	0.22	0.17
QMH77	B1.4(−2)	NONAGR. INVEST(−2)				−0.11	−0.16		−0.14	−0.15	−0.16		
QMH77	B1.4(−3)	NONAGR. INVEST(−3)				−0.11	−0.16	−0.13	−0.22	−0.24	−0.16		
QMH77	B1.4(−4)	NONAGR. INVEST(−4)						−0.22	−0.23	−0.24			
QMH77	B1.4(−5)	NONAGR. INVEST(−5)						−0.22	−0.13	−0.14			
QMH77	B1.7	NONAGR. INVEST : average					0.29	−0.13	−0.13	−0.13	−0.19	−0.17	−0.14
JCMH	A1.0	INTERCEPT		0.27	0.27	0.27							
PPNF	A2.0	INTERCEPT	−0.68										
PPNF	A2.5	JIPM/JCAP : weighted average	0.82										
PPNF	A2.6	JCMH—QMH77 rate of change	0.83										
M72	C13.0	INTERCEPT				0.21	0.38	0.83	1.46	1.76	0.78		−0.10
M72	C13.1	LOG(GNP72)			−0.10	−0.33	−0.60	−1.31	−2.32	−2.80	−1.25	−0.12	0.16
M72	C13.3	LOG(M72(−1))			−0.10	−0.33	−0.60	−1.31	−2.32	−2.79	−1.25	−0.28	0.16
JCAP	F3.0	INTERCEPT						−0.21	−0.28	−0.28	−0.30	−0.28	−0.21
JCAP	F3.3	NONRES. INVEST						−0.14	−0.19	−0.19	−0.20	−0.19	−0.14
JCAP	F3.4	CAPACITY * NONRES. INVEST							−0.11	−0.11	−0.12	−0.11	
JCAP	F3.5	LOG(JCAP(−1))					0.11	0.38	0.52	0.52	0.55	0.52	0.39
JIPM	F2.0	INTERCEPT						−0.40	−0.37	−0.17			
JIPM	F2.1	FSMF72			0.15	0.22	0.26	1.30	1.22	0.57	0.20		
JIPM	F2.5	JIPM(−1)			0.17	0.24	0.28	1.39	1.30	0.61	0.21		
JIPM	F2.6	CN72				0.14	0.16	0.80	0.74	0.35	0.12		
JIPM	F2.7	FSNMF72						0.11	0.10	0.10	0.15		
CDO72	C5.4	CDO72(−1)						0.11	0.17	0.20	0.15		
CDFE72	C4.6	CDFE72(−1)					0.12	0.29	0.45	0.52	0.46	0.30	0.11
CN72	C6.0	INTERCEPT					0.12	0.29	0.47	0.53	0.24		
CN72	C6.2	YD72(−1)					0.11	0.27	0.44	0.50	0.22		
CN72	C6.3	PCN(−1)/PC(−1)						−0.21	−0.35	−0.39	−0.17		
CN72	C6.5	CN72(−1)				0.26	0.47	1.10	1.79	2.03	0.90		−0.16
CDAO72	C3.6	CDAO72(−1)						0.10	0.15	0.17	0.10		
AUTOS	C1.2	AUTOS(−1)						0.12	0.19	0.19			
IBFNC72	C9.4	IBFNC72						0.22	0.34	0.38		−0.41	−0.49
IINV72	C10.1	FS72(−1)—SERVE72(−1)			0.10	0.16	0.18	0.71	0.66	0.21	−0.17	−0.12	

IINV72	C10.2	SINV72(−1)	−0.13							
IRC72	C11.5	IRC72(−1)		−0.15	−0.58	−0.54	−0.17	0.14	0.17	
IRC72	C11.6	IRC72(−2)		0.17	0.40	0.67	0.82	0.55		
IPDO72	C14.1	IPDO72			0.25	−0.15	−0.18	−0.12	−0.14	
IPDO72	C14.4	DEPR.—INV. TAX CREDIT			0.14	0.37	0.36			
IPDO72	C19.1	IPDO72(−1)				0.20	0.20			
IPDO72	C19.2	GNPAVEQ(−2)		0.14	0.34	0.49	0.44	−0.22	−0.44	−0.26
IPDO72	C19.3	GNPAVEQ(−3)		−0.13	−0.31	−0.45	−0.40	0.20	0.40	0.24
M1BPLUS	E16.1	M1BPLUS(−1)/M2PLUS(−1)				−0.17	−0.17	−0.78	−1.03	−0.58
M1BPLUS	E16.2	M1BPLUS(−2)/M2PLUS(−2)						0.16	0.22	0.12
RTB	E2.0	INTERCEPT				0.11	0.11	0.20		
RTB	E2.4	LOG(RDIS)				−0.11	−0.21	−0.40		0.12
RTB	E2.5	LOG(RDIS(−1))					0.11	0.22		
RTB	E2.6	LOG(MBASE)				0.12	0.22	0.42	0.10	−0.13
RTB	E2.7	LOG(M1BPLUS)				−0.17	−0.31	−0.60	−0.15	0.19
RTB	E2.8	LOG(RTB(−1))						−0.11		
RCD	E15.1	RTB					−0.14	−0.24	−0.10	
RCD	E15.8	RCD(−1)						−0.12		
RAAA	E11.8	RAAA(−1)					0.19	0.55	0.55	0.28
RAAA	E11.7	PPNF/PPNF(−2)					0.10	0.30	0.30	0.15
RAAA	E11.2	RTB(−1)						−0.12	−0.12	
RAAA	E11.1	RTB						0.12	0.12	
RAAA	E11.0	INTERCEPT						−0.29	−0.29	
YPDIV	D7.2	YPDIV(−1)						0.13		−0.14

Notably missing from the own dynamics, but present in coefficients of other right-hand side variables, are two equations that one might expect to affect PPNF—wage rate (JCMH) and productivity (QMH77). The JCMH intercept A1.0 shows up in period 2 but vanishes after period 5. An investment term B1.4 in QMH77 has moderate consequences through period 12 that decline afterwards. Many lagged investment terms appear in periods 6 to 12. However, the largest elasticities are elsewhere, principally in final demand for imports (M72), nondurable demand (CN72), and the index of industrial production for manufacturing (JIPM). Lags for a money demand (M1BPLUS) component and money supply (RTB) are relatively strong in period 12 and afterwards.

The dominant right-hand side variables are final demand variables, such as GNP72, disposable personal income, and final sales in the nonmonetary sectors. Intercepts appear several times. In the monetary sector a M1BPLUS to RTB effect as well as RDIS and MBASE influences appear relevant.

Thus we have arrived at an economically consistent picture of how parameter perturbations reveal the links between model structure and inflation. Starting with wages in the short run, the medium-term emphasis then shifts to GNP components, especially imports and consumption demand. Finally, in the longer run $\Delta \ln$ PPNF responds mainly to monetary and investment variables. Although the coefficients of the autoregressive terms from other equations tend to dominate responses, other coefficients also count, mainly aggregate output (sometimes averaged) and intercepts.

Attention now shifts to characteristic roots, of which table 8.3 is a summary. Nearly 40 percent of the magnitudes (counting each complex pair as a single entity) exceed 0.90, a fact that is consistent with sluggish dynamics or, mildly explosive ones at times. Most imaginary roots—which are particularly relevant for price dynamics—are concentrated in the medium-size to swiftly responding (smaller) roots.

"Partial characteristic root decompositions," described algebraically by equation (8.17), will now be used to decompose each period's parameter response into weights (entries from the C matrix), characteristic roots, and coefficient changes. The last are single, initial period 1 percent perturbations. By summing across all the coefficient perturbation responses of all $\Delta \ln$ PPNF responses for one root in a given period, we obtain the *net* impact of that characteristic root-period outcome for the variable in ques-

Table 8.3
MQEM characteristic roots for A matrix

Root magnitude	Total	Real	Imaginary pairs
1.01–1.036	10	10	0
0.99–1.01	24	24	0
0.90–0.99	7	6	1
0.80–0.89	4	3	1
0.70–0.79	8	4	4
0.60–0.69	13	1	12
0.50–0.59	13	3	10
0.40–0.49	9	7	2
0.30–0.39	5	3	2
0.20–0.29	6	6	0
0.10–0.19	3	2	1
	102	69	33

tion. This amounts to reporting the net effect of components of equation (8.17) by individual roots (with $\Delta x_t \equiv 0$).

Table 8.4 contains 34 net root responses for $\Delta \ln PPNF$ which exceeded the 0.10 cutoff. This cutoff captures one-third of the root total, which should be adequate to give a fair picture of what is happening. These have been tabulated from the largest to smallest root magnitudes. As algebraic logic dictates (barring exceptional C matrix elements), small roots matter only in the short run. Thus of the 20 smaller imaginary roots (ones with magnitude less than 0.70) 19 had only nominal influence beyond the four period. Some root magnitudes between 0.70 and 0.80 exceeded the cutoff through period 12. Roots in excess of 0.80 often showed up strongly through periods 16 or 24. Pronounced long-term effects are concentrated in the large real roots with the exception of imaginary root 45. Borderline explosive characteristic roots 32 and 33 matter a great deal to $\Delta \ln PPNF$ in period 24 (although they have partially offsetting effects), and real root 36 is associated with borderline instability and has a 0.96 magnitude. Note that the largest 31 roots are absent. Of more relevance for our purposes, only a small subset really matters.

Since root 36 shows up most strongly in the net root elasticity computations, we will look more closely at its elasticities with respect to linearized coefficients (see equation 8.18 and related text).

The root elasticities for the real part of this complex root, shown at the top of table 8.5, are most influenced by price dynamics for PCN, PCS, PG,

Table 8.4
Partial elasticity parameter perturbation-root response of $\Delta \ln$ PPNF: filter 0.10, 1 percent initial impulse

Root information			Partial parameter responses					
Root index	Root magnitude	Imaginary component	Period 2	Period 4	Period 8	Period 12	Period 16	Period 24
32	1.00	—	−0.75	−0.73	−0.68	−0.61	−0.54	−0.42
33	1.00	—	1.33	1.29	1.20	1.07	0.94	0.72
36	0.96	0.05	3.18	2.09	0.41	−0.64	−1.17	−1.32
37	0.94	—	0.13	0.12	—	—	—	—
38	0.93	—	0.98	0.83	0.58	0.40	0.26	0.12
39	0.91	—	−0.95	−0.78	−0.51	−0.33	−0.20	—
42	0.88	—	−1.08	−0.82	−0.47	−0.26	−0.14	—
45	0.79	0.28	−5.77	−1.80	1.12	0.33	−0.11	—
46	0.78	—	0.22	0.13	—	—	—	—
47	0.77	0.11	4.20	2.86	0.98	0.22	—	—
48	0.77	—	0.88	0.50	0.16	—	—	—
50	0.74	0.01	−5.53	−2.92	−0.80	−0.21	—	—
51	0.71	—	0.92	0.45	0.11	—	—	—
52	0.71	0.43	−2.93	0.47	—	—	—	—
53	0.69	0.35	0.19	0.12	—	—	—	—
54	0.69	0.60	4.89	−1.96	0.51	—	—	—
55	0.69	—	−0.12	—	—	—	—	—
56	0.66	0.50	−2.08	−1.00	0.11	—	—	—
57	0.65	0.01	2.05	0.86	0.15	—	—	—
58	0.64	0.63	1.55	−0.63	—	—	—	—
59	0.63	0.52	−0.58	0.27	—	—	—	—
61	0.63	0.19	1.40	0.45	—	—	—	—

62	0.62	0.60	−2.78	0.78	—	—	—	—
63	0.61	0.58	0.26	—	—	—	—	—
64	0.61	0.23	0.44	−0.31	—	—	—	—
65	0.60	0.55	0.51	0.30	−0.11	—	—	—
66	0.60	0.43	−1.31	0.90	—	—	—	—
67	0.60	0.32	1.22	0.48	—	—	—	—
68	0.60	—	0.82	0.29	—	—	—	—
69	0.59	0.48	0.54	−0.73	—	—	—	—
70	0.59	0.59	—	−0.13	—	—	—	—
71	0.58	0.11	−1.23	−0.29	—	—	—	—
72	0.58	0.57	0.29	—	—	—	—	—
73	0.57	0.44	−0.64	—	—	—	—	—

Table 8.5
Sensitivity of root 36 with respect to the A matrix

Modulus root 36

	CS72(−1)	JCAP(−1)	M1BPLUS(−1)	PCN(−1)	PCS(−1)	PG(−1)	PINC(−1)	YPWS(−1)	PCS(−2)	Sum
CS72	0.140	—	—	—	—	—	—	—	—	0.133
JCAP	—	0.346	—	—	—	—	—	—	—	0.335
M1BPLUS	—	—	0.176	—	—	—	—	—	—	0.135
PCN	—	—	—	0.125	—	—	—	—	—	0.127
PCS	—	—	—	—	−0.381	—	—	—	0.145	−0.204
PG	—	—	—	—	—	0.303	—	—	—	0.298
PINC	—	—	—	—	—	—	0.260	—	—	0.200
YPWS	—	—	—	—	—	—	—	−0.282	—	−0.260
PCS(−1)	—	—	—	—	0.129	—	—	—	—	0.129
Sum	0.133	0.335	0.135	0.127	−0.204	0.298	0.200	−0.260	0.129	—

Period root 36

	JCMH(−1)	PC(−1)	PCN(−1)	PCS(−1)	JCMH(−2)	JCMH(−3)	JCMH(−4)	PCS(−2)	Sum
JCMH	19.483	—	—	—	—	—	—	—	18.424
PCN	—	—	10.921	24.843	—	—	—	—	8.804
PCS	—	—	—	24.843	—	—	—	−7.866	16.587
JCMH(−1)	−5.332	—	—	—	—	—	—	—	−5.332
JCMH(−2)	—	—	—	—	−4.821	—	—	—	−4.821
JCMH(−3)	—	—	—	—	—	−4.821	—	—	−4.821
JCMH(−4)	—	—	—	—	—	—	−4.838	—	−4.838
PC(−1)	—	−4.625	—	—	—	—	—	—	−4.625
PCS(−1)	—	—	—	−7.703	—	—	—	−7.703	−7.703
Sum	18.424	−1.735	8.804	16.587	−5.332	−4.821	−4.821	−7.703	—

and PINC. Real final demand of consumption services, CS72, manufacturing capital stock JCAP, and money supply M1BPLUS also enter. A characteristic of MQEM is that prices and the real sector interact quite strongly. On the other hand, the imaginary root sensitivities in the lower part of table 8.5 are dominated by the wage rate JCMH, its lags, and two final consumption prices PCN and PCS. So this powerful imaginary root is dominated by wages and prices, with some influence evident from the real and monetary sectors.

8.3   A Compressed Model

We summarize the diverse elements presented here by using information about influential parameters and equations to construct a smaller macro-model derived from MQEM. This is intended to make understanding price, wage, and productivity behavior easier and, where practical, other economic sectors as well. First, the process of moving from MQEM to its reduced version, MINI 1, is explained. MINI 1's equations and coefficients were mainly selected according to influential parameters. Simulation comparisons with common inputs are the main way to corroborate how effectively linear-systems methods pick out accurate (relative to MQEM) compressed models.

Model Reduction Process

Static Identity Removal   As one preliminary, we eliminated seven particularly simple, uninteresting static identities. Forty-nine identities remain along with the original 61 behavioral equations, so this nominally altered version of the complete MQEM has 110 equations.

Model Reduction   Table 8.6 records the final results of equation reduction for MINI 1: half the behavioral equations remain along with a third of the identities. The last third of table 8.6 shows in relative terms where changes occurred. Most of the behavior equations in consumption and investment remain whereas most of the income sector behavior equations vanish. Half of the fourteen wage-price behavior equations were eliminated, as were six of seven price-wage identities. Finally, five of the eleven monetary equations stay while all six identities are dropped. The broad impression is that relative to our objectives, the reduced version of MQEM is a model driven by final demand with a condensed monetary sector and, for the analysis of inflation of course, the central price-wage-productivity elements.

Table 8.6
MQEM equations remaining in MINI 1

Sector	MQEM			MINI 1			Equation percent remaining in MINI 1		
	Behavior	Identity	Total	Behavior	Identity	Total	Behavior	Identity	Total
Wages & prices	14	7	21	7	1	8	50%	14%	38%
Productivity and employment	3	3	6	1	2	3	33%	66%	50%
Consumption and investment	15	19	34	14	8	22	93%	42%	65%
Income flows	15	14	29	2	5	7	13%	35%	24%
Monetary	11	6	17	5	0	5	45%	0	29%
Output composition	3	2	3	3	0	3	100%	—	100%
Total	61	49	110	32	16	48	52%	33%	44%

We next describe the process of creating MINI 1. First, "primary" equations—PPNF, JCMH, and QMH77—were kept intact. It might be argued that all equations in the model should be treated the same and that, by leaving the three equations unchanged, we are biasing the results in our favor. But, since the model MQEM and its condensed version are a set of simultaneous dynamic equations, simultaneous interaction of the wage-price-productivity sector can significantly modify behavior. If the model is only weakly coupled and cross-equation dynamics are weak, then the compressed model results are bound to be close to the full model. This still serves our purpose, which is to arrive at a compressed model that closely mimics the responses of the original large model. Second, other equations and/or parameters were retained that had a sensitivity elasticity for parameter perturbations or multipliers exceeding 0.10 in at least one of the three central equations: price, wage, or productivity. The responses for prices (PPNF) are in table 8.2. The equations for which such variables appeared on the left-hand side were retained, although coefficients were eliminated (barring minor exceptions) if they dropped below the standard 0.10 minimum elasticity for one of the three central equations.

The exceptions mentioned parenthetically mainly occur where equations are needed to complete the model. Indirect links between an influential coefficient and variables (ones that satisfied the 0.10 elasticity criterion or appeared in one of three basic equations) include two productivity variables, QHT1 and a smoothed version of it, QMHT, which appears in the PPNF equation. These in turn are derived from the behavioral equation QMH77, which exerts strong influences on $\Delta \ln$ PPNF. Other direct links were needed to complete an investment equation, and total constant dollar consumption (C72) was needed to satisfy the definition of GNP72 with UCKPDQ remaining to complete the definition of UCAVEQ.

Several otherwise uninfluential variables were also retained for completeness. To construct YD72, PC (which originally was made up of all consumption price indexes, half of which were eliminated) was necessary to deflate YD to obtain YD72, and PC is also part of the JCMH equation. In this and similar instances we propose a simple mechanical rule to create the missing variable. Thus PC was defined to be a weighted average of PCS and PCN, which are the main consumption price equations that remain in the reduced model.[5] So in these instances "pseudobehavioral" relations replace the original relation for uninfluential variables.

Table 8.7
Percent of variables and coefficients retained in MINI 1 relative to MQEM

Sector	Variables	Coefficients
Wages and prices	38	51
Productivity and employment	59	29
Consumption and investment	59	67
Income flows	18	15
Monetary	29	49
Output composition	65	69
Total	40	50

Table 8.7 contains the percent of remaining variables and the percent of remaining coefficients in MINI 1 compared with MQEM, offering much the same impression as table 8.6. Final demand—consumption and investment—is the largest sector, reinforcing the impression that MQEM remains substantially what it started out to be two decades ago, a final demand model. The monetary sector loses a high proportion of variables, but the retained equations are lengthy so that the coefficient proportion drops much less.

At this stage it is impressive that so few equations matter for inflation behavior even when we apply what seems to be a conservative criterion for a one-tenth or more elasticity response in at least one period and do not eliminate other relations for reasons of model completeness. For the central inflation relations, half the behavior equations and two-thirds of the definitions are redundant. The uneven distribution of the remainder—some price and monetary equations and most of final demand—already conveys much information about the full model's structure. Other facets of MQEM, especially how influential dynamic responses migrate from sector to sector as the time span lengthens, were described earlier.

Comparative Model Behavior

The comparison between MQEM and its MINI 1 counterpart will be over the period 1973-2 to 1980-4. Graphic comparisons are the basis for judging visually whether or not divergences are large. Simulations for these comparisons use common inputs (exogenous variables, initial conditions) based on smoothed inputs that earlier generated the smoothed outputs of the MQEM prior to linearization. Their merit for purposes of comparison has a comparable rationale, namely that transitory variations of inputs will not obscure normal model behavior. We will concentrate on time plots of eight major variables: $\Delta\ln PPNF$, $\Delta\ln JCMH$, $\Delta\ln QMH77$, and RTB, GNP72, C72, IBFNC72, and IINV72.

If the original and reduced model time paths are close, we can consider that the information contained in the linear procedures has been corroborated. More concretely, if price-wage-productivity behavior in both original and reduced versions has small discrepancies, our methods have served their main purpose. If, in addition, other important variables also have small deviations, a second objective has been achieved, which is to arrive at a reduced model with acceptable behavior (judged relative to the original model).

The graphs in figure 8.4 for the selected eight variables show highly similar movements and levels so that the "corroborative" evaluation is favorable. MINI 1 tracks the full MQEM especially closely for $\Delta\ln PPNF$ and $\Delta\ln QMH77$ throughout the twenty-four quarters and does only slightly worse with $\Delta\ln JCMH$. Major macroeconomic aggregates GNP72, C72, and IINV72 track well. RTB also shows similar movements in both versions since at their worst, discrepancies are only thirty basis points. IBFNC72 alone shows a rapidly growing divergence between the two models, but even for it, the first ten to twelve quarters appear reasonably close. Since MINI 1 paths are generally so close to MQEM, we have confirmed that the excluded equations and coefficients were unimportant in this context.

8.4 Summary

Our main goal is to understand the most important elements of a medium-size macromodel: this led us to study the inflationary behavior of the Michigan Quarterly Econometric Model of the United States using linear systems analysis methods.[6] Where an earlier study with similar methodological intent used nonlinear parameter perturbations (Kuh and Neese 1982) with some quite useful results, the additional insights obtainable from characteristic roots and vectors seem definitely worthwhile. In this case, since the MQEM is not highly nonlinear (see Kuh, Neese, and Hollinger 1985), such methods are applicable. In a more nonlinear setting more frequent linearization and evaluation would be required than in the

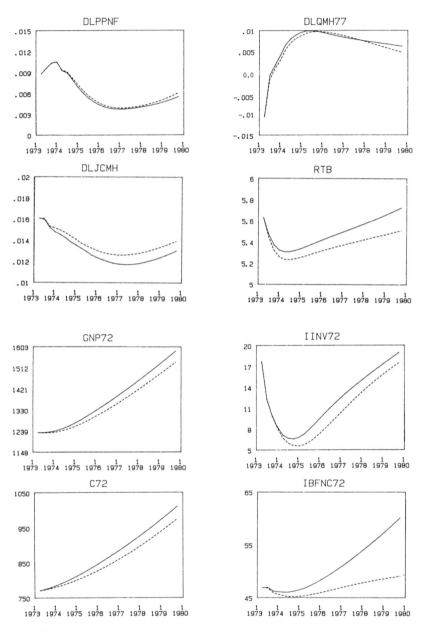

Figure 8.4
Time paths of MQEM and MINI 1 endogenous variables: smooth inputs (solid line for
MQEM variables and dashed line for MINI 1 variables)

present instance, and of course some models could be so intrinsically non-linear that the methods used here would be useless. In a nutshell, we found that for our goal of analyzing the wage-price-productivity sectors of the MQEM, half the original model could be eliminated through the use of linear-systems methods. Interestingly the remaining condensed model tracked the full MQEM well, not only for this one sector, but for most other sectors as well.

The condensed model, "what really counts," comprises the wage, price, and productivity equations, much of final-demand sector, and a stripped-down monetary sector. We also found that various sectors affected price dynamics at different times: wages in the short run, consumer final demand in the middle term, and investment and monetary variables in the longer run. This would have been hard, if not impossible, to establish in the absence of linear-systems analysis. It would also have been difficult or impossible to trace the source equations and parameters of inflation dynamics had we not had access to linear-systems methods.

Notes

Valuable assistance has been provided us especially by Karen Martel, David Gay, Steve O'Connell, Sean Doyle, Martin Shell, and Micky DuPree in various indispensible ways. An earlier version of this chapter was presented to the IFAC/IFORS Conference, Linear Analysis of Large Nonlinear Models and Model Simplification, in Washington, D.C., and appears in *4th IFAC/IFORS/IIASA Conference on the Modeling and Control of National Economies*, McGregor & Werner, Inc., June 1983.

1. We appreciate the willingness and help of Saul Hymans and Philip Howrey, University of Michigan, in making their model available to us.

2. This is a weighted average of six endogenous consumption sector prices of MQEM.

3. For our purposes the state variable representation is most conveniently obtained by augmenting the endogenous variables of the original structural model with definitions for all endogenous variable lags greater than one; similarly, we have constructed additional definitions so that exogenous variables have no lags. Thus predetermined variables appear explicitly as variable vectors y_{t-1} and x_t.

4. We will assume that A possesses a full set of G characteristic roots and vectors, for the exposition would be needlessly complicated by considering the defective case. G is the row or column dimension of the square dynamics matrix A.

5. Similarly the algebraic sum of TSIP, YFP, YNFP, and YOL (income sources or tax payments) are elements of personal income YP. This sum was defined to be proportional to YPWS plus YGWS (private plus public wage and salary income). Finally, CDAN72, which was *not* influential, is part of C72. It is defined to be proportional to CDAO72, which *is* influential and hence included in the reduced model.

6. This study extracts a handful of results from a much more complete one (Kuh, Neese, and Hollinger 1985), so a number of qualifications and extensions have necessarily been ignored here. Anyone interested in a more complete treatment of this subject is referred to that source.

References

Kuh, E., and J. Neese, 1982. Econometric Model Diagnostics. *International Symposium on Criteria For Evaluating the Reliability of Macroeconomic Models*. G. Chow and P. Corsi, eds. Wiley, New York.

Kuh, E., 1983. Linear Analysis of Large Nonlinear Models and Model Simplification. In *4th IFAC/IFORS/IIASA Conference on the Modeling and Control of National Economies* (June). McGregor & Werner, Washington, D.C.

Kuh, E., J. Neese, and P. Hollinger, 1985. *Structural Sensitivity in Econometric Models*. Wiley, New York.

Linear Model Analysis (LIMO), 1983. MIT, Center for Computational Research in Economics and Management Science. Technical Report no. 34. Cambridge, Mass.

Smith. B. T., J. M. Boyle, J. H. Dongarra, B. S. Garbow, Y. Ikebe, V. C. Klema, and C. B. Moler, 1976. *Matrix Eigensystem Routines, EISPACK Guide*. 2nd ed., Springer-Verlag, New York.

Wilkinson, J. H., 1965. *The Algebraic Eigenvalue Problem*. Oxford University Press, Oxford, England.

Index